GOOD CARB, BETTER CARB COOKBOOK

from the editors of
THE LOW-CARB BIBLE

Publications International, Ltd.

Contributing Writer: Cathy Leman, R.D., is a registered, licensed dietitian, certified personal trainer, and owner of NutriFit, a company specializing in corporate wellness programming, nutrition counseling and consulting, and in-home personal training. She has published several articles on fitness and nutrition and is a member of Cardiovascular and Wellness Nutritionists (SCAN) and the IDEA Health and Fitness Association.

Nutritional Analysis: Linda R. Yoakam, M.S., R.D., L.D.

The nutritional information that appears with each recipe was submitted in part by the participating companies and associations. Every effort has been made to check the accuracy of these numbers. However, because numerous variables account for a wide range of values for certain foods, nutritive analyses in this book should be considered approximate.

Acknowledgments:
Page 15: "Do You Eat Enough Fiber in a Day?" from *The American Dietetic Association Complete Food and Nutrition Guide Second Edition,* Roberta Larson Duyff, M.S., R.D., F.A.D.A., C.F.C.S. Copyright © 2002 The American Dietetic Association. Reprinted by permission of John Wiley & Sons, Inc.

All recipes that contain specific brand names are copyrighted by those companies and/or associations, unless otherwise specified.

Photo Credits:
Copyright © 2004 Abbott Laboratories: 44; © Fleischmann's® Yeast: 21; © FoodPix: 38; © National Turkey Federation: 17; © USA Rice: 46, 320; © California Poultry Federation, 193

Front cover center and upper-right photography, plus photography on pages 110, 111, 113, 115, 145, 147, 155, 179, 183, 247, 249, 281, 285, 287, 289, and 293 by Chris Cassidy Photography, Inc.

Photographer: Chris Cassidy

Studio Manager: Nancy Cassidy

Photographer's Assistant: Marlene Rounds

Food Stylists: Janice Bell, Lezli Bitterman, and Stephanie Samuels

Some of the products listed in this publication may be in limited distribution.

Pictured on the front cover: *(clockwise from top):* Whole Wheat Popovers *(page 114),* Chicken & Wild Rice with Indian Flavors *(page 182),* and Southwestern Omelet Wrap *(page 150).*

Pictured on the back cover *(bottom, left to right):* Spicy Roasted Chick Peas *(page 292)* and Italian Eggplant with Millet and Pepper Stuffing *(page 154).*

Microwave Cooking: Microwave ovens vary in wattage. Use the cooking times as guidelines and check for doneness before adding more time.

Contents

Introduction

Low carb, lower carb, carb friendly, carb free, carb lite, reduced carb. . . carb this and carb that! It's impossible to escape carb talk these days. Everyone knows at least one person who's on a low-carb diet and several others who are considering starting one. To meet consumer demand for low-carb fare, food manufacturers are producing more and more low-carb products, and restaurants are adding low-carb alternatives to their menus.

But if you've picked up the *Good Carb, Better Carb Cookbook,* you've probably started to wonder about the low-carb epidemic. Or perhaps you've always been skeptical. Is it really possible that pears and watermelon, potatoes and rice, and corn and carrots are bad for you? Can the secret to weight loss and good health really be to avoid the very foods that contain the most vitamins, minerals, phytochemicals, and fiber?

The answer, of course, is no. Carbohydrates are essential nutrients. They are the body's preferred source of energy, and when eaten in the form of whole grains, legumes, and whole fruits and vegetables, they are significant sources of fiber. Fiber keeps cholesterol in check and your digestive system functioning properly, and it plays an important role in weight management by filling you up and helping you stay full longer.

You don't need to eliminate carbs from your diet or drastically reduce them. In fact, you shouldn't do either. (Well, reducing the number of jelly donuts is probably a good idea.) Your long-term health and weight control depend on a diet filled with a variety of carbohydrate foods. But you do need to understand how carbohydrates work in the body and how to choose the most nutritious among them.

The *Good Carb, Better Carb Cookbook* is designed to end your carbohydrate confusion. The first chapter explains the fundamental role carbohydrate plays in human nutrition. It breaks down carbohydrate into its component parts, explains how carbohydrate is digested, and describes how different kinds of carbohydrate are utilized to produce energy. It also looks at fiber and how food processing has gradually eliminated a considerable amount of fiber from our diets. Finally, it talks about the climbing rate of obesity in this country and how diet trends have fueled the increase.

The second chapter goes into more depth about simple and complex carbohydrates. It details carbohydrate's effect on blood sugar, including a discussion of weight gain, binge eating, and the glycemic index and glycemic load. It also discusses carbohydrate's role in disease prevention and management. You'll even find instructions for using carbohydrate foods to power your exercise routine according to the time of day that you work out.

The third chapter will open up a whole new world of carbohydrate foods to you. This is the chapter that shows you how to apply what you've learned about choosing good and better carbohydrates to your home cooking and your menu selections away from home. This chapter is chock-full of suggestions for ways to substitute good and better carbs for "empty" carbs in your diet, and it shows you how to adapt your recipes for smart-carb cooking.

We've also included a nutrient counter that contains carbohydrate, fiber, and other nutrient values for hundreds of foods. And to make it even easier to pick out the foods that are your best carbohydrate bets, we've highlighted those that are good carbs and those that are even better carbs within each food group.

Of course, this wouldn't be a cookbook if it didn't have recipes. The *Good Carb, Better Carb Cookbook* is brimming with delicious recipes for meals, snacks, side dishes, appetizers, desserts, and soups that will boost your smart-carb intake while tantalizing your taste buds.

So, say good-bye to carbophobia today. The *Good Carb, Better Carb Cookbook* will introduce you to the palate-pleasing, waistline-slimming, and health-promoting wonders of carbs.

Getting to Know Carbohydrates

Are you carbophobic? Do you shun the bread basket and pick tiny pieces of pasta out of minestrone soup? This section will help you understand that carbohydrate foods are not the enemy. In fact, we can't live without them. Once you know how carbs work in the body and how to choose the most nutritious ones, you'll see that you can have your carbs, maintain good health, and control your weight, too.

Carbohydrate Basics

Many people make the mistake of thinking that carbohydrate means only bread and pasta—and perhaps cereals and rice. Of course these are carbohydrate foods, but they are by no means the lone sources of carbohydrate. All fruits and vegetables contain carbohydrate, and carbs can also be found in some dairy products. In fact, every plant-based food has carbohydrate in it. Through the process of photosynthesis, plants store carbohydrate as their main energy source.

The foods that contain carbohydrate (grains, beans, fruits, vegetables, and some dairy) are all quite different from each other. But the one thing they have in common, substantial doses of healthy carbohydrate, is something that humans can't live without.

It's easiest to understand carbohydrate and its role in human nutrition if we break it down to its least common denominators.

BREAKING DOWN CARBOHYDRATE

Carbohydrates are made up of a combination of carbon, hydrogen, and oxygen. The word carbohydrate is formed from those words: *carbo* meaning carbon and *hydrate* meaning water, which is made of hydrogen and oxygen. Carbohydrates all have these three basic component parts. It's how they are put together that makes each one unique.

Carbohydrates are categorized as either simple or complex. The simple carbohydrates are made of a single unit of various arrangements of the three elements (carbon, hydrogen, oxygen). Each unit has the same number of carbon, hydrogen, and oxygen atoms; the different arrangements of them account for their distinct properties, such as sweetness and solubility. Complex carbohydrates are made of different arrangements of these single units that are linked together in various patterns that can be from two to tens of thousands of units long. The more units linked, the more complex the carbohydrate. Simple carbohydrates are sugars; complex carbohydrates are starches, fiber, glycogen, and dextrin.

Simple carbohydrates

There are two kinds of simple carbohydrates: monosaccharides and disaccharides. Each type is quite easily broken down by the body to create the glucose the body uses for energy.

MONOSACCHARIDES. These are the simplest form of carbohydrate ("mono" means one, "saccharide" means sugar). Glucose, fructose, and galactose, the monosaccharides that are found in fruits, vegetables, and milk, make up approximately 10 percent of the carbohydrate in our diet. Glucose is often called blood sugar because it is the main form of carbohydrate that travels through the bloodstream to provide energy to the body's cells. It's found naturally in fruits, vegetables, and honey. Fructose, also known as fruit sugar, is found naturally in many different fruits as well as honey. Galactose is a monosaccharide that is the end result of the digestive breakdown of a disaccharide called lactose (the sugar found in milk).

DISACCHARIDES. These are made of two single sugar units (monosaccharides) that are linked together. The different types of disaccharides ("di" means two) are created through various combinations of monosaccharides. Here are some examples of disaccharides you might recognize and how they are formed:

glucose + fructose = sucrose (disaccharide)
glucose + galactose = lactose (disaccharide)
glucose + glucose = maltose (disaccharide)

Sucrose is the most common disaccharide; it's commonly known as table sugar. Lactose is the disaccharide found in milk. Maltose is the least common disaccharide; it's created during digestion by enzymes that break down large molecules of starch and is a product of cereal grain germination.

Complex carbohydrates

Complex carbohydrates are assembled from single sugar units, including glucose, fructose, and galactose, or pairs of single sugars (the disaccharides, including sucrose, lactose, and maltose) that are linked together. Here's how complex carbs are formed:

POLYSACCHARIDES. Polysaccharides ("poly" means more than one) are also known as complex

Is it simple or complex?
How do you know if a food contains simple or complex carbohydrates? The words simple and complex aren't listed on food labels. Some foods, like fruits and vegetables, don't have nutrition labels, and many foods we eat are "combination foods" that provide both simple and complex carbohydrates. If you're trying to keep your intake of simple carbohydrates to a minimum, keep this guideline in mind: The higher the amount of fiber listed, the more complex carbohydrate the food contains.

carbohydrates and include starch, fiber, glycogen, and dextrin. Although complex carbohydrates are built from many single sugar units, they don't taste sweet. Joining these sugar units together creates the new, complex carbohydrate—either starch, glycogen, or cellulose (fiber). Starch is found in plants (starch is their storage form of carbohydrate), glycogen is the storage form of carbohydrate in humans and animals, and cellulose, an indigestible form of carbohydrate that's better known as fiber, provides structure for all plants. A fourth type of polysaccharide, dextrin, is produced as a result of breaking down long chains of starch into shorter chains during digestion. All of these complex carbohydrates are more stable and less soluble than the simple carbohydrates. However, the body can still break them down fairly easily into simple sugars and finally into glucose, the simple sugar that the body uses directly for energy.

CARBOHYDRATES: WHAT ARE THEY GOOD FOR?
Carbohydrate is one of three macronutrients (protein and fat are the other two) that our body requires, and it comprises the bulk of the calories

Label lingo

The nutrition facts label can help you get a handle on how much and what type of nutrients you're eating. When searching for carbohydrate info, do you know what to look for? Here's a primer:

- **Total Carbohydrate:** The amount is expressed in grams. The total consists of all carbohydrate, including the fiber and sugar listed below it. There is no distinction between simple or complex.
- **Dietary Fiber:** The amount is expressed in grams. Fiber is a complex carbohydrate. It has no calories and isn't digested by the body. Occasionally you'll see soluble and insoluble fiber amounts listed as well.
- **Sugars:** The amount is expressed in grams. The total consists of sugars naturally present in the food, such as the lactose in milk and fructose in fruits, as well as sugar that's been added to the food, such as table sugar, corn syrup, and dextrose.

we eat. In fact, 45 to 60 percent of the typical American diet comes from carbohydrate sources. In some parts of the world, particularly in developing countries, carbohydrate consumption may be closer to 80 percent.

Plants are rich in carbohydrate, as that is their storage form of energy. When we eat plant-based foods, we ingest this stored energy and put it to use within the body. Although we can use protein and fat to produce energy, carbohydrate is the source of fuel that is easiest for the body to use, and so it is preferred. This is due primarily to the basic chemical structure of carbohydrate—those units of carbon, hydrogen, and oxygen. Monosaccharides, the simple carbohydrates, are absorbed directly into the bloodstream. But complex carbohy-

drates are also relatively easy for the body to disassemble, creating glucose that can be shuttled off to cells to provide energy. In fact, the body actually begins to break down carbohydrates in the mouth with the help of an enzyme that is found in saliva.

Eating an abundance of carbohydrate is essential because it provides a steady and readily available supply of energy to the body. In fact, it is the main source of energy for the brain and the central nervous system. A constant supply of glucose is necessary for the brain and nerve tissues to function properly. If you don't eat enough carbohydrate, the body will turn to other sources, such as fat, to meet its energy needs. While our body has the ability to use alternative sources (including protein) for fuel, it's ill-advised to reduce carbohydrate intake enough to force the body into this state. That's why the strategy behind some low-carbohydrate diets—to encourage the body to burn fat for fuel—may sound like a good idea but in actuality is not.

We need fat in our diets, but also in and on our body—within limits of course. Dietary fat provides a concentrated source of energy (9 calories per gram). It makes us feel fuller longer, as it tends to leave the stomach slowly, and it transports and supports absorption of the fat-soluble vitamins A, D, E, and K. In the body, fat is the primary form in which humans store excess long-term energy. Fat is not a readily available energy source like carbohydrate; rather, it's meant to sustain us in times of starvation, self-imposed or otherwise. That's one reason why it's so difficult to lose body fat, especially when you cut calories too low. Our body views fat as a source of protection, and it's reluctant to give it up easily. Throughout the body, fat is

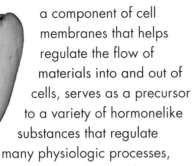

a component of cell membranes that helps regulate the flow of materials into and out of cells, serves as a precursor to a variety of hormonelike substances that regulate many physiologic processes, acts as an insulator against heat loss, and protects vital organs such as the kidneys and heart.

Protein's power is often underestimated. Sure, protein is made up of amino acids, which the body uses to build new and repair old body tissue and muscle. But protein is a workhorse—it's part of every body cell and tissue (including organs, skin, bone, and muscle), supports the body's immune functions, aids in the transport of nutrients, serves as a buffer to maintain a stable blood pH, and as enzymes and hormones, works to regulate body processes.

When there isn't enough readily available glucose from the breakdown of carbohydrate, the body first turns to stored carbohydrate reserves (glycogen). If there's still no new intake of carbohydrate and the reserves are depleted, the body is forced to use alternative sources (fat and protein) for energy. When this happens, protein is diverted from its intended job and there isn't much left over to support muscle repair, so muscles can become smaller and weaker.

In extreme cases, such as when a person is on a zero-carb diet, the body can break down muscle to convert into glucose. However, your heart—the body's main muscle—is usually protected. The energy needs of the brain and heart are the body's first priority, and it works hard to prevent damage to these and other major organs.

STOKING OUR ENGINES

Even if we eat sufficient amounts of carbohydrate every day to fuel our energy needs, we don't eat continuously. Yet our bodies need glucose all the time, not just at mealtimes or when we feel like having a snack. So how does the body manage to keep providing a constant supply of glucose to the cells?

Our bodies have an amazing ability both to use glucose and to conserve it for future needs. There

Carbohydrate math

Does the term "net carbs" throw you for a loop? If so, you're not alone. "Net carbs" is a term that manufacturers are including on food labels as a marketing tool, but it hasn't yet been defined by the Food and Drug Administration (FDA).

The idea behind net carbs is pretty simple. It's a way of showing the number of carbohydrates that are actually digested and have an effect on blood sugar and weight as opposed to the total number of carbohydrates in a product. Sugar alcohols (substitute sweeteners) such as sorbitol or mannitol have few calories and a minimal effect on blood sugar, while fiber has no calories and a favorable effect on blood sugar. Both are carbohydrate sources, but manufacturers reason that they can be subtracted from total carbohydrate amounts because they have so little effect on blood sugar and on weight.

Here's an example of how to come up with the "net carb" number:

Suppose you see a label that reads Net Carbs: 10 grams. The nutrition facts label will look like something like this:

Total Carbohydrate: 20 grams
Dietary Fiber: 5 grams
Sugar Alcohol *(specific name of ingredient used)*: 5 grams

Add the amount of sugar alcohol and fiber (5 + 5 = 10), then subtract from total carbohydrate to get "net carbs" (20 − 10 = 10).

Breaking the fast

If you're a die-hard breakfast skipper, this may change your mind. You know that the body stores carbohydrate (glycogen) in the liver and muscle so it can function even when the supply of carbohydrate dips too low. But just how long can you go before it's time to refuel? After 12 to 18 hours of fasting, the liver stores become depleted. So if you don't usually make time for breakfast but feel like you're running on fumes by lunch, it's because you truly are!

is a delicate regulatory system that maintains tight control over the level of glucose in the blood.

The regulatory system works like this: When you eat a carbohydrate-containing food or meal, the carbohydrate is absorbed from your digestive tract, causing blood sugar (glucose) levels to rise. Insulin, a hormone released from your pancreas, helps glucose enter your cells, where it is used to produce energy. Your body doesn't turn all of its blood sugar into energy at the same time. Insulin works to both clear glucose from the blood for use by cells and to store any excess in your liver and muscles. This storage form of glucose is called glycogen. Some glucose may also be converted to body fat if you eat more calories than your body needs.

If blood sugar levels drop too low, another hormone called glucagon triggers the conversion of glycogen from the liver back to glucose through a process called glycogenolysis (the breakdown of glycogen). This interplay between insulin and glucagon, in concert with several other physiologic control systems, works to keep blood sugar levels within a normal range at all times. Your body relies on a steady supply of glucose around the clock because your organs never stop working. In fact, a steady supply of glucose is so important that we can produce glucose by an alternate method dur-

ing periods when we have low glycogen stores or an inadequate intake of carbohydrate. Through a process called gluconeogenesis, protein, and to a lesser extent fat, can be called on to supply glucose to the body, although this is a much more complicated, "fuel expensive," and inefficient process and not the preferred method of obtaining glucose.

Choosing the best fuel

If you've ever experienced a headache, grouchy feeling, or lack of concentration because you were too hungry, you can appreciate how important it is to eat every few hours. Skipping meals won't keep your energy level up, but it's important not to grab just anything. Does it really matter what foods you eat? Absolutely! Some foods will raise your blood sugar levels too quickly and drop them like a rock in short order. These foods are the simple carbs, particularly the highly refined foods, such as white bread and candy. Simple carbs are quickly disassembled and absorbed into the bloodstream. While they can temporarily boost your energy, the effect is fleeting because they are used up so quickly. That's why snacking on a candy bar to overcome that mid-afternoon energy slump will likely have the opposite effect. Following a simple carb snack, you may soon experience a significant dip in energy or a return of hunger.

Remember the moral of Aesop's story about the tortoise and the hare? Slow and steady wins the race. The hare's burst of energy at the start of the race put him in the lead. But he couldn't maintain the pace and fell behind. The tortoise, on the other hand, plodded along steadily and ended up winning. You can think of simple carbohydrates as the hare and complex carbohydrates as the tortoise. If you supply your body with plenty of complex

The whole story about whole grain

Choosing whole-grain products isn't as easy as buying the brown loaf of bread instead of the white one. Many manufacturers would like you to believe that brown automatically means whole grain. But don't be fooled. Even when a label says "multigrain," it may be made from refined flour. Be sure to check the ingredients label. If the first ingredient is whole-wheat flour or another whole-grain flour, then you know you're getting the complex carbohydrates you want. If it just says wheat flour, you're getting refined flour, and that deep brown color may have come from added caramel coloring.

What exactly are whole grains? They are the entire seed grain, or the entire edible portion of any grain, including corn, oats, rice, and others. The whole grain contains three parts: the bran, endosperm, and germ. The bran makes up the outer layers of the grain, the endosperm is the innermost part of the grain, and the germ is the smallest part, otherwise known as the wheat embryo or wheat germ. Together these three parts provide B vitamins, trace minerals, fiber, proteins, phytonutrients, and carbohydrate.

During the milling process, the endosperm is separated from the bran and germ, then ground to the desired consistency, producing white, or refined, flour. For whole-grain flour, the bran and germ are returned to the flour at the end of the process, making it more nutritious. Despite its lack of nutrients, white flour is popular because it produces lighter, airier baked goods.

carbohydrates (whole grains, fruits, vegetables, and legumes) rather than simple carbohydrates, your blood sugar levels will rise more slowly, and they will stay steadier. That means you'll have a more constant supply of energy—and you'll be a winner every day.

The fiber factor

What complex carbohydrates have going for them that many simple carbohydrates do not is fiber. Complex carbohydrates are naturally rich in fiber, and fiber has been shown to slow down the absorption of glucose into the bloodstream. This helps maintain a steady feed of energy into the cells. After eating a food that has a lot of fiber, you won't get hungry again as quickly, and your energy level will remain higher. Another plus: Complex carbohydrates are naturally low in fat and calories, and they supply lots of vitamins and minerals.

It would be hard to overestimate the importance of having enough fiber in your diet. In addition to helping control blood sugar, fiber plays a role in preventing many health conditions and diseases. Although research has been controversial, high-fiber, plant-based diets may offer protection against colon cancer, the number-two cancer killer. Rich in phytonutrients and other cancer-fighting nutrients, fiber-rich foods are delicious weapons in the war on cancer. (For more on disease prevention, see pages 25–29.) Fiber also helps keep you feeling fuller longer.

Fiber comes in two varieties, soluble and insoluble. Foods that are fiber rich are normally a combination of soluble and insoluble fibers. You'll get plenty of both with an overall increased intake of whole, minimally processed foods. But soluble and insoluble fiber have specialized jobs to do in the body, so let's take a look at how each one works.

SOLUBLE FIBER. Soluble fiber is found in oats, barley, most fruits and vegetables, flaxseed, and psyllium. It dissolves into a gummy substance with a gooey, gelatinous consistency. Its job is to grab "bad" cholesterol (LDL) and remove it from the

Fiber: going, going, gone

What happens to healthy, nutrient-packed carbohydrate foods that end up over-processed and shipped out to grocer's shelves? Here are two examples:

Apple, medium, raw with skin	80 calories	3.7 grams of fiber
Applesauce, ½ cup, sweetened	97 calories	1.5 grams of fiber
Apple juice, from frozen concentrate, ½ cup	84 calories	0 grams of fiber
Corn, ½ cup, frozen	66 calories	2.0 grams of fiber
Corn flakes, 1 cup	102 calories	1.1 grams of fiber
Corn syrup, 1 tbsp	60 calories	0 grams of fiber

body. This is important to your health because LDL circulates through the body, depositing cholesterol along the way. High LDL levels are associated with an increased risk of heart disease. Eating foods high in soluble fiber, then, helps reduce LDL levels and can help prevent heart disease. As a result, some foods that are high in soluble fiber are allowed to carry health claims on their labels indicating that they have the potential to reduce the risk for heart disease and some cancers. Look for this health claim on whole-grain cereals, oat bran, and oatmeal. Soluble fiber can also help stabilize blood sugar following a meal. In fact, it's recommended that people with diabetes eat fiber-rich foods as a way to help keep blood sugar in check.

INSOLUBLE FIBER. Insoluble fiber, also known as cellulose, does not dissolve in water. Instead, it soaks up water, adding bulk and softness to the stool and increasing pressure against the intestinal wall, stimulating it to contract and speed the contents through your system. These properties make insoluble fiber especially good at helping you maintain regularity and prevent constipation, and they are critical in the prevention and treatment of many gastrointestinal conditions and diseases, particularly diverticulosis. Insoluble fiber also contributes to feelings of fullness after eating, a boon to people who are trying to lose weight. Good sources of insoluble fiber include lentils and most other dried beans or legumes, green peas, spinach, sweet potatoes, berries, dried figs, barley, and bran cereal.

But even though fiber is critical to your health, not to mention your weight-control efforts, most Americans don't get nearly enough in their daily diet. According to the American Dietetic Association, Americans average around 14 grams of fiber per day, far short of the recommended 20 to 35 grams. One of the best reasons to replace refined carbohydrate foods with whole grains and round out your diet with plenty of vegetables, fruits, and legumes is to increase intake of dietary fiber.

OUR COMPLEX CARB HISTORY

Long before processed foods, 24-hour convenience marts, and grocery stores that carry thousands of foods under one roof, humans ate foods in their natural, whole state. Foods that were good sources of fiber and other complex carbohydrates, including fruits, vegetables, nuts, and seeds, were a significant part of the human diet. We ate what nature provided, the way nature provided it.

That began to change with the advent of new technologies that allowed us to process foods in a way we never had before. Not only did we learn to mill whole grains in volume to feed an ever-growing population, but we also learned how to refine them even further into white flour. While pricey, the white flour gave breads and other baked goods more visual and textural appeal. This was not lost on the upper class, who flaunted their higher social status by serving foods prepared with refined, white flour.

As revolutionary as this new food processing method was, there was an unfortunate side effect that people weren't aware of immediately. Refinement stripped the grains of most of the nutrients that Mother Nature had built in. But it wasn't just grains that technology was processing. Oranges, a luxury item by themselves, were even more prized in their processed juice form. This unique imported food was advertised in local newspapers, and the

upper class bought it, too, as a sign of social status. Unfortunately, some of the nutrients available in whole oranges, particularly fiber, disappeared in processing. Food processing increased the choices available to consumers, but at a nutritional price.

As merchants responded to the need for a year-round food supply by carrying larger inventories, they also needed a way to extend shelf life. Food manufacturers were happy to comply and quickly discovered the profitability of adding preservatives. Fortunately, they also discovered the need to add back nutrients lost in processing, and they developed the ability to do that through enrichment and fortification of their products. (For more on enrichment and fortification, see "Making Food Healthier," page 16.)

Through the years, many of the ingredients used to extend shelf life, improve palatability, and decrease production costs to manufactured foods have come under fire for their negative impact on the quality of human nutrition. Stripping foods of their natural vitamin, fiber, and mineral package

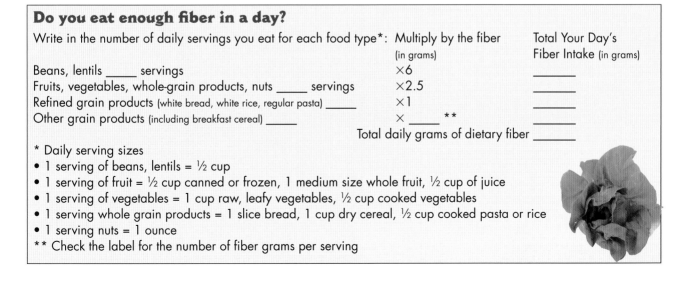

Do you eat enough fiber in a day?

Write in the number of daily servings you eat for each food type*:	Multiply by the fiber (in grams)	Total Your Day's Fiber Intake (in grams)
Beans, lentils _____ servings	×6	_____
Fruits, vegetables, whole-grain products, nuts _____ servings	×2.5	_____
Refined grain products (white bread, white rice, regular pasta) _____	×1	_____
Other grain products (including breakfast cereal) _____	× _____ **	_____
	Total daily grams of dietary fiber	_____

* Daily serving sizes
• 1 serving of beans, lentils = ½ cup
• 1 serving of fruit = ½ cup canned or frozen, 1 medium size whole fruit, ½ cup of juice
• 1 serving of vegetables = 1 cup raw, leafy vegetables, ½ cup cooked vegetables
• 1 serving whole grain products = 1 slice bread, 1 cup dry cereal, ½ cup cooked pasta or rice
• 1 serving nuts = 1 ounce
** Check the label for the number of fiber grams per serving

Making food healthier

More than 90 percent of ready-to-eat cereals and breads, as well as almost all types of processed foods, are enriched or fortified with vitamins, minerals, or fiber. Fortification and enrichment are two of the most effective methods for improving health and preventing nutritional deficiencies that cause disease. In the United States, diseases such as goiter, rickets, beriberi, and pellagra have been virtually eliminated because of these processes.

Originally, the goal of enrichment was simply to replenish the nutrients lost during food processing. Enriched means that nutrients are added back to foods. For instance, white flour is enriched with B vitamins and iron, which are removed from wheat flour when it is refined.

The concept was later expanded to include adding other substances that were not present in the food before processing. The aim of fortifying foods was to eradicate nutritional deficiencies associated with diseases. Fortified means nutrients that are often lacking in typical diets have been added. For example, salt is often fortified with iodine because there are few dietary sources of it.

While vitamins and minerals are still added to processed foods to maintain or improve our current nutritional health, the use of fortification today helps to reduce and prevent devastating and sometimes fatal diseases, such as spina bifida and anencephaly. Fortification of bread, pasta, and other cereal grains with folic acid has been directly responsible for the 26 percent annual decrease in these two birth defects.

Fortification and enrichment may even be new weapons in the fight against heart disease. The amino acid homocysteine is being increasingly accepted as a marker for heart disease risk. High homocysteine and low B vitamin concentrations have been linked to increased risk of cardiovascular disease. Although the role that folic acid and other B vitamins play in heart disease protection still needs to be confirmed, there is encouraging research indicating that fortifying cereals and other foods with folic acid and other B vitamins may help protect against heart disease risk by lowering homocysteine levels.

while adding artificial colors, sweeteners, and other additives is not the healthiest or wisest use of technological advancement. Partly out of interest in prevention and partly in response to the steady increase in type 2 diabetes and obesity, as well as the high rate of heart disease and certain cancer diagnoses, the pendulum has slowly begun to swing in the opposite direction. While it's impossible as well as impractical to return to the days when food wasn't refined or preserved in any way, there is increasing recognition that eating fewer highly refined processed foods and more whole grains and whole fruits and vegetables is better for our health and for controlling weight.

CHANGING DIET TRENDS

The link between nutrition, health, and disease grows stronger daily. In the early 1970s, much of the nutrition research linked fat, particularly saturated fat, to heart disease and obesity. But even as the evidence continued to accumulate throughout the 1980s, there seemed to be a disconnect in the message delivery: Americans were growing as well! In fact, according to the Centers for Disease Control, in the last ten years obesity rates have increased by more than 60 percent among adults. Since 1980, obesity rates have doubled among children and tripled among adolescents.

During the mid- to late-1980s, food scientists and manufacturers began working to become part of the solution to the growing obesity problem by developing fat-free and low-fat foods. Since fat has more than double the calories found in protein and carbohydrate, it seemed reasonable to assume that cutting fat in foods was a good way to cut calorie consumption overall. Consumers eagerly jumped on the bandwagon, buying lots of fat-free products.

However, much to everyone's surprise, obesity rates continued to climb at an alarming rate. Why? The fat-free products contained considerably more refined carbohydrate (sugar) to substitute for the loss of flavor from fat. The products may have been fat free, but they weren't calorie free. But people acted as if they were, consuming huge quantities of processed fat-free cookies, crackers, and other goodies.

When fat-free foods didn't appear to be the answer to the skyrocketing obesity rate, people began looking for the next solution. The focus eventually shifted from counting fat grams to counting carbohydrate grams. The theory was the fewer carbohydrates the better. Where fat was concerned, however, all caution was thrown to the wind. As long as people could build a meal around a miniscule amount of carbohydrate, they could eat as much fat and protein as they liked, and the weight was guaranteed to come off. And for some it did come off. But there were unpleasant side effects: Many people who cut carbs significantly felt less energetic and experienced constipation and bloating. And when they ceased to adhere closely to a

reduced-carb diet, the weight crept back on. Obesity rates continued to climb. Heart disease remains the number-one killer, and type 2 diabetes is becoming epidemic.

As you can see, it's a mistake to blame carbohydrate alone for obesity and nutrition-related diseases. It is absolutely true, however, to say that the type as well as the amount of carbohydrate that we eat is crucial to good health. We all know that a jelly donut is a carbohydrate food, but it's worlds apart from a whole-wheat bagel in terms of good nutrition. That's what we're talking about here: keeping carbohydrates in the diet but choosing the most nutritious among them.

The first low-carb diet

Diets are not a modern invention. As far back as 1087, when William the Conqueror tried to reduce his bulk by lying in bed and consuming nothing but alcohol, the first recorded "liquid diet," people realized there was a link between food and body size. Back then, however, people didn't understand the connection between food and weight gain, only that they would waste away if they didn't eat and maintain or gain weight when they did. People thought that it didn't matter what you ate—as long as you ate something, you'd stay alive and relatively healthy.

Even low-carb dieting isn't new. In the late 1800s it was called "banting," named for London undertaker William Banting, who lost 50 pounds on a high-protein regimen consisting of lean meat, dry toast, soft-boiled eggs, and vegetables. Banting was so delighted with his newfound health and slim appearance that he penned a bestseller, *Letter on Corpulence, Addressed to the Public*. As word of the diet traveled widely, an American physician learned of the method and instructed her overweight patients to begin following the regimen. They experienced great success, fueling the excitement and information surrounding "banting," and for a time "banting" became America's principal weight-loss method.

Choosing Good and Better Carbs

True or false: A carb is a carb is a carb. If you answered "true," you might think all carbohydrate-containing foods are created equal because they all break down into glucose. But they're not all the same. Some carb foods are better for you than others. Knowing how to make better carbohydrate choices means you'll be eating healthier and are likely to have more energy and find it easier to lose weight.

When choosing carbs, it's particularly important to keep in mind the distinction between simple and complex carbs. Simple carbs are digested more quickly and raise blood sugar levels faster and

more dramatically. Complex carbs, on the other hand, take the digestive system longer to break down, and so they enter the bloodstream more slowly, raising blood sugar levels gradually.

CARBS AND WEIGHT GAIN

Why should you care whether your blood sugar remains steady or has some peaks and valleys? After all, there are all kinds of bodily processes that we remain blissfully unaware of. And we have that regulatory system that we talked about in the first chapter to take care of our blood sugar's ups and downs.

There are lots of reasons to be concerned and aware of blood sugar levels. But since the vast majority of us today are looking for weight-loss strategies that work, let's first take a look at the role carbohydrate plays in weight gain and weight loss.

Remember, carbohydrate foods contain sugar, starch, and fiber in various amounts. Simple carbohydrates (such as table sugar and apple juice) only contain sugar, while complex carbohydrates (such as whole grains) contain starch and fiber.

The binge cycle

You probably don't realize it, but a rapid rise in blood sugar, which is the result of eating a highly refined carbohydrate food, can be a key factor in binge eating and weight gain. Eating any type of carbohydrate food triggers the release of insulin to clear the excess glucose from the bloodstream. But eating a highly refined carbohydrate, particularly a substantial portion of white pasta or a large bagel, can cause the pancreas to pump out even greater amounts of insulin to help restore normal blood sugar levels. If the insulin clears the glucose too quickly, blood sugar levels plummet. When blood sugar levels drop precipitously, the stomach and brain send out hunger signals that compel you to eat more food (glucose) to raise blood sugar levels again. If you once again choose to satisfy your hunger with a simple carbohydrate, you will crave even more sweets. But instead of feeling full and satisfied, you will feel constantly hungry. Ultimately, a diet that contains lots of simple carbs can lead to a vicious cycle of hunger, overeating, and weight gain.

When it comes to losing weight (or preventing weight gain), then, you should primarily eat complex carbohydrates. Complex carbohydrates have many advantages over simple carbs. Complex carbohydrates take longer to be digested, and so they elicit a different type of blood sugar response. They enter the bloodstream more slowly and therefore raise blood sugar levels more gradually. As a result, blood sugar levels tend to remain stable, which means your brain won't get a hunger signal for a much longer period of time. And complex carbohydrates contain fiber (simple carbs do not). Fiber, as you know, isn't digested, so it costs you

The fat-free food fallacy

Nutrition and weight-management experts agree that keeping hunger under control is one of the keys to successful weight loss and maintenance. During the mid-1990s, at the height of the fat-free, processed-foods rage, dieters would often reach for these "diet" foods to help them stay on their weight-loss plan. Unfortunately, since those foods were usually high in sugar and refined flour, they caused unsuspecting dieters to experience roller coaster energy swings and increased hunger. Instead of being a weight-management solution, these products contributed to the weight-control problem. Even now, many dieters don't realize they need to be wary of fat-free products and to eat them only in moderation.

What consumers also didn't realize—or conveniently forgot—was that "fat free" is not synonymous with "calorie free." Consumers behaved as if the fat-free products had put unlimited quantities of previously forbidden foods, such as cookies and ice cream and chips, back on the dieting menu. They could have their fat-free cake and eat it, too, believing that as long as it was fat free, they would be, too. And they didn't stop at eating just a couple of cookies; they ate the whole box. While patiently waiting for their favorite treat to be restocked on the grocer's shelves, dieters forgot about the one basic weight-loss premise that never changes: Too many calories in and not enough out = weight gain.

If these foods were fat free, why weren't they also calorie free? Why did some of the fat-free varieties pack even more calories than the original version? When manufacturers remove the fat, which adds flavor and mouthfeel to food, they must replace it with something to keep the food tasty. For sweets that replacement is sugar. While it's true that sugar is fat free, it still has lots of calories, so eating a gallon of fat-free ice cream will never help you lose that excess weight.

Another reason many people overate fat-free foods is that often, no matter how hard they tried, manufacturers just couldn't match the flavor of the original version. People felt unsatisfied regardless of how much they ate. After polishing off a box of fat-free candies, it was typical for dieters to go searching for "the real thing" in order to feel satisfied. In the end people ate more calories than if they'd had a few of the originals in the first place. Fat-free foods have their place, but they're a weight-loss tool only if used properly. And they're definitely not the answer.

nary a calorie. Not only that, but fiber adds bulk to your food, so you feel more full and satisfied after eating.

Keep in mind, too, that you're unlikely to overeat vegetables or grains, all of which have an abundant supply of complex carbohydrate. You'd be hard-pressed to binge on a bowl of carrots or lentil soup. And even if you did, these are still low-calorie foods. The carbohydrate foods that con-tribute significantly to weight gain are the simple sugars that are usually part of a high-fat package: donuts, cookies, cake, candy, and ice cream. It's not just the carbohydrate in those foods that is

responsible for packing on the pounds, it's the fat content, too.

KEEP IT LOW FAT. One caveat: It is certainly possible to turn a low-calorie, complex carbohydrate such as whole-wheat pasta or a baked potato into higher-calorie fare. In fact, it happens all the time. Just spoon some Alfredo sauce on the pasta or add sour cream and butter to the potato. Adding fat to low-calorie, complex carbs does just what it says: It adds fat! Fat, you may recall, has more than twice the number of calories per gram (9) as carbohydrate and protein (both 4). If you serve up fat-laden complex carbs in extra-large portions, you will expand your waistline just as you will with the less nutritious simple carbohydrate foods. By eating the complex carbs, though, you'll still benefit from the vitamins, minerals, and other nutrients they contain. Highly refined carbs have nothing to offer except for calories and whatever nutrients were added back through the enrichment process (see "Making food healthier," page 16, for more on the enrichment and fortification process).

GETTING CHOOSY: USING THE GLYCEMIC INDEX

You know the general guidelines for choosing the most beneficial carbohydrates: Pick complex car-bohydrates that are packed with nutrients and raise your blood sugar levels gradually. In general, that means choosing whole grains, vegetables, and fruits and avoiding foods with added sugars. But to make the best carbohydrate choices, there is a more precise way to know how a particular food will raise your blood sugar levels. You can use the

---

Simple vs. complex: It's not so simple!

You may have gotten the idea that you should always choose complex carbohydrates over simple carbohy-drates. But the fact is, you need both in your diet; you just have to choose wisely. There are some complex carbohydrates that aren't so healthy, and there are some simple carbohydrates that are very healthy. How do you figure out which ones to eat and which to avoid? Use the list below for a little guidance:

HEALTHY SIMPLE CARBS
Fruit	Pudding
Fruit-flavored yogurt	Milk

NOT-SO-HEALTHY SIMPLE CARBS
Fruit-flavored drinks	Soft drinks
Fruit-flavored gelatin	Fruit roll ups

HEALTHY COMPLEX CARBS
Corn	Green peas
Beans (legumes)	Sweet potato

NOT-SO-HEALTHY COMPLEX CARBS
Potato chips	Soda crackers
Plain white bread	Rice cakes

glycemic index (GI), which is a ranking of foods by how quickly they raise blood sugar levels compared to other foods.

Developed 20 years ago by researchers at the University of Toronto, the GI was originally created to help people with diabetes select foods that would help them better manage their chronic condition. It was well-established that stable blood sugar levels helped reduce the likelihood of developing complications associated with diabetes, such as hypoglycemia (low blood sugar) or hyperglycemia (high blood sugar), kidney disease, nerve damage, and blindness. But at the time, the conventional wisdom was that all carbohydrate foods had exactly the same effect on blood sugar, even though some studies showed that this was not the case. The researchers set out to show that some carbohydrate foods impact blood sugar more than others.

We now know that while all digested carbohydrates become glucose, different carbohydrate foods have different effects on blood sugar. For people with diabetes, eating a specific amount of total carbohydrate each day helps them maintain blood sugar levels as close to normal as possible. However, the type of carbohydrate is particularly important. And even if you don't have diabetes, it's wise to choose complex carbohydrates because they're better at keeping blood sugar levels stable.

In recent years, research has begun to focus on other uses for the GI. It may help guide weight-loss efforts and has potential as a component of dietary intervention for cardiovascular disease. In fact, the GI is being discussed in the mainstream media, as well as in clinical situations, in connection with the treatment and management of heart disease, stroke, and high blood pressure as well as diabetes. Although additional research is needed, scientific evidence is mounting that a diet of high glycemic-index foods may increase the risk of these and possibly other diseases.

How the glycemic index works

The glycemic index ranks foods according to their immediate effect on blood sugar levels in comparison to other foods. The ranking is done by establishing the effect of 50 grams of available carbohydrate (the total amount of carbohydrate minus fiber) in a control food on blood sugar levels. The control food, originally white bread, was assigned the number 100. Once that was established, researchers tested equal amounts (50 grams of available carbohydrate) of various foods and compared blood sugar response to the control food. Any food that raised blood sugar levels more than white bread had a higher number, while foods that raised blood sugar less than white bread had a lower number.

Today, some researchers have chosen to use glucose as the control food instead of white bread. Glucose, then, is given the value of 100 and all foods are compared to its effect on blood sugar instead. When white bread is used as the control food, the GI rank of glucose is 140, since it raises

Don't get confused

You'll see that the term glycemic index (GI) is also used to identify the individual GI value of a particular food. Though glycemic index is used both for the name of the index and for the individual food values within the index, it really isn't confusing. You can tell from the context which is which.

Buyer beware!

There are some foods now sporting a low-carb label that have always been naturally low in carbohydrate. Natural peanut butter (the kind without added sugar) is a good example. In general, nuts come by their low-carb title without any help from food manufacturers. Cashews have a bit more carbohydrate than other varieties, but when compared to other natural foods, such as honey, the carbohydrate content is minimal.

Many other foods also need no help from manufacturers to earn a low-carb title. These include lettuce; berries; cruciferous vegetables such as broccoli and cauliflower; protein foods such as lean meats, chicken, fish, cheese, and soy products; cantaloupe; honeydew melon; and tomatoes.

If you see a low-carb label on any of the products listed above, don't be fooled into thinking they're somehow more low-carb than they would be without the label. Eaten on their own (meaning not part of combination dishes where carbohydrates from other foods come into play), these are simply low-carb foods.

Another way that manufacturers attempt to fool you is by taking a low-carb product, reducing the carbs by a small amount, and then labeling it low carb. For instance, one particular brand of ketchup currently on the market boasts a one-carb label. It contains 1 gram of carbohydrate and 5 calories, yet the original version only has 4 grams of carbs and 15 calories—not a significant difference for either one. However, the original version sells for $1.59 while the one-carb version is 30 cents more. Be sure to compare nutrition facts labels (as well as price tags). You may be better off with the original!

There are some foods naturally low in carbohydrate that become higher in carbs because of the way they are manufactured. Yogurt is a good example. Plain yogurt has little or no carbohydrate, only 15 grams in 8 ounces, and this is from naturally occurring milk sugar. However, many yogurt products contain added sugar, giving them unnaturally high carb counts. You should also realize that added sugar increases the calorie count as well as the total carbohydrate. When a yogurt is marked low carb, it may be worth considering because it's likely that all or a great portion of the sugar has been replaced with an artificial sweetener or a lesser amount of a natural sweetener such as fruit juice. These substitutes are better for your waistline and for your blood sugar levels.

blood sugar levels more than glucose. For you to use the GI index, though, it doesn't matter which method was used in testing the foods, as the idea is the same. The GI value of a food lets you compare its effect on your blood sugar relative to other foods. That can help you make wiser food choices, including choosing better, healthier carbohydrates.

There are only a few nutrition research groups in the world that have tested the glycemic response and compiled GI values. They use a very strict testing protocol to determine the GI value of each food. Let's say they want to find out the GI value of dried apricot. Researchers use a test food and a control food. In this case, dried apricots would be the test food, and white bread or glucose would be the control food. The subjects (usually 8 to 10 participants) are given enough dried apricots to provide 50 grams of available carbohydrate (approximately 27 apricot halves). Their blood sugar response is then tested and plotted on a graph every 15 minutes during the first hour and every 30 minutes during the second hour. The same procedure is used after they ingest 50 grams of available carbohydrate from glucose or white bread (the control food). The two values are compared, and the data pulled from the graph is calculated using a computer program. Finally, the average GI from all the test subjects for the test food is calculated from the collected data.

In general, low-GI foods have scores below 55. Moderate-GI foods score between 55 and 70, while high-GI foods score above 70. As you can see, the lower the GI, the slower the blood glucose response to that food. Using the GI, you can select foods that elicit a slow, steady rise in blood sugar resulting in stable blood sugar levels that keep energy high and stave off hunger.

Tips for using the glycemic index

Using the GI in real-life situations may sound complicated at first. But you just need to get a feel for the groups of foods that have low to moderate scores. Then choose those foods more often. Keep the following in mind:

1. The GI wasn't designed to reduce the total amount of carbohydrate people consume daily but rather to help individuals select carbohydrate foods that elicit a slower insulin response.
2. Place greater focus on GI food categories rather than individual foods, selecting foods from the low and moderate categories more often than from the high category.
3. Keep in mind that foods are normally eaten in combination with other foods. The amount of fat and/or protein, as well as the carbohydrate in a food, and the addition of toppings, spreads, dressings, and sauces can all influence the effect of carbohydrate on blood glucose levels.
4. A simple way to moderate blood glucose response is by replacing one high-GI food with one low-GI food at each meal or snack. This is also much more realistic than totally eliminating all high-GI foods.
5. It's perfectly acceptable to include high-GI foods in the diet. However, the higher the GI, the smaller the portion should be.
6. Eating high-GI foods following a hard workout will help replenish glycogen stores.
7. The GI is not meant to be used in isolation but rather as one component of an overall healthy eating plan that considers other nutrients (protein, fat, and fiber), portion size, and timing of meals and snacks.

Glycemic load and the glycemic index

While the GI is a useful tool when choosing between carbohydrates, there's another ranking system that may be more practical. The GI system ranks individual foods, which allows you to compare one to another in isolation. Yet we rarely eat only one single food at a time, and that's where the GI system has some limitations. Many factors can affect the rate at which a carbohydrate is digested and raises blood glucose levels. For instance, if you eat protein and fat along with carbohydrate, it is digested more slowly and raises blood sugar levels more gradually. Other factors that can have an impact on the GI of any food are:

• Degree of ripeness. For example, the more ripe a banana is, the higher its GI. This typically applies to all fruits that continue to ripen once harvested.
• Acids in foods. When acid is present in food, it slows the rate at which your body digests that particular food. Slower digestion means slower

Getting acquainted with GI and GL values

The following gives both the GI and GL of some sample foods. The foods are organized by their GI ranking. The GL rankings are as follows:
Low GL = 10, Moderate GL = 11–19, and High GL = 20+
(per 50 g of available carbohydrate)

	GI	GL
Low GI (< 55)		
Low-fat yogurt with artificial sweetener	14	2
Lentils	28	5
Apple	36	6
All-Bran cereal	38	8
Tomato juice	38	4
Spaghetti	41	20
Canned baked beans	48	7
Orange, raw	48	5
Sourdough rye bread	48	6
100% stone-ground whole-wheat bread	53	6
Sweet potato	54	17
Moderate (55–70)		
Brown rice	55	16
Oatmeal cookies	55	9
Moroccan couscous	58	23
Peach, canned in heavy syrup	58	9
Cheese pizza	60	16
Sweet corn	60	9
Split pea soup	60	16
Raisins	64	28
Grapenuts	67	15
Cranberry juice cocktail	68	24
Whole-wheat bread	69	9
High (> 70)		
Toaster pastry	70	26
Skittles	70	32
Wonder, enriched white bread	71	10
Watermelon	72	4
Cheerios	74	15
Long-grain white rice, quick cooking	75	25
French fries	76	22
Russet potato, baked without fat	78	78
Jelly beans	80	22
Pretzels	83	19
French baguette	95	15

absorption and a more favorable effect on blood sugar.

- Individual differences in rate of carbohydrate digestion. Test five people and each will respond differently to the same food. Use the GI as a guide, but monitor the effect carbohydrate foods have on you, especially if you have diabetes.
- Type of flour (if any) in the product. The more refined white flour in a product, the higher the GI; the more whole-grain flour, the lower the GI.
- Cooking time. The cooking process makes starch molecules swell and also softens food (the longer the cooking time, the softer the food) making it easier (faster) to digest. GI numbers typically increase with cooking time.
- Other ingredients. If a high-GI food is packaged with foods containing protein or fat (such as prepared fettuccine Alfredo), the carbohydrate will have a lower GI effect than it would alone because the fat and protein slow down its digestion. By the same token, foods such as beans (legumes), which have a naturally low GI, can produce a higher GI when canned with sugar and other ingredients, as in the case of baked beans.

Another limitation of the GI is that it requires participants to consume 50 grams of available carbohydrate for comparison purposes. For some foods, that's a reasonable amount to eat, but for others, it's not. For example, watermelon has a GI of 72, which puts it into the high-GI category. Knowing that might lead you to avoid eating watermelon, even though it's a healthy food and a great source of phytochemicals such as lycopene. What the GI doesn't tell you is that it takes a little more than 4½ cups of watermelon to provide the 50 grams of available carbohydrate on which watermelon's GI is calculated. That's nine times the amount in a typical ½ cup serving.

When you calculate the glycemic load (GL), however, you get a very different picture. The glycemic load is used in conjunction with the GI. It reflects the amount of available carbohydrate in a typical serving size of a particular food, so it is more grounded in the real world of eating. The GL is calculated using a formula that multiplies the amount of available carbohydrate in a typical serving size by the food's GI and then divides the result by 100.

Let's take the watermelon example from above. We know it has a high GI. Let's see what happens when we calculate its glycemic load. A typical serving size of watermelon is ½ cup, the amount of available carbohydrate in it is 5.75, and its GI is 72. The GL for this food is calculated like this: 5.75×72÷100. If you calculate correctly, you get 4.14, which is rounded to get its glycemic load rating of 4. Watermelon doesn't seem like a high-GI food anymore, does it? That's what happens when you use the carbohydrate in a reasonable serving size to determine the effect on blood sugar. Using the GL shows that it is possible to include high-GI foods in meal planning (more on this

later). Remember, eliminating individual foods from your diet, especially fruits, vegetables, whole grains, and beans that may have a high GI, means you'll miss out on lots of vitamins, minerals, and fiber. You can find in-depth information on the glycemic index and search for the GI and GL of individual foods at www.glycemicindex.com.

CARBOHYDRATES AND YOUR HEALTH

So far, we've been concentrating on how to choose good and better carbohydrates for weight control. But selecting good and better carbs also affects your health. Choose wisely, and you may avoid the onset of some life-threatening health conditions as well as take control of others you already have.

Carbohydrate's role in disease prevention and management

Complex carbohydrates are the all-stars of disease prevention and disease management. That's

Keeping it low cal

Take one 7-ounce baked potato without the skin (145 calories), add 2 tablespoons of butter (216 calories) and 2 tablespoons of sour cream (52 calories), and you end up with a 413-calorie side dish. And that's if you add the toppings only in the small amounts we've used here. It's an example of turning a complex carbohydrate that is relatively low in calories and high in nutrients on its own into a high-calorie, not to mention high-fat, carbohydrate. An alternative is to eat half the potato with half the amount of toppings and take double helpings of anything green, yellow, or red. You'll decrease the overall total intake of carbohydrate and fat while getting an abundance of healthy carbs, fiber, and phytochemicals.

because of their high fiber content as well as the abundance of vitamins, minerals, and phytonutrients they contain. Here's a look at how eating a diet filled with complex carbohydrates can prevent or improve a variety of health conditions and diseases.

HEART DISEASE. The traditional approach to treating or preventing cardiovascular disease (CVD) has long been a low-fat, high-carbohydrate diet. The connection between fat, especially saturated fat, and heart disease was established years ago. Saturated fat, found in particularly high amounts in red meat and full-fat dairy products, raises LDL cholesterol levels (the "bad"

cholesterol). Researchers concluded that if people reduced the overall amount of fat in their diet, the amount of saturated fat would also drop. Since fat has more than twice as many calories as carbohydrate and protein (9 calories per gram for fat compared to 4 calories per gram for carbohydrate or protein), reducing the amount of fat in the diet and increasing the amount of carbohydrate would mean eating fewer calories. Excess body weight is a contributing factor for heart disease, so maintaining a healthy weight works to reduce CVD risk.

Typically, carbohydrate foods are naturally low in fat. When minimally processed, they contain fiber that helps reduce cholesterol levels by removing LDL from the body. Health professionals included carbohydrates in their recommendations for heart-healthy eating. However, people were not always counseled to eat more of the "healthy" carbs and fewer of the "less healthy" carbs and filled up on large portions of fat-free and refined carbohydrates. They may have been taking in less fat but certainly not fewer calories!

To help reduce the risk of heart disease, the American Heart Association (AHA) currently recommends a diet rich in fruits; vegetables; legumes (beans); whole, unrefined, complex carbohydrates; low-fat dairy products; fish; lean meats; and poultry. The AHA also recommends reducing the amount of saturated and hydrogenated (trans) fats in the diet. Nutrition counseling

Best and worst fiber bets
(g = gram)

GOOD SOURCES OF FIBER:		
Oatmeal, old fashioned	½ cup dry	3.7 g
Shredded wheat	2 biscuits	5.0 g
Popcorn, oil popped	2.6 cups	2.8 g
Chili with beans	1 cup	11.0 g
Tofu, firm	½ cup	2.9 g
Blueberries	1 cup raw	3.9 g
Avocado	1 med raw	8.5 g
Green peas	½ cup	4.4 g
Peanuts, dry roasted	1 ounce	3.0 g
Minestrone soup	1 cup	5.8 g
Baked beans	1 cup	13.9 g
LOW-FIBER FOODS:		
Puffed rice cereal	1 cup	.2 g
Cream of rice cereal	½ cup	.2 g
Pork rinds	1 ounce	0 g
Macaroni and cheese	1 cup	1.0 g
Beef and vegetable stew	1 cup	1.0 g
Apple juice	8 ounces	.2 g
Fruit roll up	1 roll	0 g
Lettuce, romaine	½ cup	.5 g
French fries	10 pieces	1.6 g
Chicken noodle soup	½ cup	1.0 g
Raisin bread	1 slice	1.1 g

and education recommendations from the American Dietetic Association, the AHA, and other organizations focus on the distinction between heart-healthy fats and the importance of "healthy" carbohydrates.

GASTROINTESTINAL DISEASE. Complex carbohydrates, such as whole fruits and vegetables, beans, and whole grains, are particularly helpful for improving overall gastrointestinal health. These foods are high in fiber, which plays a pivotal role in reducing the incidence of constipation and diverticulosis, a condition in which tiny pouches form inside the colon. Fiber may also reduce the risk of colon, stomach, and gallbladder cancers. But that's not the only benefit of these nutrient-rich foods. Increased intake of intact grains and other fiber-rich, whole, complex carbohydrate foods helps decrease pressure inside the intestinal tract and may help prevent diverticulosis as well as diverticulitis, the painful inflammation of the pouches. Many of these complex carbohydrate foods also pack vitamins and minerals, such as iron, zinc, magnesium, and a host of B vitamins, as well as antioxidants such as vitamins E and C, selenium, and beta carotene. The phytic acid found in whole grains may help reduce cancer risk by decreasing free radicals. Free radicals, molecules formed as a byproduct of various biochemical processes in your body, can damage

The scoop on low-carb products

The fat-free craze of the 1990s didn't have quite the impact on obesity that was expected. It's too early to tell for certain, but some experts are predicting the same outcome for low-carb and carb-free products.

How do manufacturers make foods low carb? It's all about the substitution of ingredients. The particular type of product dictates which substitute is used. Some substitutes include soy flour, xanthan gum, psyllium husk, and artificial sweeteners.

By using a flour, such as soy flour, that contains more protein or fiber than refined white flour does, manufacturers reduce the total carbohydrate in a product. Sometimes they substitute all the flour in a product, and sometimes they substitute only a portion of it.

Xanthan gum, a natural product, is used to replace gluten (a type of protein found in flour) and acts as a substitute binder in products that don't use flour. Baked goods require gluten for structure (breads require the most; cookies the least), and so low-carb products that contain less flour or no flour need a substitute to prevent them from crumbling or falling apart. For instance, a mixture of finely ground nuts and sweetener can

stand in as a low-carb crust, but the final product will be crumbly and won't hold together well. Instead of adding flour, which also adds carbs, manufacturers of low-carb products add a small amount of xanthan gum.

High-fiber psyllium is sometimes added to low-carb foods to increase their fiber content. That helps reduce the amount of "net carbs" (the marketing term manufacturers use) because net carbs are calculated by deducting fiber from the amount of total carb. If a product has more fiber, it contains fewer net carbs and has less effect on blood sugar and weight gain.

The sugar replacers used in low-carb foods, such as the artificial sweetener Splenda or the sugar alcohols mannitol or sorbitol, add sweetness without the carbohydrate and calories from sugar.

All of these substitutions, used either alone or together, do produce a decrease in total carbohydrate. However, how substantial the reduction is varies from product to product. Sometimes the reduction is so small that it has a negligible effect.

cells. Reducing the amount of free radicals can in turn reduce the risk of cancer.

DIABETES. It's still unclear whether diabetes can be prevented by eating complex carbohydrates that have a low-GI ranking. One prevailing theory is that long-term intake of lots of high-GI carbohydrates increases the risk of type 2 diabetes. This is thought to result from either insulin resistance (see below) or by exhausting the pancreas as it works to produce constant, high levels of insulin. There is good evidence, however, that a diet filled with complex carbohydrates can help treat and manage diabetes. We've known for quite some time that people with diabetes don't need to stay away from all carbohydrate. The body processes all forms of carbohydrate the same way, turning them into sugar (glucose). It's the speed with which the carbohydrate is processed and its corresponding effect on blood sugar that is important in diabetes management. Since simple, refined carbohydrates raise blood sugar more dramatically than do complex carbohydrates, people with diabetes should eat low-GI carbohydrates rather than refined, high-GI carbs. Eating low-GI foods throughout the day—at meals and for snacks—can go a long way toward controlling blood sugar levels.

INSULIN RESISTANCE. Insulin resistance is a condition that may make it difficult for some people to process simple carbohydrates, especially large portions of them at one time. Overwhelming or flooding the body with large intakes of carbohydrate forces the body to work extra hard to clear the glucose from the blood. In the case of insulin resistance, the body's tissues are not receptive to the message that insulin is there to unlock the cell and let glucose in to do its job. The result is high levels of glucose circulating in the bloodstream for extended periods of time. This causes the pancreas to work harder to crank out more insulin to shuttle all of the extra glucose into cells. Overworked pancreatic cells may eventually wear out and decrease insulin production, which is an early sign of type 2 (or non-insulin-dependent) diabetes. One way to reduce your chances of developing insulin resistance is by eating plenty of low-GI complex carbohydrates and fewer high-GI, refined, simple carbohydrates.

OBESITY. You may not think of obesity as a health condition, but being considerably overweight puts you at risk for a number of different health problems. And people who are overweight typically respond differently to carbohydrates than people who are not. A diet of high-GI, refined carbohydrates may have a much more adverse effect on an obese person's health. For example, in the ongoing Nurses' Health Study, established at Brigham and Women's Hospital in 1976 with funding from the National Institutes of Health, the odds of having a heart attack are increased for overweight women who eat lots of

simple (easily digested) carbohydrates. Additionally, volunteers following high-carbohydrate, low-fat diets experienced unhealthy changes in levels of HDL (the good cholesterol), triglycerides (a type of fat), blood sugar, and insulin—the changes being most pronounced in overweight, inactive people. People who are lean and active may be better able to handle a high-carbohydrate intake for a number of reasons. First of all, being overweight makes it more difficult for insulin to do its job helping glucose get into the cells to provide energy. Secondly, people who are more active require more fuel for energy and are particularly efficient at burning carbohydrate, which is the body's preferred source. This allows active people to burn excess carbohydrate for energy instead of storing it as fat. Finally, when you have less fat tissue and more muscle, the body is more efficient at processing and digesting food, including carbohydrates. Whole grains, legumes, fruits, and most vegetables are naturally low in fat and contain healthy carbohydrates and significant amounts of fiber, all of which contribute to an overall healthy eating plan. Human studies have produced mixed results in the low-GI/weight-loss arena, but it certainly isn't harmful to employ the GI when making daily food choices. Some people may experience weight loss as a result.

FUELING EXERCISE WITH CARBOHYDRATES

Whether you currently exercise on a regular basis or have been giving some thought to getting started, don't even think about skimping on the carbohydrates. Carbohydrates are the fuel your body needs and prefers to power any type of exercise. Regardless of your choice of activity—aerobic dance, running, strength training, yoga, swimming, bicycling, or walking—you'll perform at your best by including a variety of carbohydrates in your diet.

People often begin an exercise program when they go on a diet. They know that increased physical activity helps burn calories and tone muscle. What they may not consider is that when you cut calories, whether by extreme reductions in food intake or occasionally skipping meals, energy levels can take a nosedive. If you happen to be following a diet that cuts out or drastically reduces carbohydrate, remember that the conversion of protein to energy is a much slower and more difficult process for the body to complete. Following a high-protein diet may make you feel weak and tired. You'll end up skipping your workout entirely or cutting it short because you're too worn out—neither of which helps you reach your weight-loss goals.

There are also considerations for carbs and timing of meals that depend on when you work out. Whether it's first thing in the morning, during your lunch hour, late afternoon, or after work, make sure you're not sabotaging your efforts by giving yourself either too little or the wrong kind of food.

Early birds

If you're an early riser who likes to work out while most everyone else is still sleeping, congratulations! This is the best time to work out—not necessarily in terms of burning more calories but because it's done and out of the way. Not much conflicts with a 5:30 A.M. workout. You're less likely to blow it off than if you save it for after work when long-running meetings, family commitments, or socializing with coworkers can get in the way.

How do you feel before you begin your morning workout? Do you wake up hungry? If that's the

The best workout fuel

PRE-WORKOUT (LOW-GI) CARBOHYDRATE CHOICES:

Apple
Apricots, dried
Garbanzo beans
   (chickpeas)
Grapefruit
Lentils

Low-fat, fruited
   yogurt
Pear
Skim milk,
   plain or
   chocolate

POST-WORKOUT (HIGH-GI) CARBOHYDRATE CHOICES:

Bagel
Corn flakes
Graham crackers
Potato, baked
Pretzel

Raisins
Watermelon
White rice, long grain,
   quick cooking

case, you definitely need to eat something before you exercise. There's no one perfect food for everyone, so experiment with different food choices. One thing is certain, a small amount of a carbohydrate-rich food will do the trick to get you going and keep you going. Since glycogen (carbohydrate) stores are used while you sleep to keep your heart, brain, and other organs functioning, you need to top off those stores in the morning, particularly if you're hungry first thing.

Some people do just fine exercising in the morning on an empty stomach; in fact, they may feel discomfort if they DO eat. Again, pay attention to your own hunger cues to see how you feel. If you're one of these folks, you may be ravenous after you wrap up your workout. This is an especially good time to bring on the carbohydrates! Immediately following a workout, your muscle cells are most receptive to taking up carbohydrate—sort of like sponges soaking up all that glucose and storing it for the next bout of exercise.

What if you have no appetite before you exercise and still don't feel hungry when you're fin-

ished? Try a liquid form of carbs, such as a fruit smoothie or a sports drink. This will still get the carbohydrate to your muscles within an optimal time frame and help prevent the extreme hunger that often follows a delayed appetite. Sometimes your appetite kicks in when you don't have access to food, and you end up overly hungry.

Lunchtime warriors

Working out during lunchtime can break up the day while relieving stress. Before you work out, however, think back a few hours: Did you eat breakfast or skip it? If you ate breakfast, how many hours has it been? That light breakfast eaten in the predawn hours is long gone, and you may feel the effects in the form of low energy once you hit the gym. If you've skipped breakfast altogether, well, by now you know the consequences of that!

If a midday workout is your standard routine, make certain you're up to the challenge by eating a mid-morning, carbohydrate-rich snack. Remember that most people need to eat every 3 to 4 hours. Topping off your tank an hour or so before you exercise will get you through your workout with energy to spare. Once you're finished, don't think skipping lunch will aid in your weight-loss efforts. Replenish carbohydrates, fluid, and protein to refill glycogen

Actively seeking carbs

When it comes to physical activity powered by muscle glycogen stores, there are many variables to consider, such as the size of the individual and intensity of the activity. However, on average, we store enough carbohydrate for only 2 to 3 hours of physical exertion. As long as you eat consistently throughout the day with an eye toward variety and balance of macronutrients (protein, fat, and carbohydrate) and don't skimp on calories, you'll have plenty of fuel to get you through your daily workout. Unless you're participating in an ultra-endurance distance sporting event, you don't have to worry about running out of fuel completely!

stores, cool and rehydrate your body, and begin to rebuild muscle. All are equally important for your next workout!

Evening exercisers

If you save your workout until the end of the day, it's particularly important to do a fuel check. It may have been hours since you last ate. Just as you wouldn't expect your car to run without gas, you can't expect your body to perform optimally with-

out fuel. Evening exercisers need to be diligent about their food intake all day long. A large coffee and pastry for breakfast, and a salad and diet soft drink for lunch will barely get you through the day, much less an evening distance run or toug h aerobics class. If you've added strength training to your workout routine and feel frustrated that you're not as strong or defined as you'd like, you may not be eating enough calories, including fat, protein, and carbohydrate. Carbohydrates aren't reserved for runners only!

Consider eating five to six times during the day (meals and snacks), and include protein and carbohydrate each time. This eating strategy helps fill in nutrient gaps, maintain a steady blood sugar level, and won't leave you empty at the end of the day when your workout depends on adequate calories.

For some people, foods with a high glycemic index may produce a quick surge in blood sugar followed by a quick drop to a too-low level. Use those foods in moderation before and during a workout. High-GI foods typically are best saved for replenishing glycogen after a workout.

Better-Carb Eating: At Home and When Dining Out

Applying what you've learned about choosing healthy carbs to home cooking as well as restaurant meals is much easier than you may think. In this section we'll show you just how quick and simple it is to plan meals and alter recipes using the best carb ingredients. And we'll give you insight into making the healthiest carbohydrate choices when dining out, too.

Although it's tempting to try, don't expect to overhaul your diet and change all your eating habits overnight. Experts say it takes 21 days for new behavior to become a habit. What you want to do is gradually change from your old ways to your new smart-carb way of eating. That way your dietary changes are more likely to stick.

HOME CARB COOKERY

Nothing beats sitting down to a home-cooked meal. Yet at the end of a hectic day, the drive-through can be awfully appealing. When you're the cook, though, you're in control. You choose the dish that sounds most appetizing, and you pick the amount and type of ingredients used. The availability of seasonal produce and other ingredients, personal preference, and health and nutrition concerns are all considerations, and you're free to address any or all of them when you're wearing the apron.

Don't feel constrained by a recipe. Use it as an outline, then improvise. Just be aware that baking is a bit trickier because the outcome is much more dependent on correct proportions of ingredients. But even in baking there's room for improvisation, particularly when it comes to boosting nutrition.

Starting with a whole-grain tutorial, and moving on to the inside story on beans, fruits, and vegetables, we'll add some inspiration, throw in a few tricks for tempting picky eaters, and voila—you'll be the star of your own healthy kitchen. Sit back and get ready to collect the compliments!

Switching tip

It's common to experience resistance from family members, or even your own taste buds, when making ingredient changes. Remember when you made the switch from whole milk to skim? You probably thought you'd never get used to the flavor or the mouthfeel. However, you've most likely reached the point where you can't imagine downing a glass of whole milk! Substituting whole-wheat pasta and brown rice can take you down a similar path. One of the best ways to overcome resistance is to make the switch gradually. Try mixing two-thirds white and one-third whole-wheat pasta, and do the same with rice. Over time, decrease the amount of white and increase the whole grain. Some pasta manufacturers have even begun marketing pasta made from $\frac{1}{2}$ white flour and $\frac{1}{2}$ whole-wheat flour, an excellent choice for those just starting to make the switch.

Whole-grain primer

Most of us tend to stick to the same old grains. But if you venture beyond the usual white rice and whole-wheat bread, you'll find a whole new world of delicious and nutritious grains. There are plenty of tasty discoveries to be made. The following list will get you started.

AMARANTH. A lesser-known grain, amaranth is high in protein and a good source of calcium. Most often eaten as cooked cereal, it's also available as flour and as an ingredient in ready-to-eat cereals. Add extra nutrition to baked goods by substituting 10 to 20 percent of the all-purpose flour in recipes with amaranth flour.

BARLEY. This is a hardy, nutty-tasting grain that dates back to the Stone Age. Barley is available in a variety of forms, including hulled, pearled, flakes, grits, and even quick cooking. Toss a large handful of the quick-cooking variety into a pot of chili or bean soup to add protein, iron, and fiber.

BUCKWHEAT. Often offered as a pancake selection on restaurant menus, buckwheat is technically an herb of the buckwheat family. Originating in Asia, where for thousands of years people have eaten noodles made from buckwheat flour, it can be found in a variety of baked goods including breads, muffins, cookies, crackers, and waffles. Toasted buckwheat groats (the hulled, crushed kernels) are known as kasha. Combine buckwheat with other grains and serve as a healthy side dish or pilaf, or add the flour to baked goods.

BULGUR. A form of wheat, this nutritious grain is a staple in Middle Eastern/Mediterranean cooking. In fact, bulgur forms the basis of tabbouleh, a delicious Middle Eastern dish. Bulgur is made from steamed or boiled wheat kernels

(also called wheat berries) that first have been dried, then crushed. Combine hot, cooked bulgur with oatmeal and dried fruit for a powerhouse breakfast; mix with brown rice, herbs, and olive oil to make a pilaf; or add cooked bulgur to ground beef or turkey for burgers or meat loaf.

BROWN RICE. The unmistakable brown color, distinct nutty flavor, and chewy texture of brown rice are the result of removing only the inedible outer husk. Brown rice takes a bit longer to cook than white, so cook up extra, and store it in the freezer. As a quick, convenient alternative, buy instant brown rice; it cooks up in only 10 minutes. It's just as nutritious as long-cooking brown rice; it's just precooked to decrease cooking time. A good source of fiber and vitamin E, brown rice can be substituted anywhere you would use white rice.

CORN. Yes, corn is a grain. From the most basic corn on the cob to grits, cornmeal, corn flour, or popcorn, this Native American staple is fiber rich and contributes small amounts of iron and vitamin C to the diet. Canned, frozen, or

Bulk tryouts

Most health food stores and now even many mainstream grocers have some foods available for bulk purchase. Bulk foods are usually stored in barrels or plastic containers; you simply scoop the amount you need into plastic bags that are provided. They're weighed at the checkout register. Grains and beans are two foods commonly sold in bulk. This is a wonderful opportunity for cooks who need a small amount of a particular ingredient for a recipe. Purchasing only the amount you need prevents wasting any extra you don't use. It's also a terrific way to try new varieties of the foods we're discussing here. You can experiment to find your favorites while buying as much or as little as you'd like.

fresh, it's unbelievably versatile. Corn mixes well with any type of canned bean (black and pinto are especially tasty), enhances many foods as a quick side dish, and can be tossed into soups, salads, and muffins with equal ease.

COUSCOUS. Not technically a whole grain, couscous is a type of pasta made from semolina (coarsely ground durum wheat). However, couscous is available in a whole-wheat version that provides protein, fiber, and small amounts of iron. Due to its exceptionally quick cooking time (5 minutes!) it's a wonderful way to add a good source of healthy carbohydrates to the diet. Use as a base for salads and casseroles or cook in vegetable or chicken broth and serve as a speedy, flavorful side dish.

MILLET. Commonly sold as bird food in the United States, millet is a crunchy, nutty-flavored grain that is a staple in other parts of the world, especially Asia and Africa. Millet swells enormously when cooked, requiring about five parts water to one part millet. Incredibly nutritious,

it provides protein, fiber, potassium, vitamin B1, and iron. Millet is often eaten as a hot cereal and is delicious in breads, muffins, pilaf, pancakes, soups, and stews.

OATS. Full of phytochemicals, not to mention good taste, oats are one of the most popular grains. They're extremely versatile and are used in cookies, muffins, cakes, breads, and breakfast cereals. Oats contain soluble fiber, a powerful cholesterol-reducing agent. They come in several varieties, all relatively easy to locate at your local grocery store. When serving oatmeal for breakfast, it's best to choose the least processed variety; flavored instant oatmeal contains added sugar and sodium.

QUINOA. A staple of the Incas, quinoa is one of the oldest cultivated grains. It's a nutritional powerhouse because it contains all the essential amino acids. That makes it equivalent in protein content to beef or eggs yet without cholesterol or saturated fat. Quinoa is lower in carbohydrate than most grains and can be used in the same manner as rice. Quinoa looks like a tiny bead but expands to nearly four times its size when cooked. Use it as a base for salads or as a side dish, or add quinoa flour to baked goods.

RYE. Rye can be purchased as a cereal grain (most often in combination with other grains), as berries (similar to wheat berries), and as flour. You'll find plenty of baked goods, including bread, bagels, and rolls, that

contain rye. Often referred to as a "peasant grain," rye is a hardy plant that can grow practically anywhere. Lower in gluten (the protein that helps bread rise) than most grains, rye flour is normally combined with a high-protein flour when used in bread making. Use rye flour in your baking, and seek out rye breads and other baked goods that include rye.

SPELT. Another ancient cereal grain that is native to southern Europe, spelt is a cousin to wheat. Spelt can be used any place you would use regular wheat, yet due to its higher protein content, even people with wheat allergies can include spelt in their diet. Spelt is often combined with other grains in hot cereal and granola mixtures or used in salads, soups, and casseroles. In baking, spelt flour can be used in place of wheat flour.

TRITICALE. A hybrid mixture of wheat and rye, triticale has a nutty sweet flavor. Found in many forms, including whole berries, flakes, flour, and cereal, triticale is an extremely nutritious grain. Use it in a variety of dishes, from casseroles to pilaf. Lower in gluten, triticale flour is best used in combination with wheat flour when baking to produce a more lightly textured product.

The magic bean

There are many parts of the world where it's unheard of for a day to go by without eating beans in one form or another. Other cultures include beans in unusual ways, such as grinding them into flour to be used in a variety of indigenous foods. Even in the United States, there are particular regions as well as cultures where bean dishes are more common than others. For instance, the main ingredients in the southern classic Hoppin' John are black-eyed peas and rice. Season-

ings and various other ingredients used in it are as diverse as the cook stirring the pot. The vegetarian and vegan community wholeheartedly embrace beans and the unparalleled plant-based, protein-rich nutrition they contribute to a diet that excludes meat. But vegetarians and folks with southern roots needn't be the only beneficiaries of these nutrition powerhouses. Without question, we need to include beans on our list of healthy carbohydrates.

There are literally hundreds of different varieties of beans. If you can, sample them all! Here's an overview of some of the most common kinds.

ADZUKI (aka Azuki and Aduki). A cousin to the larger red kidney bean, Adzuki beans likely originated in China and Japan. Adzukis are sweet and commonly used in desserts. They can be found in Asian markets, where they're sold either whole or powdered.

Celebrating with beans

Throughout the world, all sorts of holidays and other momentous occasions are celebrated with food starring the humble bean. For instance, a southern New Year's Day meal isn't complete without a dish of black-eyed peas symbolizing luck and prosperity in the new year. Often the beans are served as Hoppin' John, but could just as easily be found as a side dish on their own. In Japanese culture, black soybeans served during the new year celebration are for energy and to be industrious in the coming year. During the celebration of Chinese New Year, dried bean curd (tofu) symbolizes happiness.

BLACK (aka turtle bean or frijoles negros). Native to South and Central America, black beans are a staple in Latin American dishes. Cuba, Puerto Rico, Brazil, and Spain all boast a wide variety of delicious dishes starring this beautiful, oval-shaped bean. Black beans form the base of dips and salads, as well as the classic black bean soup.

CANNELLINI. Less flavorful than their cousin, the red kidney bean, cannellinis are often used in minestrone soup and other Italian dishes.

CRANBERRY (aka shell bean, Roman, October, borlotti). Often used in Italian dishes, this oval-shaped bean is streaked with red, both inside and out. They have a delicious flavor, often described as earthy or nutty, and are available fresh during the summer or dried throughout the remainder of the year.

GREAT NORTHERN. This large white bean has a slightly nutty, intriguingly distinctive, mild, delicate flavor. It makes a delicious base for herb-flavored bean spreads and is superb in pasta dishes, particularly those that include green vegetables such as broccoli. Great northerns are also commonly used in baked beans and added to soups. They can serve as a substitute in most recipes that call for navy beans or any white bean.

LENTILS. Lentils are often used as a versatile meat substitute and star in a variety of salads, soups, stews, dips, spreads, and ethnic dishes such as East Indian *dal*. Most supermarkets carry the standard brown lentil and occasionally the red and yellow varieties as well. Middle Eastern or East Indian markets are sure to carry the more unusual varieties. Lentils are delicious served whole, puréed, or mixed with vegetables and spices.

LIMA. Succotash (a mix of corn and lima beans), the side dish with a fun name, is a high-protein, traditional way to serve lima beans. Called butter beans in the South, lima beans have a pale green color and slight kidney shape. The bean was named for Lima, Peru, where it was discovered in the early 1500s. They're available fresh from June to September and frozen at any time of the year. They make a great side dish and are occasionally used in soups.

NAVY (aka Boston, Yankee, pea bean). This small, white version of the Great Northern bean has been served as a versatile staple by the U.S. Navy since the mid-1800s. Navy beans are often used by commercial producers of many different brands of pork and beans. Navy beans require long, slow cooking, making them the perfect addition to a long-simmering pot of soup on the stove top.

PINTO. Pinto means "painted" in Spanish, a fitting description for this artistic-looking staple of Mexico and the American Southwest. Refried beans and chili con carne are both made with pinto beans. They're also often served with rice and found in dips, soups, and stews.

RED KIDNEY. Kidney beans are a perennial favorite. They're full flavored with a soft texture and a kidney shape, from which the bean derives its name. They retain this distinctive shape even during long periods of cooking time, hence their popularity in chili and other soups. Chili con carne or red beans and rice wouldn't be the same without kidney beans, but they're also found in sandwiches, dips, the ubiquitous three-bean salad, and salad bars around the country.

SOYBEAN. You would be hard-pressed to find a more nutritious bean, particularly when it comes to protein. Soybeans are an economical source of protein, providing all of the amino acids typically found in animal products without the saturated fat and cholesterol. Soybeans have been cultivated in China for thousands of years and are one of the leading crops grown in the Midwest. Foods such as tofu, tempeh, miso, and edemame are all soybean based. In fact, edemame is the Japanese name for green soybeans. In their almost infinite color combinations of red, yellow, green, brown, and black, soybeans can be used like any other bean in soups, stews, casseroles, and dips.

Fantastic fruit

A glance at the glycemic index lists fruit in all three GI categories: low, moderate, and high. However, there's no question that all fruits are unbeatable sources of many vitamins, including C and A, as well as fiber and phytonutrients. While fruits have a high percentage of simple sugars, that's no reason to leave these readily available sources of healthy carbohydrate out of the diet.

Fruits eaten whole contribute all of the good things listed above, yet there's another compelling reason to include whole versions. Many nutrition researchers agree that the "synergy" of whole foods such as fruits, vegetables, whole grains, and beans is what appears to confer protection against cancer and other diseases. Synergy is the interactive way vitamins, minerals, phytochemicals, and other components work to produce a much stronger effect than they do individually. Including whole fruits in your diet on a regular basis ensures you'll get the optimal health benefits in a delicious package.

It's easy to toss an apple or banana into a lunch box or briefcase, but this can get boring. Increase your intake of whole fruits by featuring them in a wide variety of entrées and desserts. You can even serve them disguised as fun foods. Rest assured that the antioxidant power of blueberries is not what people think about as they dip into a dish of warm blueberry cobbler. It's not that healthy foods aren't fun on their own, but if you're feeding a reluctant crowd or trying to pad the diets of your loved ones with a few more healthy foods, a little enticement can work in your favor.

Vary the fruit you use depending on the season. For instance, eat pumpkin, apples, and cranberries in the fall and nectarines and blueberries in summer. Start with a fruit base, then use tried-and-true tricks to make the recipe as nutritious as possible: Substitute low- or nonfat dairy products for full-fat varieties, use whole-wheat flour in place of white flour, and substitute applesauce for some of the fat. You can even cut the sugar by ⅓ without negatively impacting the outcome.

Use the following list of tasty ideas as a starting place to add more fruit to your family's diet. You're only limited by your imagination!

- Cobblers
- Crumbles
- Layered fruit and yogurt
- Baked apples
- Frozen fruit ice pops
- Fruit soups
- Sautéed bananas
- Fruit puddings (pumpkin, banana)
- Add dried fruits to drop cookies
- Bar cookies filled with figs or other fruit
- Fruit tarts
- Fruit-filled crepes
- Fruit smoothies
- Blueberry/apple/raspberry pancakes
- French toast topped with fruit compote
- Fruit-based muffins
- Fruit breads (banana, pumpkin, cranberry, etc.)
- Fruit dipped in chocolate (strawberries, apricots, oranges, cherries, etc.)

Label lingo

You can trust the nutrient content claims that describe the level of a nutrient in a food product (terms such as *free, high,* and *low)* or that compare the level of a nutrient in a food to that of another food (terms such as *more, reduced,* and *lite).* These claims are regulated by the Food and Drug Administration (FDA) to ensure validity. Any nutrient claim that the FDA has not defined is prohibited.

But you need to be careful about terms on labels that intimate the product is low carb. Currently, the term *low carb* has not been defined by the FDA. Food manufacturers and restauranteurs are using terms like "carb aware," "carb smart," and "carb friendly" to give the impression that the food is low carb without making the actual claim. It helps them boost sales while still complying with FDA regulations. Some have also interpreted the rule to mean that *low carb* can be

used as a descriptor, which technically might not be considered a nutrient claim.

Food manufacturers also mislead the public by placing a low-carb or carb-friendly label on a food that has always been low in carbohydrate. For instance, ranch salad dressing is naturally low in carbohydrate. A two-tablespoon serving of one brand-name ranch dressing contains only two grams of carbohydrate. But another brand offers a low-carb ranch dressing with zero carbs. The difference in carbs isn't significant, but the difference to your pocketbook may be. Products that claim to have fewer or no carbs often cost more than their regular counterparts.

Variations on veggies

The idea of synergy applies to vegetables as well as fruits, but when serving these nutrition powerhouses you may need to disguise them using the "fun food" approach. People are very particular about their vegetables, from which varieties they prefer to preparation methods to size and shape. Eating more vegetables is so important that you should pull out all the stops to make them delicious. If the only way you'll eat green veggies is to sauté them in a bit of butter, do it! If you love cauliflower and broccoli nestled under cheese sauce, just try to find the healthiest version of cheese sauce you can and be judicious in the amount you use. The benefits of eating more vegetables far outweighs any bit of topping you might add. For some, nothing beats the flavor of unadorned vegetables, where their true flavors stand on their own. Particularly during the summer when fresh vegetables are at their peak, try to experiment with steaming, microwaving, and munching veggies raw.

A discussion of carbohydrate and vegetables would be incomplete without touching on the starchy varieties. These complex carbohydrates are often avoided because "they turn to sugar" after you eat them. While that's true, as all carbohydrates break down into glucose (a form of sugar) following digestion, that doesn't make them unhealthy. Where folks get into trouble is by eating huge servings of less healthy versions of starchy vegetables, such as super-size orders of french fries. Healthy people shouldn't avoid starchy vegetables. They should be included in the diet as a solid source of energy and because of their many beneficial nutrients. If you're managing diabetes, be sure to count the carbohydrate in these foods in your daily total to help keep blood sugar in line.

As far as the glycemic index goes, keep in mind that starchy vegetables are rarely eaten on their own. It's not too often that you sit down to a huge bowl of plain mashed potatoes. If you've monitored your own reaction to these high-GI foods and find your blood sugar surging, then plummeting, eat smaller portions and always accompany them with a source of protein. Complement them with double helpings of nonstarchy vegetables. Include them in other dishes as well, such as muffins, breads, or burritos, where you'll still score the nutrition benefits.

Starchy vegetables:

- Potatoes
- Corn
- Green peas
- Sweet potato
- Yam
- Winter squash

ADAPTING NEW AND EXISTING RECIPES

Take a look through some of your favorite recipes. We all have an old standby that's foolproof, quick to throw together, and requested often. Could any of these tried-and-true dishes use a healthy-carbohydrate makeover? What about new recipes you'd like to try? Here's how you can make those home-cooked favorites carb friendly.

Breadcrumbs or crushed cereal toppings and fillers

Recipes that call for breadcrumbs and/or crushed cereal use them in a couple of ways. They're either sprinkled on top to add a crunchy texture or mixed into the main recipe to add bulk or holding/forming power. If you purchase ready-made breadcrumbs, it may be difficult to find anything other

Spotting carbohydrate

Do you think you can spot all of the carbohydrate in foods just by reading an ingredient label? It seems so simple: Flour or sugar scream carbohydrate. But carbohydrates go by many other names, so if you're looking to cut down on them it's helpful to know what to look for on a food label.

All of the following ingredients are carbohydrates. When perusing a product label, check to see if any of these appear on it. If they do, look to see whether they're one of the first ingredients (which means it's a main ingredient) or one of the last (which means that little of it is used). Then you can judge whether the product fits into your healthy carb plan.

Cane syrup
Corn starch
Corn syrup
Dextrose
Fructose
Golden syrup
High fructose corn syrup
Honey
Invert sugar
Jaggery
Lactose
Maple syrup
Milk
Molasses

Pulled sugar
Rock sugar
Sorghum
Spun sugar
Sucrose
Treacle

than white bread as the base. Whether the recipe calls for a small sprinkling or a larger measured amount, whole-grain crumbs are a better choice since they contain some fiber and additional nutrients. You can make your own by tossing the heels of whole-grain bread into the food processor (many people throw these out anyway). Give them a whirl and store in plastic freezer bags or containers for future use. When a recipe calls for breadcrumbs, you can add them directly from the freezer (no need to thaw) or mix in a variety of herbs and spices or other flavorings as dictated by the recipe. If you're trying to reduce carbohydrate even further, try mixing chopped nuts and breadcrumbs. This works best for coating foods rather than as a filler. For cereal toppings, use a high-fiber (at least five grams of fiber per serving) cereal rather than a variety that contains only one gram or less. Unless you're preparing a dessert-type dish, be sure the cereal is unsweetened.

Pasta dishes

This may seem like an obvious place to make a healthy carb change, but it's easy to get into the habit of always doing things the same way because they've always been done that way. In fact, many people don't even consider substituting whole-grain pasta for white-flour pasta just because they never have. But it only requires a bit of forethought. It's easier than ever to find whole-wheat pasta in a wide variety of shapes. Whatever the pasta dish, from macaroni and cheese to linguini and clam sauce, there's no need to ban it from your dinner table; just use whole-wheat pasta in place of the white. Regardless of the type of pasta you use, refrain from eating excessive portion sizes. Serve pasta in smaller, salad-size bowls, and round out the meal with extra vegetables and a salad.

Rice dishes

Any dish that calls for rice—unless it's something unique such as sushi—can accommodate the substitution of brown rice. Pay attention to cooking times, as brown rice takes longer to cook than white. Be sure to allow for such adjustments.

Tortillas

Whether cradling savory burrito fillings or the contents of a tempting taco, or serving main duty in any number of vegetable- or meat-filled wraps, tortillas lend themselves well to a variety of dishes. Corn and whole-wheat tortillas both contain more fiber and nutrients than the white flour variety, and they're getting easier to find even on the shelves of mainstream grocery stores. Corn tortillas aren't normally made with fat. But when buying any type of tortilla other than corn, scan the ingredient list for shortening or lard and only buy tortillas that contain neither.

Bread

In recipes that call for bread, such as an egg-rich strata or baked French toast, substitute 100 percent whole-grain bread for the kind you usually use. Just like substituting whole-wheat pasta for white, you need to plan ahead to make the substitution; otherwise you'll just use the same white bread you've always used.

SUMMING IT UP

Cooking with healthy carbohydrates really comes down to including plenty of four main ingredients: whole, intact grains; legumes (dried beans of any variety); vegetables; and fruits. These foods (with the exception of a few varieties of fruit) naturally score low on the glycemic index rating, so they're kind to blood sugar levels, and they help you feel full and provide vitamins, minerals, and phyto-chemicals.

Many of the popular low-carb diets push excessive amounts of protein complemented by only small amounts (if any) of good carbs. You may be tempted to try one of these diet plans if you've been living on large quantities of processed carbo-

hydrate foods and have experienced the dramatic energy dips, uncontrollable cravings for sweets, and weight gain associated with that kind of diet. Instead, try substituting healthier carbohydrate choices and monitor how your body responds—you'll probably find you feel much better! Pair moderate portions of lean cuts of red meat, poultry, fish, or plant-based proteins such as soy or legumes with plenty of veggies and whole grains, and you'll be consuming less unhealthy cholesterol and saturated fat as well.

Many of the carbohydrate choices people grab on the run or include in ready-to-eat, grab-and-go meals are high in sugar, low in fiber, and loaded with additives and/or preservatives. By cutting out these foods and replacing them with the foods we talked about above, many people will experience weight loss, maintain stable blood sugar levels, and manage and possibly prevent a multitude of diseases.

HEALTHY CARB CHOICES WHEN DINING OUT

It's easy to monitor what ends up on your plate and in your mouth when you're cooking at home.

Low carb, not low cal

Does eating low carb equal eating low calorie? In a word—no! The low-carb foods crowding supermarket shelves and highlighted on restaurant menus still have calories. Many people discovered during the '90s low-fat, no-fat craze that it's possible to eat fat-free cookies and still get fat! So it goes with low- and no-carb foods. A large chicken Caesar salad (without the croutons of course) is absolutely low carb, but it can still pack close to 1,000 calories. In today's sedentary world any extra calories, regardless of where they come from, can lead to weight gain. It also pays to read labels carefully: Look for the small print that can clarify misleading information related to portion size and carbohydrate amount.

Dining out presents new challenges. Many restaurants, though, have begun to pay attention to diet trends and help customers eat more healthfully. You'll find some menu choices marked with special icons designating healthier choices. And some restaurants have begun to offer low-carb options. Just remember, what you want to do is include more healthy carbohydrates in your diet, not eliminate most carbohydrates.

A few tips to keep in mind when scanning menus for healthy carbs. Meat, poultry, and seafood do not contain carbohydrate—none whatsoever. The same goes for most types of cheeses. But even those cheeses that do have carbohydrate, such as feta, have very small amounts. Keep cholesterol and saturated fat levels in check by ordering lean cuts of red meat, choosing poultry and fish more often, and limiting the amount of cheese.

Dishes that are heavy in animal protein and smothered in cream sauce or cheese may be low in carbohydrate, but they're certainly not heart healthy.

Instead order dishes that have more vegetables—or order more vegetables as side dishes—since vegetables naturally contain very low amounts of carbohydrates. And don't shy away from fruit: The carbohydrates in fruit come with lots of nutrients. Whole-grain and bean-based dishes provide fiber, protein, and healthy carbs. And as always, keep portion sizes in check. When it comes to weight gain, it's not the number of carbohydrate grams in a meal that's important, it's how many calories you take in. If you consume more calories than you need, you will gain weight.

Asian

Whether you opt for Japanese, Chinese, or Thai, Asian restaurants are a mecca for healthy carbohydrate dining. Many of the dishes are built around seafood, vegetables, and soy protein (such as tofu), and the chances of finding noodles made from whole grains or alternatives to white flour are much greater. Some Chinese restaurants even offer brown rice instead of white.

If sushi is one of your favorites, don't worry about the small amount of white rice accompanying the fish. The protein and heart-healthy fats in the fish slow down the absorption of the carbohydrate, and the total amount of rice isn't that significant unless you eat sushi by the boatload. Choose dishes that are vegetable-heavy, with small amounts of protein added for flavor. If you've wanted to taste tofu but were never quite sure how to prepare it, Asian restaurants are the place to give it a try. You can experience this wonderfood prepared in a variety of delicious ways while reaping the health benefits of soy protein: fiber, healthy carbohydrates, and plenty of phytonutrients.

Eclectic American

If you're not a particularly adventurous eater or live in an area with few ethnic restaurant choices, good old American standbys probably make up the majority of your meals. If you're following any of the fad low-carb/no-carb diets, it's relatively simple to order a large portion of meat with a salad or a side of vegetables. Unfortunately, you'll most likely get tired of eating this way long before your weight has settled (and stays) at a number that makes you happy. There are healthier ways to cut back on carbs. Use these pointers to include the carbohydrates so crucial for energy and overall good health while maintaining the variety so critical to success and changing eating habits for the better.

ORDER RED MEAT LESS OFTEN. You've heard this before but may not know why it's recommended. Red meat has the same amount of protein as poultry and fish, but (depending on the cut) it has much more saturated fat and cholesterol. Poultry and fish do have cholesterol, but in lower amounts. We make all the cholesterol we need in our livers, so try not to add excess cholesterol in your diet. Lower-fat cuts of beef

include eye of the round, top round, round tip, top sirloin, bottom round, top loin, and tenderloin. It may be difficult to locate these cuts on restaurant

Low-carb menu madness

Many restaurants have embraced the low-carb revolution and now offer low-carb menu selections. Sometimes the change brings superior nutritional choices. That's the case if a restaurant's take on low carb is to pair a protein food (such as lean meat, poultry, fish, or legumes) with vegetables. Unfortunately, too many restaurants interpret low carb to mean extra large protein portions smothered in cheese and high-fat sauce served with a tiny side of vegetables or burgers wrapped in lettuce instead of a bun.

Don't get taken in by "new" low-carb menu selections that aren't new at all. Foods such as bacon, eggs, ham, and sausage are menu standards and have always been low carb. Meat and eggs just don't contain any carbohydrate. In some cases, the only difference between an old menu item and a new low-carb item is that high-carb foods such as potatoes and bread are swapped for a vegetable or another high-protein food such as cottage cheese. In these cases, restaurants are responding to customer ordering trends such as requests to hold the pancakes, toast, or potatoes that accompany egg dishes. There's nothing wrong with that. In fact, a veggie omelet accompanied by a double order of tomatoes or grilled chicken with heaping sides of vegetables are both healthy choices. The swapping is only an issue when restaurants take advantage of consumers by charging more for menu items tagged "low carb" than they do for the regular version of that item. Usually there's no reason to charge more for these specially marked offerings.

menus, so if they're not available, order the smallest, leanest cut you can find (or poultry, fish, or seafood in its place), and concentrate on always serving the "skinny" cuts at home.

HAVE SAUCES AND DRESSINGS SERVED ON THE SIDE. They add flavor and very few carbs but lots of calories and saturated fat. Use the "dip" method: Dip (not dunk!) your fork into the sauce or dressing before spearing a bite of food to get the full flavor of the sauce in smaller, less damaging doses.

DOUBLE UP ON VEGETABLES AND SALADS. Instead of having protein as the center of your meal, push it to the side (unless of course it's vegetable-based protein such as soy or beans), and load up on green, yellow, orange, and red foods. Don't skimp on the veggies! They're naturally low carb, full of flavor and nutrients, and guaranteed to fill you up, not out. Vegetables don't have to be flavorless; just avoid drowning them in butter, cheese, or cream sauce. Look for (or ask for) vegetables that are roasted, sautéed with

Completely vegetarian

The diet in many other countries is vegetarian based, but they're not missing out on essential nutrients. Far from it! Vegetarian diets can easily supply all the nutrients the body needs. Vegetarian diets are rich in fiber and complex carbohydrates from vegetables, fruits, whole grains, and beans. And vegetarians get their protein and fat from alternative sources such as soy, beans, eggs, dairy products, and oils. Although it was once thought that vegetarians need to carefully combine alternative protein sources at each meal to make "complete" protein, we now know that's not necessary. Vegetarians just need to eat a variety of vegetables and whole grains on a daily basis. The amino acids from all the foods work together to supply adequate protein.

herbs, prepared with olive oil, or prepared with garlic. If the dish you're ordering doesn't come with a vegetable you like, scan the menu for one you do. Ask the server to substitute a different veggie from another dish. Restaurants are usually more than happy to oblige.

DON'T MAKE BREAD "THE MEAL BEFORE THE MEAL." You don't have to forgo the bread basket, just don't overdo it. If you just can't stop at one piece, select the darkest, most hearty-looking piece in the basket and ask the waitstaff to remove the rest. Eat your piece of bread when you most enjoy it—on its own while waiting for your dinner, as an accompaniment to your salad, or with your main meal. Then savor every bite. As a rule, foccacia-type breads are higher in fat and calories. The plainer the item, the fewer calories, fat, sodium, and other additives there are.

DON'T SKIP DESSERT. There's no reason to skip dessert, but there's also no reason to consume a piece of chocolate cake large enough to feed several people. You need a strategy. Remember the tips from earlier in this chapter about including fruit as dessert? Now's the time to use them. First, scan the menu for anything that's fruit-based—even if it's pie. You can always eat just the fruit and the bottom crust. Sorbet with fruit, a fruit crumble or crisp, or even an apple tart all contribute some nutrients. And they're all healthier than a bowl of chocolate mousse, which is primarily fat and sugar. Second tip: share!

Indian

Whether you've been dying to try Indian food or have long been a fan, healthy carbohydrate selections await. The third most popular cuisine in the world is much more than curry dishes, the first dish that comes to the mind of many Westerners when considering Indian food. The rich, complex blends of spices add the depth and flavor so unique and crucial to Indian cuisine. Vegetarian dishes are plentiful, particularly in southern India. Meat dishes are more common in the north, particularly the healthfully prepared tandoori chicken, fish, and meats, which are marinated in herbs and baked quickly at high temperatures in a clay oven. Dishes prepared with yogurt, lentils, and flours made from ground beans such as garbanzo; roasted meats, chicken, or fish with vegetable sauces; and an abundance of fruit, both tropical and temperate, are all good carbohydrate choices.

Italian

When dining à la Italiano, the bread basket and huge servings of pasta are the bad guys. As we've already pointed out, foods made from refined white flour are quickly broken down and absorbed into the bloodstream. In fact, white bread, pasta, and potatoes are often the first carb foods to be slashed on low-carb diets due to their high glycemic index and "bad carb" status. But how often do you go to an Italian restaurant and eat just plain bread and pasta? Remember, carbohydrate-based foods that are eaten in combination with protein or fat enter the bloodstream more slowly.

If you're in the mood for pasta, first ask if the restaurant serves the whole-wheat variety. This could be a long shot, but if you're dining in an urban area or more upscale restaurant, you're more likely to find this option. If not, select a protein-based entrée, preferably chicken or fish; grilled, sautéed, or steamed vegetables; and a salad and a small side order of pasta. Stick to olive oil or tomato-based sauces, and skip the cream/butter/cheese-based types. You'll satisfy your craving for pasta without overdoing it and round out the meal with heart-healthy protein and lots of antioxidants and fiber.

Mediterranean

Mediterranean countries such as Greece, Morocco, Spain, Turkey, Italy, and France (particularly the southern region) have long been studied by nutrition researchers. That's because these countries boast a cuisine that some say is unrivaled in its nutritional superiority. The diet is rich in olive oil, vegetables, and herbs, and it uses only the freshest ingredients prepared as simply as possible. This diet baffles many Americans, though, because of its high fat content. How can a diet that is close to 40 percent fat produce such good health and longevity and have a reputation for causing fewer heart attacks? The secret is that much of the fat in the Mediterranean diet comes from high-quality, heart-healthy olive oil. The cuisine also includes fish, rice and other whole grains, hearty breads, olives, small amounts of cheese, nuts, and red wine, as well as

PLAN ON CARB SWAPPING

Now that we've had such a thorough discussion of carbohydrates, it's time to put what you've learned into practice. Here's an example of what one full day of meals and snacks would look like if it were built around healthy carb choices. We've compared the new improved version to a day that includes less healthy carbs—see where your diet fits and where there's room for improvement!

Old Carbs	New Carbs
BREAKFAST	
1 cherry Danish	100% whole-wheat bagel with peanut butter
12 ounces orange juice	6 ounces orange juice
Coffee	Coffee
MID-MORNING SNACK	
½ jelly donut	Low-fat yogurt
Whole-grain crackers	Whole-grain crackers
LUNCH	
Chicken noodle soup	Lentil soup
Small Caesar salad	Small Caesar salad
Iced tea	Whole-grain roll
	Unsweetened iced tea
MID-AFTERNOON SNACK	
Pretzels	Whole-grain pretzels with hummus (bean spread) dip
Cranberry juice	Strawberries
Oatmeal cookie	
DINNER	
Grilled chicken breast	Grilled chicken breast
Baked potato	Brown and wild rice pilaf
Salad	Sautéed broccoli and walnuts
Iced Tea	Spinach salad with mandarin orange slices
	Unsweetened iced tea
SNACK	
Ice cream	Oatmeal cookie
	Fat-free milk

fruit for dessert. The low-stress environment, the importance of gathering with family and friends to enjoy meals, and the reverence for food have also been noted as contributing factors in the good health of people in this region. It's possible that it's the combination of the Mediterranean diet and the Mediterranean lifestyle that promotes good health. Something for all of us to consider!

Mexican

Even though most Mexican restaurants serve white rice, the combination of rice and beans is an unbeatable protein source that is blood sugar friendly. Many restaurants now serve vegetarian refried beans, so if they're available, go for that option to eliminate cholesterol and saturated fat. Healthy carb choices are veggie burritos and chicken, steak, shrimp, or veggie tacos or fajitas (ask for corn tortillas and order the sour cream on the side). The bottomless tortilla chip basket found at every Mexican restaurant is best left untouched. Better yet, ask the waitstaff to remove it unless you can limit yourself to a handful of chips. These restaurants are notorious for offering cheese-smothered dishes, many of which have first been deep-fried: low carb yes, heart healthy no!

Middle Eastern

Middle Eastern restaurants are another wonderful choice for enjoying healthy carbohydrates prepared in the most delectable ways. These restaurants serve lots of beans (legumes) and whole grains such as bulgur and couscous. Lentils often stand in as the main protein in a meal, pushing meat to the side of the plate. Tangy hummus spread (a dip made from garbanzo beans, garlic, olive oil, and sesame paste), tabbouleh (bulgur wheat mixed with tomatoes, parsley, mint, olive oil, and lemon juice), chilled yogurt soup, and rice dishes are just a few of the menu options that fit the carbohydrate profile you're looking for. Food from the Middle East also has a high fiber content, including lots of vegetables and grains that make it extremely filling. The bonus to you? You'll eat smaller portions, leave feeling more than satisfied, and have scrumptious leftovers for tomorrow's lunch!

The Nutrient Counter

Life is full of decisions—

especially when it comes to food. But when you're trying to eat healthier and lose weight, there's more to the decision-making process than figuring out what you're in the mood to eat. Choose well, and your health, your waistline, and your taste buds will all benefit. The nutrient counter will show you how.

Understanding the Nutrient Counter

Wouldn't it be great if all foods came with a nutrition label to guide you? Then you could be certain which were the best carbohydrate choices. Of course, after reading this book you know quite a bit about carbohydrate—definitely enough to tell the difference between empty carbs (those with little nutritional value or fiber) and more nutritious ones.

But that isn't always enough to go on when you're deciding between one food and another. For many foods, the carbohydrate content isn't obvious, nor is the kind of carbohydrate, which is even more important. When you're at the bagel counter and have narrowed your choice to cinnamon raisin or oat bran, do you know which is better?

That's why we've included this nutrient counter. It lists the nutrient values for hundreds of foods with varying amounts of carbs, so you can compare foods side by side. For each food item, the counter lists the number of grams of total carbohydrate, fiber, protein, total fat, and saturated fat in a portion. (While the total carbohydrate value for a food includes its fiber content, we've broken out the number of fiber grams where available so you can see how many of a food's carb grams came from this beneficial and indigestible component.)

Values have been rounded to the nearest whole number. If "Tr" (which stands for trace) appears in a column, it means there's less than half a gram of that nutrient in a single portion of that food. If "NA" appears, that means the value was not available to us. When comparing foods, remember to check the portion sizes listed to be sure you're comparing equal portions of each food.

We've added a new feature to the traditional nutrient counter to help you choose the best carbohydrate foods. We've highlighted good- and better-carbohydrate choices in each food group where applicable. Good choices are highlighted in cream, and better choices are highlighted in green. If a food that contains carbohydrate isn't highlighted, that doesn't mean you shouldn't eat it. You just need to be aware of how it fits into your diet. Just be sure to choose the good and better carbs more often than those that aren't highlighted.

Thank you, Uncle Sam

This nutrient counter was adapted from: U.S. Department of Agriculture, Agricultural Research Service. 2004. USDA Nutrient Database for Standard Reference, Release 16-1. Nutrient Data Laboratory Home Page, http://www.nal.usda.gov/fnic/foodcomp

How did we decide which foods were which? There were no ingredient labels for these foods, so a registered dietitian reviewed the list. She took into account the amount of fiber, the ingredients and the preparation method as indicated by the food name, and the nutrient analysis provided by the U.S. Department of Agriculture (USDA). And she used Food and Drug Administration (FDA) standards for fiber content claims as part of the mix. According to the FDA, a food is considered a "good" source of fiber if it contains 2.5 to 4.9 grams of fiber per serving and "high" in fiber if it contains 5 grams of fiber or more per serving.

Here's an example of how the good and better carb choices were determined. If you compare a slice of pecan pie to a slice of pumpkin pie, you'll see that the pecan pie has more total fiber. You'll also see that the pecan pie is higher in calories, sugar, total fat, and saturated fat—not the best for your waistline or your health. Pumpkin pie, on the other hand, is a significant source of vitamin A and has fewer calories and fat. So if you were choosing the healthier pie, pumpkin would get the vote. As you can see, while fiber content is important and often one of the most quantifiable of the criteria, it is not the only determining factor when picking out the good- and better-carb foods.

As you look through the counter, you'll see that the majority of fruits, vegetables, and legumes are highlighted as "better" carbs. An exception is fruit canned in heavy syrup. It's highlighted as a "good" carb, but you can make it even better by draining and rinsing the syrup off the fruit before eating (or buy fruit in light syrup or juice instead). In addition, when using our list, be certain to compare similar, realistic portion sizes and similar preparation methods. One tablespoon of beans, for instance, doesn't contain much fiber or nutrients, but bump that up to ½ cup—the amount you're more likely to eat—and you've got yourself a "better" carbohydrate!

There will be times when you'll have to make the best choices you can with limited options. For one meal, even for a few days, if you're healthy and not managing a nutrition-related medical condition such as diabetes, less optimal food choices won't make much of a difference to your health. It's how you eat over time that matters. When you don't have the best choices, eat as well as you can, and make up for lost ground at the next opportunity. Remember, eating healthy doesn't mean always eating perfectly!

FOOD, PORTION	TOTAL CARB (G)	FIBER (G)	CALORIES	TOTAL FAT (G)	SAT FAT (G)	PROTEIN (G)	CALCIUM (MG)	SODIUM (MG)
BAKED PRODUCTS								
Bagel, cinnamon-raisin, 3½″ dia	39	2	195	1	Tr	7	13	229
Bagel, egg, 3½″ dia	56	2	292	2	Tr	11	14	530
Bagel, oat bran, 3½″ dia	38	3	181	1	Tr	8	9	360
Bagel, plain (includes onion, poppy, sesame), 3½″ dia	56	2	289	2	Tr	11	19	561
Biscuit, mixed-grain, refrigerated dough, 2½″ dia	21	NA	116	2	1	3	7	295
Biscuit, plain or buttermilk, commercially baked, 2½″ dia	17	Tr	127	6	1	2	17	368
Biscuit, plain or buttermilk, prepared from recipe, 2½″ dia	27	1	212	10	3	4	141	348
Bread, banana, made with margarine, 1 slice	33	1	196	6	1	3	13	181
Bread, cornbread, dry mix, prepared, 1 piece	29	1	188	6	2	4	44	467
Bread, cracked-wheat, 1 slice	12	1	65	1	Tr	2	11	135
Bread crumbs, grated, plain, 1 oz	20	1	112	2	Tr	4	52	208
Bread, egg, 1 slice	19	1	115	2	1	4	37	197
Bread, French or Vienna (includes sourdough), 4″×2½″×1¾″	33	2	175	2	Tr	6	48	390
Bread, Italian, 1 slice	10	1	54	1	Tr	2	16	117
Bread, mixed-grain (includes whole-grain, 7-grain), 1 slice	12	2	65	1	Tr	3	24	127
Bread, oat bran, 1 slice	12	1	71	1	Tr	3	20	122
Bread, oat bran, reduced-calorie, 1 slice	9	3	46	1	Tr	2	13	81
Bread, oatmeal, 1 slice	13	1	73	1	Tr	2	18	162
Bread, pumpernickel, 1 slice	12	2	65	1	Tr	2	18	174
Bread, raisin, 1 slice	14	1	71	1	Tr	2	17	101
Bread, rye, 1 slice	15	2	83	1	Tr	3	23	211

Food, portion	Total Carb (g)	Fiber (g)	Calories	Total Fat (g)	Sat Fat (g)	Protein (g)	Calcium (mg)	Sodium (mg)
Bread, rye, reduced-calorie, 1 slice	9	3	47	1	Tr	2	17	93
Bread stick, plain, 7⅝″×⅝″	7	Tr	41	1	Tr	1	2	66
Bread stuffing, dry mix, 6 oz package	130	5	656	6	1	19	165	2703
Bread, wheat bran, 1 slice	17	1	89	1	Tr	3	27	175
Bread, wheat (includes wheat berry), 1 slice	12	1	65	1	Tr	2	26	133
Bread, white, 1 slice	13	1	67	1	Tr	2	38	170
Bread, white, 1 slice, no crust	6	Tr	32	Tr	Tr	1	18	82
Bread, whole-wheat, 1 slice	13	2	69	1	Tr	3	20	148
Brownies, 1 large square	36	1	227	9	2	3	16	175
Cake, angel food, commercially prepared, ¹⁄₁₂ of 12 oz cake	16	Tr	72	Tr	Tr	2	39	210
Cake, Boston cream pie, ⅙ of pie	39	1	232	8	2	2	21	132
Cake, chocolate, prepared from recipe, no frosting, ¹⁄₁₂ of 9″ dia	51	2	340	14	5	5	57	299
Cake, chocolate, with chocolate frosting, ⅛ of 18 oz cake	35	2	235	10	3	3	28	214
Cake, fruitcake, 1 piece	26	2	139	4	Tr	1	14	116
Cake, gingerbread, prepared from recipe, ⅑ of 8″ square	36	NA	263	12	3	3	53	242
Cake, pineapple upside-down, prepared from recipe, ⅑ of 8″ square	58	1	367	14	3	4	138	367
Cake, pound, ¹⁄₁₀ of cake	15	Tr	116	6	3	2	11	119
Cake, pound, commercially prepared, fat-free, 1 oz	17	Tr	80	Tr	Tr	2	12	97
Cake, shortcake, biscuit-type, prepared from recipe, 1 oz	14	NA	98	4	1	2	58	143
Cake, sponge, ¹⁄₁₂ of 16-oz cake	23	Tr	110	1	Tr	2	27	93
Cake, white, prepared from recipe, no frosting, ¹⁄₁₂ of 9″ dia	42	1	264	9	2	4	96	242

Food, portion	Total Carb (g)	Fiber (g)	Calories	Total Fat (g)	Sat Fat (g)	Protein (g)	Calcium (mg)	Sodium (mg)
Baked Products (cont.)								
Cheesecake, ⅙ of 17-oz cake	20	Tr	257	18	8	4	41	166
Coffee cake, cheese, ⅙ of 16-oz cake	34	1	258	12	4	5	45	258
Coffee cake, fruit, ⅛ cake	26	1	156	5	1	3	23	193
Cookies, animal crackers, 2-oz box	42	1	254	8	2	4	25	224
Cookies, butter, 1 cookie	3	Tr	23	1	1	Tr	1	18
Cookies, chocolate chip, prepared from recipe with butter, 1 cookie	9	NA	78	5	2	1	6	55
Cookies, chocolate chip, soft-type, 1 cookie	9	Tr	69	4	1	1	2	49
Cookies, chocolate sandwich, with creme filling, 1 cookie	7	Tr	47	2	Tr	Tr	3	60
Cookies, chocolate wafers, 1 wafer	4	Tr	26	1	Tr	Tr	2	35
Cookies, coconut macaroons, prepared from recipe, 1 cookie	17	Tr	97	3	3	1	2	59
Cookies, fig bars, 1 cookie	11	1	56	1	Tr	1	10	56
Cookies, fortune, 1 cookie	7	Tr	30	Tr	Tr	Tr	1	22
Cookies, gingersnaps, 1 cookie	5	Tr	29	1	Tr	Tr	5	46
Cookies, graham crackers, chocolate-coated, 1 cracker, 2½" sq	9	Tr	68	3	2	1	8	41
Cookies, ladyfingers, with lemon juice and rind, 1 ladyfinger	7	Tr	40	1	Tr	1	5	16
Cookies, oatmeal, commercially prepared, 1 oz	19	1	128	5	1	2	10	109
Cookies, oatmeal, prepared from recipe, with raisins, 1 cookie	10	NA	65	2	Tr	1	15	81
Cookies, peanut butter, 1 cookie	9	Tr	72	4	1	1	5	62
Cookies, peanut butter sandwich, 1 cookie	9	Tr	67	3	1	1	7	52
Cookies, raisin, soft-type, 1 cookie	10	Tr	60	2	1	1	7	51
Cookies, shortbread, 1 cookie	5	Tr	40	2	Tr	Tr	3	36

Food, portion	Total Carb (g)	Fiber (g)	Calories	Total Fat (g)	Sat Fat (g)	Protein (g)	Calcium (mg)	Sodium (mg)
Cookies, sugar (includes vanilla), 1 cookie	10	Tr	72	3	1	1	3	54
Cookies, sugar, refrigerated dough, 1 rolled cookie	10	Tr	74	4	1	1	14	72
Cookies, vanilla wafers, 1 wafer	4	Tr	28	1	Tr	Tr	2	18
Crackers, cheese, 1 cracker, 1" sq	1	Tr	5	Tr	Tr	Tr	2	10
Crackers, cheese, sandwich-type with peanut butter filling, 1 sandwich	4	Tr	32	2	Tr	1	3	46
Crackers, crispbread, rye, 1 wafer	8	2	37	Tr	Tr	1	3	26
Crackers, matzo, plain, 1 matzo	23	1	111	Tr	Tr	3	4	1
Crackers, matzo, whole-wheat, 1 matzo	22	3	98	Tr	Tr	4	6	1
Crackers, melba toast, plain, 1 round	2	Tr	12	Tr	Tr	Tr	3	25
Crackers, melba toast, wheat, 1 round	4	Tr	19	Tr	Tr	1	2	42
Crackers, rye, wafers, plain, 1 cracker	9	3	37	Tr	Tr	1	4	87
Crackers, saltines (includes oyster, soda, soup), 1 cup	32	1	195	5	1	4	54	586
Crackers, sandwich-type, with peanut butter filling, 1 sandwich	4	Tr	32	2	Tr	1	5	47
Crackers, wheat, 1 cracker	1	Tr	9	Tr	Tr	Tr	1	16
Crackers, whole-wheat, 1 cracker	3	Tr	18	1	Tr	Tr	2	26
Cream puffs, prepared from recipe, with custard filling, 1 puff	30	1	335	20	5	9	86	443
Croissants, butter, 1 croissant	26	1	231	12	7	5	21	424
Croutons, plain, 1 cup	22	2	122	2	Tr	4	23	209
Cupcake, creme-filled, chocolate with frosting, 1 cupcake	30	Tr	188	7	1	2	37	213
Danish pastry, cheese, 1 pastry	26	1	266	16	5	6	25	320
Danish pastry, fruit, 1 pastry	34	1	263	13	3	4	33	251
Doughnuts, cake-type, plain, chocolate-coated or frosted, 1 doughnut	21	1	204	13	3	2	15	184

Food, portion	Total Carb (g)	Fiber (g)	Calories	Total Fat (g)	Sat Fat (g)	Protein (g)	Calcium (mg)	Sodium (mg)
Baked Products (cont.)								
Doughnuts, cake-type, plain, sugared or glazed, 1 doughnut	23	1	192	10	3	2	27	181
Doughnuts, yeast-leavened, glazed (includes honey buns), 1 doughnut	27	1	242	14	3	4	26	205
Doughnuts, yeast-leavened, with creme filling, 1 doughnut	26	1	307	21	5	5	21	263
Doughnuts, yeast-leavened, with jelly filling, 1 doughnut	33	1	289	16	4	5	21	249
English muffins, mixed-grain (includes granola), 1 muffin	31	2	155	1	Tr	6	129	275
English muffins, plain (includes sourdough), 1 muffin	26	2	134	1	Tr	4	99	264
English muffins, raisin-cinnamon (includes apple-cinnamon), 1 muffin	28	2	139	2	Tr	4	84	255
English muffins, wheat, 1 muffin	26	3	127	1	Tr	5	101	218
English muffins, whole-wheat, 1 muffin	27	4	134	1	Tr	6	175	420
French toast, frozen, ready-to-heat, 1 piece	19	1	126	4	1	4	63	292
French toast, prepared from recipe, made with 2% milk, 1 slice	16	NA	149	7	2	5	65	311
Hush puppies, prepared from recipe, 1 hush puppy	10	1	74	3	Tr	2	61	147
Ice cream cones, cake or wafer-type, 1 cone	3	Tr	17	Tr	Tr	Tr	1	6
Ice cream cones, sugar, rolled-type, 1 cone	8	Tr	40	Tr	Tr	1	4	32
Muffins, blueberry, 1 medium	54	3	313	7	2	6	64	505
Muffins, corn, 1 medium	58	4	345	9	2	7	84	589
Muffins, oat bran, 1 medium	55	5	305	8	1	8	71	444
Muffins, plain, prepared from recipe, made with 2% milk, 1 muffin	24	2	169	6	1	4	114	266

Food, portion	Total Carb (g)	Fiber (g)	Calories	Total Fat (g)	Sat Fat (g)	Protein (g)	Calcium (mg)	Sodium (mg)
Pancakes, blueberry, prepared from recipe, 1 pancake, 6" dia	22	NA	171	7	2	5	159	317
Pancakes, buttermilk, prepared from recipe, 1 pancake, 6" dia	22	NA	175	7	1	5	121	402
Pancakes, plain, dry mix, complete, prepared, 1 pancake, 6" dia	28	1	149	2	Tr	4	97	484
Pancakes, plain, prepared from recipe, 1 pancake, 6" dia	22	NA	175	7	2	5	169	338
Pancakes, whole-wheat, dry mix, prepared, 1 pancake, 6" dia	38	4	268	8	2	11	323	738
Phyllo dough, 1 sheet dough	10	Tr	57	1	Tr	1	2	92
Pie, apple, ⅛ of 9" dia	58	NA	411	19	5	4	11	327
Pie, banana cream, ⅛ of 9" dia	47	1	387	20	5	6	108	346
Pie, blueberry, ⅛ of 9" dia	44	1	290	13	2	2	10	406
Pie, chocolate creme, commercially prepared, ¼ of 6" pie	33	2	301	19	5	3	36	135
Pie crust, standard-type, dry mix, prepared, ⅛ of 9" crust	10	Tr	100	6	2	1	12	146
Pie, lemon meringue, ⅙ of 8" pie	53	1	303	10	2	2	63	165
Pie, pecan, ⅙ of 8" pie	65	4	452	21	4	5	19	479
Pie, pumpkin, ⅙ of 8" pie	30	3	229	10	2	4	65	307
PILLSBURY Cinnamon Rolls with Icing, refrigerated dough, 1 serving	24	NA	150	5	1	2	NA	334
Pita, white, 6½" dia	33	1	165	1	Tr	5	52	322
Pita, whole-wheat, 6½" dia	35	5	170	2	Tr	6	10	340
Rolls, dinner, French, 1 roll	19	1	105	2	Tr	3	35	231
Rolls, dinner, oat bran, 1 oz roll	13	1	78	2	Tr	3	28	136
Rolls, dinner, plain, 1 oz roll	14	1	84	2	Tr	2	33	146
Rolls, dinner, pumpernickel, 1 small roll	15	2	78	1	Tr	3	19	159
Rolls, dinner, wheat, 1 oz roll	13	1	76	2	Tr	2	49	95

Food, portion	Total Carb (g)	Fiber (g)	Calories	Total Fat (g)	Sat Fat (g)	Protein (g)	Calcium (mg)	Sodium (mg)
Baked Products *(cont.)*								
Rolls, dinner, whole-wheat, 1 submarine, hoagie roll	48	7	250	4	1	8	100	449
Rolls, hamburger or hot dog, mixed-grain, 1 roll	19	2	113	3	1	4	41	197
Rolls, hamburger or hot dog, plain, 1 roll	21	1	120	2	Tr	4	59	206
Rolls, hard (includes kaiser), 3½" dia	30	1	167	2	Tr	6	54	310
SHAKE 'N' BAKE original recipe, 1 serving	22	NA	106	1	0	2	NA	795
Strudel, apple, 1 piece	29	2	195	8	1	2	11	191
Taco shells, baked, approx 5" dia	8	1	62	3	Tr	1	21	49
Toaster pastries, brown-sugar-cinnamon, 1 pastry	34	1	206	7	2	3	17	212
Toaster pastries, fruit (includes apple, blueberry, cherry, strawberry), 1 pastry	37	1	204	5	1	2	14	218
Tortillas, corn, approx 6" dia	11	1	53	1	Tr	1	42	39
Tortillas, flour, approx 6" dia	18	1	104	2	1	3	12	153
Waffles, EGGO Golden Oat Waffles, 1 waffle	13	1	69	1	Tr	2	23	135
Waffles, EGGO Lowfat Homestyle Waffles, 1 waffle	15	Tr	83	1	Tr	2	20	155
Waffles, plain, prepared from recipe, 7" dia	25	NA	218	11	2	6	191	383
Waffles, plain, ready-to-heat (includes buttermilk), 1 waffle	15	1	95	3	Tr	2	84	284
Wonton wrappers (includes egg roll wrappers), 1 wrapper, 7" sq	19	1	93	Tr	Tr	3	15	183
Beef Products								
Beef, ground, 75% lean meat /25% fat, pan-browned, 3 oz	0	0	235	15	6	22	29	79
Beef, ground, 85% lean meat /15% fat, pan-browned, 3 oz	0	0	218	13	5	24	19	76

Food, portion	Total Carb (g)	Fiber (g)	Calories	Total Fat (g)	Sat Fat (g)	Protein (g)	Calcium (mg)	Sodium (mg)
Beef, ground, 95% lean meat /5% fat, pan-browned, 3 oz	0	0	164	6	3	25	8	72
Beef, ground, patties, frozen, broiled, medium, 3 oz	0	0	240	17	7	21	9	65
Bottom round, braised, 3 oz	0	0	181	8	3	26	4	43
Breakfast strips, cured, cooked, 3 slices	Tr	0	153	12	5	11	3	766
Brisket, whole, braised, 3 oz	0	0	247	17	6	23	6	55
Chuck, arm pot roast, braised, 3 oz	0	0	238	14	6	25	9	53
Chuck, top blade, broiled, 3 oz	0	0	173	9	3	22	6	58
Corned beef, brisket, cured, cooked, 3 oz	Tr	0	213	16	5	15	7	964
Eye of round, roasted, 3 oz	0	0	141	4	1	25	4	53
Flank, braised, 3 oz	0	0	224	14	6	23	5	60
Inside skirt steak, broiled, 3 oz	0	0	174	9	3	23	9	65
Liver, cooked, pan-fried, 1 slice	4	0	142	4	1	21	5	62
Loin, bottom sirloin butt, roasted, 3 oz	0	0	184	9	3	24	7	50
Rib, eye, broiled, 3 oz	0	0	174	8	3	25	14	51
Rib, prime, broiled, 3 oz	0	0	250	18	8	21	7	60
Shank crosscuts, simmered, 3 oz	0	0	224	12	5	26	26	52
Short loin, porterhouse steak, broiled, 3 oz	0	0	235	16	6	20	6	55
Short loin, T-bone steak, broiled, 3 oz	0	0	168	8	3	22	3	60
Short loin, top loin, broiled, 3 oz	0	0	174	8	3	24	15	48
Tenderloin, broiled, 3 oz	0	0	175	8	0	25	14	50
Tongue, simmered, 3 oz	0	0	236	19	7	16	4	55
Beverages								
Apple cider-flavored drink, powder, low-calorie, prepared, 8 fl oz	1	0	2	0	0	0	26	NA
Beer, light, 12 fl oz	5	0	99	0	0	1	18	11
Beer, regular, 12 fl oz	6	Tr	117	Tr	0	1	18	14

Food, portion	Total Carb (g)	Fiber (g)	Calories	Total Fat (g)	Sat Fat (g)	Protein (g)	Calcium (mg)	Sodium (mg)
Beverages (cont.)								
Chocolate syrup, 2 tbsp	25	1	109	Tr	Tr	1	5	28
Chocolate syrup, prepared with whole milk, 8 fl oz	36	1	254	8	5	9	251	133
Chocolate-flavor beverage mix, powder, prepared with whole milk, 8 fl oz	32	1	226	9	5	9	253	154
Chocolate-flavored soda, 12 fl oz	39	0	155	0	0	0	15	325
Citrus fruit juice drink, frozen concentrate, prepared with water, 8 fl oz	30	Tr	124	Tr	0	Tr	12	5
Clam and tomato juice, canned, 5.5 oz	18	Tr	80	Tr	Tr	1	20	601
Club soda, 12 fl oz	0	0	0	0	0	0	18	75
Cocoa mix, powder, 1 serving	24	1	111	1	1	2	39	141
Coffee, brewed from grounds, prepared with tap water, 8 fl oz	0	0	9	2	0	Tr	2	2
Coffee, instant, cappuccino-flavor powder, 1 serving	20	Tr	107	2	1	1	55	75
Coffee, instant, prepared with water, 6 fl oz	1	0	4	0	Tr	Tr	7	4
Cola, carbonated, 12 fl oz	40	0	155	0	0	Tr	11	15
Cranberry juice cocktail, bottled, 8 fl oz	36	Tr	144	Tr	Tr	0	8	5
Cranberry-apple juice drink, low-calorie, 8 fl oz	11	Tr	46	0	0	Tr	24	12
Cranberry-grape juice drink, bottled, 8 fl oz	34	Tr	137	Tr	Tr	Tr	20	7
Cream soda, carbonated, 12 fl oz	49	0	189	0	0	0	19	45
Daiquiri, canned, 6.8 fl oz	32	0	259	0	0	0	0	83
Eggnog-flavor mix, powder, prepared with whole milk, 8 fl oz	39	0	258	8	5	8	250	150
Fruit punch juice drink, frozen concentrate, prepared with water, 8 fl oz	30	Tr	124	Tr	Tr	Tr	17	12

Food, portion	Total Carb (g)	Fiber (g)	Calories	Total Fat (g)	Sat Fat (g)	Protein (g)	Calcium (mg)	Sodium (mg)
GATORADE Lemon Lime Mix, powder, ¾ scoop	15	NA	58	0	0	0	NA	96
Ginger ale, carbonated, 12 fl oz	32	0	124	0	0	0	11	26
Grape juice drink, canned, 8 fl oz	32	0	125	0	0	Tr	8	3
Grape soda, carbonated, 12 fl oz	42	0	160	0	0	0	11	56
Hard liquor (gin, rum, vodka, whiskey), distilled, 80 proof, 1½ fl oz	0	0	97	0	0	0	0	Tr
KOOL-AID Tropical Punch, sweetened, powder, 1 serving	16	0	64	0	0	0	28	2
Lemon-lime soda, carbonated, 12 fl oz	38	0	147	0	0	0	7	40
Lemonade, COUNTRY TIME, pink, sugar-free mix, 1 portion	2	NA	5	Tr	0	Tr	NA	Tr
Lemonade, frozen concentrate, pink, prepared with water, 8 fl oz	26	0	99	0	Tr	Tr	7	7
Lemonade, frozen concentrate, white, prepared with water, 8 fl oz	34	Tr	131	Tr	Tr	Tr	10	7
Lemonade, powder, prepared with water, 8 fl oz	27	0	103	0	0	0	71	11
Malted drink mix, powder, prepared with whole milk, 8 fl oz	27	Tr	233	10	5	10	310	209
NESTEA Ice Tea, Lemon Flavor, ready-to-drink, 8 fl oz	20	0	89	1	Tr	0	NA	0
Orange breakfast drink, ready-to-drink, 8 fl oz	27	0	110	0	0	0	10	160
Orange juice drink, 8 fl oz	33	0	132	0	0	Tr	5	5
Pepper-type cola, carbonated, 12 fl oz	38	0	151	Tr	Tr	0	11	37
Piña colada, prepared-from-recipe, 1 cocktail, 4½ fl oz	32	Tr	245	3	2	1	11	8
Pineapple and grapefruit juice drink, canned, 8 fl oz	29	Tr	118	Tr	Tr	1	18	35
RICE DREAM, canned, 8 fl oz	25	0	120	2	Tr	Tr	20	86

☐ GOOD CARB CHOICE   ☐ BETTER CARB CHOICE

FOOD, PORTION	TOTAL CARB (G)	FIBER (G)	CALORIES	TOTAL FAT (G)	SAT FAT (G)	PROTEIN (G)	CALCIUM (MG)	SODIUM (MG)
BEVERAGES (CONT.)								
Root beer, 12 fl oz	39	0	152	0	0	0	19	48
Shake, chocolate, 8 fl oz	34	3	211	6	4	6	188	161
Shake, vanilla, 8 fl oz	30	Tr	184	5	3	6	203	136
Tea, brewed, prepared with tap water, 8 fl oz	1	0	2	0	Tr	0	0	7
Tea, instant, lemon-flavored, prepared, 8 fl oz	1	0	5	0	0	Tr	7	24
Tomato cocktail, Bloody Mary mix, ready-to-drink, 8 fl oz	12	1	56	0	0	2	61	1174
Tonic water, 12 fl oz	32	0	124	0	0	0	4	15
Wine, cooking, 1 fl oz	2	0	15	0	0	Tr	3	182
Wine, table, red, 1 glass, 3½ fl oz	2	0	74	0	0	Tr	8	5
Wine, table, white, 1 glass, 3½ fl oz	1	0	70	0	0	Tr	9	5
BREAKFAST CEREALS								
APPLE CINNAMON CHEERIOS, ¾ cup	25	1	118	2	Tr	2	100	120
APPLE JACKS, 1 cup	27	1	117	1	Tr	1	8	143
BANANA NUT CRUNCH Cereal, 1 cup	44	4	249	6	1	5	21	253
BASIC 4, 1 cup	42	3	202	3	Tr	4	196	316
Bran flakes with raisins, 1 cup	46	8	187	1	Tr	5	27	360
CAP'N CRUNCH, ¾ cup	23	1	108	2	Tr	1	4	202
CHEERIOS, 1 cup	22	3	111	2	Tr	3	100	273
CINNAMON TOAST CRUNCH, ¾ cup	24	1	127	3	1	2	100	206
COCOA PUFFS, 1 cup	26	1	117	1	Tr	1	100	171
COOKIE CRISP, 1 cup	26	Tr	117	1	Tr	1	100	178
CORN CHEX, 1 cup	26	1	112	Tr	Tr	2	100	288
Corn grits, white, cooked with water, 1 cup	31	1	143	Tr	Tr	3	7	5
CORN POPS, 1 cup	28	Tr	118	Tr	Tr	1	5	120

FOOD, PORTION	TOTAL CARB (G)	FIBER (G)	CALORIES	TOTAL FAT (G)	SAT FAT (G)	PROTEIN (G)	CALCIUM (MG)	SODIUM (MG)
CREAM OF RICE, cooked with water, 1 cup	28	Tr	127	Tr	Tr	2	7	2
CREAM OF WHEAT, instant, prepared with water, 1 cup	32	1	149	1	Tr	4	154	10
CRISPIX, 1 cup	25	Tr	109	Tr	Tr	2	6	210
Farina, enriched, cooked with water, 1 cup	24	1	112	Tr	Tr	3	9	5
FIBER ONE, ½ cup	24	14	59	1	Tr	2	100	129
FROOT LOOPS, 1 cup	26	1	118	1	Tr	1	23	141
Frosted ALPHA-BITS Cereal, 1 cup	27	1	130	1	Tr	3	10	212
FROSTED FLAKES, ¾ cup	28	1	114	Tr	Tr	1	2	148
FROSTED WHEATIES, ¾ cup	27	1	112	Tr	Tr	2	100	204
GOLDEN GRAHAMS, ¾ cup	25	1	112	1	Tr	2	350	269
HONEY BUNCHES OF OATS Honey Roasted Cereal, ¾ cup	25	1	118	2	Tr	2	6	193
HONEY NUT CHEERIOS, 1 cup	24	2	112	1	Tr	3	100	269
KELLOGG'S CORN FLAKES, 1 cup	24	1	101	Tr	Tr	2	2	203
KELLOGG'S RAISIN BRAN, 1 cup	47	7	195	2	Tr	5	29	362
KELLOGG'S RICE KRISPIES, 1¼ cups	29	Tr	119	Tr	Tr	2	5	319
KIX, 1⅓ cups	26	1	113	1	Tr	2	150	267
LUCKY CHARMS, 1 cup	25	2	114	1	Tr	2	100	203
MALT-O-MEAL, plain and chocolate, cooked with water, 1 cup	26	1	122	Tr	Tr	4	5	2
MAYPO, cooked with water, 1 cup	32	6	170	2	Tr	6	125	10
MUESLIX, ⅔ cup	40	4	196	3	Tr	5	32	170
MULTI-BRAN CHEX, 1 cup	41	6	166	1	Tr	3	89	322
NESTUM, prepared with water, 1 cup	34	7	191	1	Tr	6	179	10
POST 100% BRAN Cereal, ⅓ cup	23	8	83	1	Tr	4	22	121

Food, portion	Total Carb (g)	Fiber (g)	Calories	Total Fat (g)	Sat Fat (g)	Protein (g)	Calcium (mg)	Sodium (mg)
Breakfast Cereals (cont.)								
POST Frosted Shredded Wheat Bite Size Cereal, 1 cup	44	5	183	1	Tr	4	7	10
POST GRAPE-NUTS Cereal, ½ cup	47	5	208	1	Tr	6	20	354
POST HONEYCOMB Cereal, 1⅓ cups	26	1	115	1	Tr	2	5	215
PRODUCT 19, 1 cup	25	1	100	Tr	Tr	2	5	207
QUAKER Instant Oatmeal, apples and cinnamon, 1 packet, prepared	26	3	130	1	Tr	3	110	165
QUAKER Instant Oatmeal, maple and brown sugar, 1 packet, prepared	31	3	157	2	Tr	4	109	253
QUAKER OAT LIFE, plain, ¾ cup	25	2	120	1	Tr	3	112	164
RAISIN NUT BRAN, 1 cup	41	5	209	4	1	5	20	250
RALSTON, cooked with water, 1 cup	28	6	134	1	Tr	6	13	5
ROMAN MEAL WITH OATS, cooked with water, 1 cup	34	7	170	2	Tr	7	26	10
SPECIAL K, 1 cup	22	1	117	Tr	Tr	7	9	224
TOTAL Corn Flakes, 1⅓ cups	26	1	112	Tr	Tr	2	1000	209
TRIX, 1 cup	27	1	117	1	Tr	1	100	194
WHEATIES, 1 cup	24	3	107	1	Tr	3	0	218
Whole Grain TOTAL, ¾ cup	23	2	97	1	Tr	2	1000	192
Cereal Grains and Pasta								
Amaranth, 1 cup	129	30	729	13	3	28	298	41
Arrowroot flour, 1 cup	113	4	457	Tr	Tr	Tr	51	3
Barley, 1 cup	135	32	651	4	1	23	61	22
Buckwheat, 1 cup	122	17	583	6	1	23	31	2
Bulgur, cooked, 1 cup	34	8	151	Tr	Tr	6	18	9
Corn bran, crude, 1 cup	65	65	170	1	Tr	6	32	5
Corn flour, masa, yellow, 1 cup	87	NA	416	4	1	11	161	6

Food, portion	Total Carb (g)	Fiber (g)	Calories	Total Fat (g)	Sat Fat (g)	Protein (g)	Calcium (mg)	Sodium (mg)
Corn flour, whole-grain, yellow, 1 cup	90	16	422	5	1	8	8	6
Cornmeal, self-rising, plain, bolted yellow, 1 cup	86	8	407	4	1	10	440	1521
Cornmeal, whole-grain, yellow, 1 cup	94	9	442	4	1	10	7	43
Couscous, cooked, 1 cup	36	2	176	Tr	Tr	6	13	8
Macaroni, cooked, enriched, 1 cup elbow shaped	40	2	197	1	Tr	7	10	1
Macaroni, cooked, enriched, 1 cup small shells	33	1	162	1	Tr	5	8	1
Macaroni, vegetable, cooked, 1 cup	36	6	172	Tr	Tr	6	15	8
Macaroni, whole-wheat, cooked, 1 cup	37	4	174	1	Tr	7	21	4
Noodles, Chinese, chow mein, 1 cup	26	2	237	14	2	4	9	198
Noodles, egg, cooked, enriched, 1 cup	40	2	213	2	Tr	8	19	11
Noodles, egg, spinach, cooked, enriched, 1 cup	39	4	211	3	1	8	30	19
Noodles, soba, cooked, 1 cup	24	NA	113	Tr	Tr	6	5	68
Noodles, somen, cooked, 1 cup	48	NA	231	Tr	Tr	7	14	283
Oat bran, cooked, 1 cup	25	6	88	2	Tr	7	22	2
Oats, 1 cup	103	17	607	11	2	26	84	3
Pasta, fresh-refrigerated, plain, cooked, 2 oz	14	NA	75	1	Tr	3	3	3
Pasta, homemade, egg, cooked, 2 oz	13	NA	74	1	Tr	3	6	47
Pasta, homemade, without egg, cooked, 2 oz	14	NA	71	1	Tr	2	3	42
Rice bran, crude, 1 cup	59	25	373	25	5	16	67	6
Rice, brown, long-grain, cooked, 1 cup	45	4	216	2	Tr	5	20	10
Rice flour, brown, 1 cup	121	7	574	4	1	11	17	13
Rice flour, white, 1 cup	127	4	578	2	1	9	16	0
Rice noodles, cooked, 1 cup	44	2	192	Tr	Tr	2	7	33

Food, portion	Total Carb (g)	Fiber (g)	Calories	Total Fat (g)	Sat Fat (g)	Protein (g)	Calcium (mg)	Sodium (mg)
Cereal Grains and Pasta (cont.)								
Rice, white, glutinous, cooked, 1 cup	37	2	169	Tr	Tr	4	3	9
Rice, white, long-grain, cooked, 1 cup	45	1	205	Tr	Tr	4	16	2
Rice, white, short-grain, cooked, 1 cup	53	NA	242	Tr	Tr	4	2	0
Rye, 1 cup	118	25	566	4	Tr	25	56	10
Rye flour, dark, 1 cup	88	29	415	3	Tr	18	72	1
Rye flour, light, 1 cup	82	15	374	1	Tr	9	21	2
Semolina, enriched, 1 cup	122	7	601	2	Tr	21	28	2
Spaghetti, cooked, enriched, 1 cup	40	2	197	1	Tr	7	10	1
Spaghetti, spinach, cooked, 1 cup	37	NA	182	1	Tr	6	42	20
Spaghetti, whole-wheat, cooked, 1 cup	37	6	174	1	Tr	7	21	4
Tapioca, pearl, dry, 1 cup	135	1	544	Tr	Tr	Tr	30	2
Triticale, 1 cup	138	NA	645	4	1	25	71	10
Wheat bran, crude, 1 cup	37	25	125	2	Tr	9	42	1
Wheat flour, white, bread, 1 cup	99	3	495	2	Tr	16	21	3
Wheat flour, white, cake, 1 cup	107	2	496	1	Tr	11	19	3
Wheat flour, whole-grain, 1 cup	87	15	407	2	Tr	16	41	6
Wheat germ, crude, 1 cup	60	15	414	11	2	27	45	14
Wild rice, cooked, 1 cup	35	3	166	1	Tr	7	5	5
Dairy and Egg Products								
BREAKSTONE'S FREE Fat Free Sour Cream, 2 tbsp	5	0	29	Tr	Tr	2	45	23
BREYERS LIGHT Nonfat Strawberry Yogurt, 8 oz	22	0	125	Tr	Tr	8	216	102
BREYERS Lowfat Strawberry Yogurt (1% milkfat), 8 oz	41	Tr	218	2	1	9	284	118
Butter, salted, 1 tbsp	Tr	0	102	12	6	Tr	3	82
Butter, salted, 1 stick	Tr	0	810	92	46	1	27	651

Food, portion	Total Carb (g)	Fiber (g)	Calories	Total Fat (g)	Sat Fat (g)	Protein (g)	Calcium (mg)	Sodium (mg)
Butter, whipped, with salt, 1 tbsp	Tr	0	67	8	5	Tr	2	78
Cheese, American, 1 oz	2	0	94	7	4	6	141	274
Cheese, blue, 1 cup, crumbled	3	0	477	39	25	29	713	1883
Cheese, blue, 1 oz	1	0	100	8	5	6	150	395
Cheese, brick, 1 cup, shredded	3	0	419	34	21	26	762	633
Cheese, brick, 1 oz	1	0	105	8	5	7	191	159
Cheese, Brie, 1 oz	Tr	0	95	8	5	6	52	178
Cheese, Camembert, 1 oz	Tr	0	85	7	4	6	110	239
Cheese, cheddar, 1 cup, shredded	1	0	455	37	24	28	815	702
Cheese, cheddar, 1 slice	Tr	0	113	9	6	7	202	174
Cheese, Colby, 1 cup, shredded	3	0	445	36	23	27	774	683
Cheese, Colby, 1 oz	1	0	112	9	6	7	194	171
Cheese, cream, 1 package, 3 oz	2	0	297	30	19	6	68	252
Cheese, cream, 1 tbsp	Tr	0	51	5	3	1	12	43
Cheese, cream, low-fat, 1 tbsp	1	0	35	3	2	2	17	44
Cheese, feta, 1 cup, crumbled	6	0	396	32	22	21	740	1674
Cheese, feta, 1 oz	1	0	75	6	4	4	140	316
Cheese, goat, soft type, 1 oz	Tr	0	76	6	4	5	40	104
Cheese, Gouda, 1 oz	1	0	101	8	5	7	198	232
Cheese, low-fat, cheddar or colby, 1 cup, shredded	2	0	195	8	5	28	469	692
Cheese, low-fat, cheddar or Colby, 1 oz	1	0	49	2	1	7	118	174
Cheese, Mexican, queso asadero, 1 oz	1	0	101	8	5	6	187	186
Cheese, Mexican, queso Chihuahua, 1 oz	2	0	106	8	5	6	185	175
Cheese, Monterey, 1 oz	Tr	0	106	9	5	7	211	152
Cheese, Monterey, low-fat, 1 slice	Tr	0	88	6	4	8	197	158
Cheese, mozzarella, part-skim milk, 1 oz	1	0	72	5	3	7	222	175

Food, portion	Total Carb (g)	Fiber (g)	Calories	Total Fat (g)	Sat Fat (g)	Protein (g)	Calcium (mg)	Sodium (mg)
Dairy and Egg Products *(cont.)*								
Cheese, mozzarella, whole milk, 1 oz	1	0	85	6	4	6	143	178
Cheese, Muenster, 1 oz	Tr	0	104	9	5	7	203	178
Cheese, Parmesan, grated, 1 cup	4	0	431	29	17	38	1109	1529
Cheese, Port du Salut, 1 oz	Tr	0	100	8	5	7	184	151
Cheese, provolone, 1 slice	1	0	98	7	5	7	212	245
Cheese, ricotta, part-skim milk, 1 oz	1	0	39	2	1	3	77	35
Cheese, Romano, 1 oz	1	0	110	8	5	9	302	340
Cheese, Swiss, 1 cup, shredded	6	0	410	30	19	29	854	207
Cheese, Swiss, 1 slice	2	0	106	8	5	8	221	54
Cheese, Swiss, low-fat, 1 slice	1	0	50	1	1	8	269	73
CHEEZ WHIZ cheese sauce, 2 tbsp	3	Tr	91	7	4	4	118	541
Cottage cheese, creamed, with fruit, 1 cup	10	Tr	219	9	5	24	120	777
Cottage cheese, 1% milkfat, 1 cup	6	0	163	2	1	28	138	918
Cottage cheese, 2% milkfat, 1 cup	8	0	203	4	3	31	156	918
Cream, fluid, half-and-half, 1 fl oz	1	0	39	3	2	1	32	12
Cream, fluid, heavy whipping, 1 fl oz	1	0	103	11	7	1	19	11
Cream, fluid, light (coffee or table cream), 1 fl oz	1	0	59	6	4	1	29	12
Cream, half-and-half, fat-free, 1 fl oz	3	0	18	Tr	Tr	1	29	43
Cream, sour, cultured, 1 tbsp	1	0	26	3	2	Tr	14	6
Cream substitute, liquid, light, 1 fl oz	3	0	21	1	Tr	Tr	Tr	18
Cream substitute, powdered, 1 tsp	1	0	11	1	1	Tr	Tr	4
Cream, whipped, pressurized, 1 tbsp	Tr	0	8	1	Tr	Tr	3	4
Dessert topping, pressurized, 1 tbsp	1	0	11	1	1	Tr	Tr	2
Egg substitute, liquid, 1 cup	2	0	211	8	2	30	133	444
Egg substitute, powder, 0.7 oz	4	0	89	3	1	11	65	160

Food, portion	Total Carb (g)	Fiber (g)	Calories	Total Fat (g)	Sat Fat (g)	Protein (g)	Calcium (mg)	Sodium (mg)
Egg, white, raw, fresh, 1 large	Tr	0	17	Tr	0	4	2	55
Egg, whole, cooked, fried, 1 large	Tr	0	92	7	2	6	27	94
Egg, whole, cooked, hard-boiled, 1 large	1	0	78	5	2	6	25	62
Egg, whole, cooked, poached, 1 large	Tr	0	74	5	2	6	27	147
Egg, whole, cooked, scrambled, 1 large	1	0	101	7	2	7	43	171
Egg, whole, raw, fresh, 1 large	Tr	0	74	5	2	6	27	70
Egg, yolk, raw, fresh, 1 large	1	0	55	5	2	3	22	8
Eggnog, 1 cup	34	0	343	19	11	10	330	137
ENSURE PLUS, liquid nutrition, 1 cup	50	0	355	11	2	13	199	239
Instant breakfast beverage, powder, chocolate, 1 envelope	24	Tr	131	1	Tr	7	105	142
KRAFT FREE Singles, American, nonfat, 1 slice	2	Tr	31	Tr	Tr	5	150	273
Milk, buttermilk, low-fat, 1 cup	12	0	98	2	1	8	284	257
Milk, canned, evaporated, 1 cup	25	0	338	19	12	17	658	267
Milk, chocolate, commercial, 1 cup	26	2	208	8	5	8	280	150
Milk, dry, whole, 1 cup	49	0	635	34	21	34	1167	475
Milk, fluid, 2% milkfat, 1 cup	11	0	122	5	2	8	271	115
Milk, fluid, whole, 1 cup	11	0	146	8	5	8	246	105
Milk, nonfat, fluid, 1 cup	12	0	83	Tr	Tr	8	223	108
Milk shakes, thick chocolate, 10.6 oz	63	1	357	8	5	9	396	333
Milk shakes, thick vanilla, 11 oz	56	0	351	9	6	12	457	297
Sauce, cheese, prepared from recipe, 1 cup	13	Tr	479	36	20	25	756	1198
Sour cream, imitation, 1 oz	2	0	59	6	5	1	1	29
Yogurt, fruit variety, nonfat, 8 oz	43	0	213	Tr	Tr	10	345	132
Yogurt, plain, low-fat, 8 oz	16	0	143	4	2	12	415	159
Yogurt, plain, skim milk, 8 oz	17	0	127	Tr	Tr	13	452	175

Food, portion	Total Carb (g)	Fiber (g)	Calories	Total Fat (g)	Sat Fat (g)	Protein (g)	Calcium (mg)	Sodium (mg)
Dairy and Egg Products (cont.)								
Yogurt, plain, whole milk, 8 oz	11	0	138	7	5	8	275	104
Yogurt, vanilla, low-fat, 8 oz	31	0	193	3	2	11	388	150
Fast Foods								
Biscuit, with egg and bacon, 1 biscuit	29	1	458	31	8	17	189	999
Biscuit, with egg and sausage, 1 biscuit	41	1	581	39	15	19	155	1141
Biscuit, with egg, cheese, and bacon, 1 biscuit	33	NA	477	31	11	16	164	1260
Biscuit, with sausage, 1 biscuit	40	1	485	32	14	12	128	1071
Brownie, 2" sq	39	NA	243	10	3	3	25	153
Burrito, with beans, 2 pieces	71	NA	447	13	7	14	113	985
Burrito, with beans and cheese, 2 pieces	55	NA	378	12	7	15	214	1166
Burrito, with beans and meat, 2 pieces	66	NA	508	18	8	22	106	1335
Burrito, with beans, cheese, and beef, 2 pieces	40	NA	331	13	7	15	130	991
Burrito, with beef, 2 pieces	59	NA	524	21	10	27	84	1492
Cheeseburger, large, double patty, with condiments and vegetables, 1 sandwich	40	NA	704	44	18	38	240	1148
Cheeseburger, large, single patty, with condiments and vegetables, 1 sandwich	38	NA	563	33	15	28	206	1108
Chicken, breaded and fried, boneless pieces, plain, 6 pieces	15	0	319	21	5	18	14	513
Chicken, breaded and fried, boneless pieces, with sweet and sour, 6 pieces	29	NA	346	18	6	17	21	677
Chicken, breaded and fried, dark meat (drumstick or thigh), 2 pieces	16	NA	431	27	7	30	36	755
Chicken, breaded and fried, light meat (breast or wing), 2 pieces	20	NA	494	30	8	36	60	975
Chicken fillet sandwich, plain, 1 sandwich	39	NA	515	29	9	24	60	957
Chili con carne, 1 cup	22	NA	256	8	3	25	68	1007

FOOD, PORTION	TOTAL CARB (G)	FIBER (G)	CALORIES	TOTAL FAT (G)	SAT FAT (G)	PROTEIN (G)	CALCIUM (MG)	SODIUM (MG)
Chimichanga, with beef, 1 chimichanga	43	NA	425	20	9	20	63	910
Coleslaw, ¾ cup	13	NA	147	11	2	1	34	267
Cookies, chocolate chip, 1 box	36	NA	233	12	5	3	20	188
Corn on the cob, with butter, 1 ear	32	NA	155	3	2	4	4	29
Crab cake entrée, 1 cake	5	Tr	160	10	2	11	202	491
Croissant, with egg, cheese, and sausage, 1 croissant	25	NA	523	38	18	20	144	1115
Danish pastry, cheese, 1 pastry	29	NA	353	25	5	6	70	319
Egg and cheese sandwich, 1 sandwich	26	NA	340	19	7	16	225	804
Egg, scrambled, 2 eggs	2	0	199	15	6	13	54	211
Enchilada, with cheese and beef, 1 enchilada	30	NA	323	18	9	12	228	1319
English muffin, with butter, 1 muffin	30	NA	189	6	2	5	103	386
English muffin, with egg, cheese, and sausage, 1 muffin	31	NA	487	31	12	22	196	1135
Fish fillet, battered or breaded, and fried, 1 fillet	15	Tr	211	11	3	13	16	484
Fish sandwich, with tartar sauce, 1 sandwich	41	NA	431	23	5	17	84	615
French toast sticks, 5 pieces	58	3	513	29	5	8	78	499
French toast with butter, 2 slices	36	NA	356	19	8	10	73	513
Ham and cheese sandwich, 1 sandwich	33	NA	352	15	6	21	130	771
Hamburger, large, double patty, with condiments and vegetables, 1 sandwich	40	NA	540	27	11	34	102	791
Hamburger, large, single patty, with condiments, 1 sandwich	37	2	427	21	8	23	134	731
HOT POCKETS Pepperoni Pizza, frozen, 1 serving	39	NA	367	18	7	14	280	676
Hot dog, plain, 1 sandwich	18	NA	242	15	5	10	24	670
Hot dog, with chili, 1 sandwich	31	NA	296	13	5	14	19	480

FOOD, PORTION	TOTAL CARB (G)	FIBER (G)	CALORIES	TOTAL FAT (G)	SAT FAT (G)	PROTEIN (G)	CALCIUM (MG)	SODIUM (MG)
FAST FOODS (CONT.)								
Hot dog, with corn flour coating (corn dog), 1 sandwich	56	NA	460	19	5	17	102	973
Hush puppies, 5 pieces	35	NA	257	12	3	5	69	965
JACK'S Sausage & Pepperoni Pizza, frozen, 1 serving	30	NA	348	18	7	17	225	708
JENO'S CRISP 'N TASTY, Sausage & Pepperoni, frozen, 1 serving	52	3	491	24	6	17	166	1239
Nachos, with cheese, 6–8 nachos	36	NA	346	19	8	9	272	816
Onion rings, breaded and fried, 8–9 onion rings	31	NA	276	16	7	4	73	430
Pancakes with butter and syrup, 2 cakes	91	NA	520	14	6	8	128	1104
Pizza with cheese, 1 slice	21	NA	140	3	2	8	117	336
Pizza with pepperoni, 1 slice	20	NA	181	7	2	10	65	267
Potato, baked and topped with cheese sauce, 1 piece	47	NA	474	29	11	15	311	382
Potato, baked and topped with cheese sauce and broccoli, 1 piece	47	NA	403	21	9	14	336	485
Potato, baked and topped with sour cream and chives, 1 piece	50	NA	393	22	10	7	106	181
Potato, french fried in vegetable oil, 1 medium	53	5	458	25	5	6	19	265
Potato, mashed, ⅓ cup	13	NA	66	1	Tr	2	17	182
Potato salad, ⅓ cup	13	NA	108	6	1	1	13	312
Potatoes, hashed brown, ½ cup	16	NA	151	9	4	2	7	290
RED BARON Pepperoni Pizza, frozen, 1 serving	36	NA	442	25	9	18	219	1023
RED BARON, Two Cheeses, Sausage, Pepperoni & Onions, frozen, 1 serving	32	NA	337	18	6	12	147	704
Roast beef sandwich, plain, 1 sandwich	33	NA	346	14	4	22	54	792

Food, portion	Total Carb (g)	Fiber (g)	Calories	Total Fat (g)	Sat Fat (g)	Protein (g)	Calcium (mg)	Sodium (mg)
Roast beef sandwich with cheese, 1 sandwich	45	NA	473	18	9	32	183	1633
Salad, vegetable, tossed, without dressing, 1½ cups	7	NA	33	Tr	Tr	3	27	54
Salad, vegetable, tossed, without dressing, with chicken, 1½ cups	4	NA	105	2	1	17	37	209
Salad, vegetable, tossed, without dressing, with pasta and seafood, 1½ cups	32	NA	379	21	3	16	71	1572
Salad, vegetables, tossed, without dressing, with turkey, ham, and cheese, 1½ cups	5	NA	267	16	8	26	235	743
Shrimp, breaded and fried, 6–8 shrimp	40	NA	454	25	5	19	84	1446
Steak sandwich, 1 sandwich	52	NA	459	14	4	30	92	798
STOUFFER'S French Bread Pizza with Sausage, Pepperoni & Mushroom, frozen, 1 serving	44	4	429	21	6	16	231	840
Submarine sandwich, with cold cuts, 1 submarine	51	NA	456	19	7	22	189	1651
Submarine sandwich, with roast beef, 1 submarine	44	NA	410	13	7	29	41	845
Submarine sandwich, with tuna salad, 1 submarine	55	NA	584	28	5	30	74	1293
Taco, 1 large	41	NA	568	32	17	32	339	1233
Taco salad, 1½ cups	24	NA	279	15	7	13	192	762
TOMBSTONE Pepperoni Pizza, frozen, 1 serving	28	NA	312	16	6	14	202	551
TONY'S Pepperoni Pizza, frozen, 1 serving	36	NA	406	22	8	15	215	834
Tostada, with beans and cheese, 1 piece	27	NA	223	10	5	10	210	543
Tostada, with beef and cheese, 1 piece	23	NA	315	16	10	19	217	897
TOTINO'S PIZZA ROLLS, Sausage, frozen, 1 serving	40	3	351	15	3	14	102	632

Food, portion	Total Carb (g)	Fiber (g)	Calories	Total Fat (g)	Sat Fat (g)	Protein (g)	Calcium (mg)	Sodium (mg)
Fats and Oils								
Fat, beef, 1 tbsp	0	0	115	13	6	0	0	0
Fat, chicken, 1 tbsp	0	0	115	13	4	0	0	0
Flaxseed oil, 1 tbsp	0	0	120	14	1	0	0	0
Lard, 1 tbsp	0	0	115	13	5	0	0	0
Margarine, 80% fat, stick, 1 tbsp	Tr	0	99	11	2	Tr	Tr	92
Margarine, spread, fat-free, tub, 1 tbsp	1	0	6	Tr	Tr	Tr	1	85
Margarine, spread, soybean, 1 tbsp	Tr	NA	87	10	2	Tr	1	98
Margarine, vegetable oil spread, 60% fat, stick, 1 tbsp	Tr	0	74	8	1	Tr	3	112
Margarine-butter blend, 60% corn oil margarine and 40% butter, 1 tbsp	Tr	0	102	11	4	Tr	4	127
Mayonnaise dressing, no cholesterol, 1 tbsp	Tr	0	103	12	2	0	1	73
Mayonnaise, low-sodium, low-calorie, 1 tbsp	2	0	32	3	Tr	Tr	0	15
Mayonnaise, made with tofu, 1 tbsp	1	Tr	48	5	Tr	1	8	116
MIRACLE WHIP FREE, nonfat, 1 tbsp	2	Tr	13	Tr	Tr	Tr	1	126
MIRACLE WHIP LIGHT, 1 tbsp	2	Tr	37	3	Tr	Tr	1	131
Oil, corn and canola, 1 tbsp	0	0	124	14	1	0	0	0
Oil, olive, 1 tbsp	0	0	119	14	2	0	Tr	Tr
Oil, peanut, 1 tbsp	0	0	119	14	2	0	0	0
Oil, sesame, 1 tbsp	0	0	120	14	2	0	0	0
Oil, soybean, 1 tbsp	0	0	120	14	2	0	0	0
Oil, vegetable, canola, 1 tbsp	0	0	124	14	1	0	0	0
Oil, vegetable, corn, 1 tbsp	0	0	120	14	2	0	0	0
Oil, vegetable, palm, 1 tbsp	0	0	120	14	7	0	0	0
Oil, vegetable, safflower (over 70%), 1 tbsp	0	0	120	14	1	0	0	0

FOOD, PORTION	TOTAL CARB (G)	FIBER (G)	CALORIES	TOTAL FAT (G)	SAT FAT (G)	PROTEIN (G)	CALCIUM (MG)	SODIUM (MG)
Oil, vegetable, sunflower, 1 tbsp	0	0	120	14	2	0	0	0
Salad dressing, bacon and tomato, 1 tbsp	Tr	Tr	49	5	1	Tr	1	163
Salad dressing, Caesar, 1 tbsp	Tr	Tr	78	8	1	Tr	4	158
Salad dressing, Caesar, low-calorie, 1 tbsp	3	Tr	17	1	Tr	Tr	4	162
Salad dressing, French, 1 tbsp	2	0	73	7	1	Tr	4	134
Salad dressing, French, fat-free, 1 tbsp	5	Tr	21	Tr	Tr	Tr	1	128
Salad dressing, Italian, 1 tbsp	2	0	43	4	1	Tr	1	243
Salad dressing, Italian, fat-free, 1 tbsp	1	Tr	7	Tr	Tr	Tr	4	158
Salad dressing, peppercorn, 1 tbsp	Tr	0	76	8	1	Tr	3	143
Salad dressing, Russian, 1 tbsp	2	0	74	8	1	Tr	3	130
Salad dressing, sweet and sour, 1 tbsp	1	0	2	0	0	Tr	1	33
Salad dressing, Thousand Island, 1 tbsp	2	Tr	59	6	1	Tr	3	138
Salad dressing, vinegar and oil, 1 tbsp	Tr	0	72	8	1	0	0	Tr
Shortening, household, lard and vegetable oil, 1 tbsp	0	0	115	13	5	0	0	0
Vegetable oil-butter spread, reduced calorie, 1 tbsp	0	0	60	7	2	0	1	76
FINFISH AND SHELLFISH PRODUCTS								
Anchovy, European, canned in oil, drained, 1 anchovy	0	0	8	Tr	Tr	1	9	147
Bass, freshwater, cooked, dry heat, 3 oz	0	0	124	4	1	21	88	77
Bluefish, cooked, dry heat, 3 oz	0	0	135	5	1	22	8	65
Carp, cooked, dry heat, 3 oz	0	0	138	6	1	19	44	54
Catfish, breaded and fried, 3 oz	7	1	195	11	3	15	37	238
Catfish, farmed, cooked, dry heat, 3 oz	0	0	129	7	2	16	8	68
Caviar, black and red, 1 tbsp	1	0	40	3	1	4	44	240
Clam, breaded and fried, 20 small	19	NA	380	21	5	27	118	684
Clam, canned, drained, 3 oz	4	0	126	2	Tr	22	78	95

Food, portion	Total Carb (g)	Fiber (g)	Calories	Total Fat (g)	Sat Fat (g)	Protein (g)	Calcium (mg)	Sodium (mg)
Finfish and Shellfish Products (cont.)								
Cod, Atlantic, cooked, dry heat, 3 oz	0	0	89	1	Tr	19	12	66
Crab, Alaska king, cooked, moist heat, 1 leg	0	0	130	2	Tr	26	79	1436
Crab, Alaska king, imitation, made from surimi, 3 oz	9	0	87	1	Tr	10	11	715
Crab, blue, cooked, 3 oz	0	0	87	2	Tr	17	88	237
Crab, dungeness, cooked, 3 oz	1	0	94	1	Tr	19	50	321
Crab, queen, cooked, 3 oz	0	0	98	1	Tr	20	28	587
Crayfish, mixed, wild, cooked, 3 oz	0	0	70	1	Tr	14	51	80
Dolphinfish, cooked, dry heat, 3 oz	0	0	93	1	Tr	20	16	96
Fish sticks, frozen, preheated, 1 stick	7	Tr	76	3	1	4	6	163
Flatfish (flounder and sole), cooked, dry heat, 3 oz	0	0	99	1	Tr	21	15	89
Grouper, mixed, cooked, dry heat, 3 oz	0	0	100	1	Tr	21	18	45
Haddock, cooked, dry heat, 3 oz	0	0	95	1	Tr	21	36	74
Halibut, Atlantic and Pacific, cooked, dry heat, 3 oz	0	0	119	2	Tr	23	51	59
Herring, Atlantic, cooked, dry heat, 3 oz	0	0	173	10	2	20	63	98
Herring, Pacific, cooked, dry heat, 3 oz	0	0	213	15	4	18	90	81
Lobster, northern, cooked, 3 oz	1	0	83	1	Tr	17	52	323
Mackerel, king, cooked, 3 oz	0	0	114	2	Tr	22	34	173
Mussel, cooked, moist heat, 3 oz	6	0	146	4	1	20	28	314
Octopus, cooked, moist heat, 3 oz	4	0	139	2	Tr	25	90	391
Oyster, Pacific, cooked, moist heat, 3 oz	8	0	139	4	1	16	14	180
Oyster, wild, cooked, moist heat, 3 oz	7	0	116	4	1	12	77	359
Perch, ocean, cooked, dry heat, 3 oz	0	0	103	2	Tr	20	116	82
Pike, northern, cooked, dry heat, 3 oz	0	0	96	1	Tr	21	62	42

Food, portion	Total Carb (g)	Fiber (g)	Calories	Total Fat (g)	Sat Fat (g)	Protein (g)	Calcium (mg)	Sodium (mg)
Roe, mixed, cooked, dry heat, 3 oz	2	0	173	7	2	24	24	99
Roughy, orange, cooked, dry heat, 3 oz	0	0	76	1	Tr	16	32	69
Salmon, Atlantic, wild, cooked, 3 oz	0	0	155	7	1	22	13	48
Salmon, Chinook, smoked, 3 oz	0	0	99	4	1	16	9	666
Salmon, pink, canned, solids with bone and liquid, 3 oz	0	0	118	5	1	17	181	64
Sardine, Atlantic, canned in oil, drained solids with bone, 2 sardines	0	0	50	3	Tr	6	92	121
Scallop, breaded and fried, 2 large	3	NA	67	3	1	6	13	144
Shrimp, imitation, made from surimi, 3 oz	8	0	86	1	Tr	11	16	599
Shrimp, mixed, breaded and fried, 3 oz	10	Tr	206	10	2	18	57	292
Shrimp, mixed, cooked, moist heat, 3 oz	0	0	84	1	Tr	18	33	190
Snapper, mixed, cooked, dry heat, 3 oz	0	0	109	1	Tr	22	34	48
Squid, mixed, cooked, fried, 3 oz	7	0	149	6	2	15	33	260
Surimi, 3 oz	6	0	84	1	Tr	13	8	122
Swordfish, cooked, dry heat, 3 oz	0	0	132	4	1	22	5	98
Trout, cooked, dry heat, 3 oz	0	0	162	7	1	23	47	57
Trout, rainbow, wild, cooked, dry heat, 3 oz	0	0	128	5	1	19	73	48
Tuna, bluefin, cooked, dry heat, 3 oz	0	0	156	5	1	25	9	43
Tuna, light, canned in oil, drained, 1 can	0	0	339	14	3	50	22	605
Tuna, light, canned in water, drained, 1 can	0	0	191	1	Tr	42	18	558
Tuna salad, 3 oz	8	0	159	8	1	14	14	342
Walleye, cooked, dry heat, 3 oz	0	0	101	1	Tr	21	120	55
Whitefish, mixed, cooked, dry heat, 3 oz	0	0	146	6	1	21	28	55

Fruits and Fruit Juices

Food, portion	Total Carb (g)	Fiber (g)	Calories	Total Fat (g)	Sat Fat (g)	Protein (g)	Calcium (mg)	Sodium (mg)
Apple juice, canned or bottled, unsweetened, 1 cup	29	Tr	117	Tr	Tr	Tr	17	7

Food, portion	Total Carb (g)	Fiber (g)	Calories	Total Fat (g)	Sat Fat (g)	Protein (g)	Calcium (mg)	Sodium (mg)
Fruits and Fruit Juices (cont.)								
Apples, canned, sweetened, sliced, 1 cup	34	3	137	1	Tr	Tr	8	6
Apples, frozen, unsweetened, heated, 1 cup slices	25	4	97	1	Tr	1	10	6
Apples, raw, with skin, 1 medium	19	3	72	Tr	Tr	Tr	8	1
Applesauce, canned, sweetened, 1 cup	51	3	194	Tr	Tr	Tr	10	8
Apricots, halves, juice pack, with skin, solids and liquids, 1 cup	30	4	117	Tr	Tr	2	29	10
Bananas, raw, 1 medium	27	3	105	Tr	Tr	1	6	1
Blackberries, canned, heavy syrup, solids and liquids, 1 cup	59	9	236	Tr	Tr	3	54	8
Blackberries, raw, 1 cup	14	8	62	1	Tr	2	42	1
Blueberries, canned, heavy syrup, solids and liquids, 1 cup	56	4	225	1	Tr	2	13	8
Blueberries, raw, 1 cup	21	3	83	Tr	Tr	1	9	1
Boysenberries, canned, heavy syrup, 1 cup	57	7	225	Tr	Tr	3	46	8
Cantaloupe, raw, ⅛ of melon	8	1	35	Tr	Tr	1	9	16
Casaba, raw, 1 cup, cubes	11	2	48	Tr	Tr	2	19	15
Cherries, sour, light syrup pack, solids and liquids, 1 cup	49	2	189	Tr	Tr	2	25	18
Cherries, sweet, juice pack, solids and liquids, 1 cup, pitted	35	4	135	Tr	Tr	2	35	8
Cherries, sweet, raw, 1 cup, with pits	19	2	74	Tr	Tr	1	15	0
Cranberries, raw, 1 cup, whole	12	4	44	Tr	Tr	Tr	8	2
Cranberry juice, unsweetened, 1 cup	31	Tr	116	Tr	Tr	1	20	5
Cranberry sauce, canned, sweetened, 1 cup	108	3	418	Tr	Tr	1	11	80
Figs, dried, uncooked, 1 fig	5	1	21	Tr	Tr	Tr	14	1
Figs, raw, 1 fig	10	1	37	Tr	Tr	Tr	18	1

FOOD, PORTION	TOTAL CARB (G)	FIBER (G)	CALORIES	TOTAL FAT (G)	SAT FAT (G)	PROTEIN (G)	CALCIUM (MG)	SODIUM (MG)
Fruit cocktail (peach, pineapple, pear, grape, cherry), juice pack, solids and liquids, 1 cup	28	2	109	Tr	Tr	1	19	9
Fruit salad, (peach, pear, apricot, pineapple, cherry), juice pack, solids and liquids, 1 cup	32	2	125	Tr	Tr	1	27	12
Grapefruit, canned, juice pack, solids and liquids, 1 cup	23	1	92	Tr	Tr	2	37	17
Grapefruit juice, white, canned, sweetened, 1 cup	28	Tr	115	Tr	Tr	1	20	5
Grapefruit, raw, pink and red, ½ fruit	9	1	37	Tr	Tr	1	18	0
Grapefruit, raw, white, Florida, ½ fruit	10	NA	38	Tr	Tr	1	18	0
Grape juice, frozen concentrate, prepared, sweetened, 1 cup	32	Tr	128	Tr	Tr	Tr	10	5
Grapes, red or green, raw, 1 cup, seedless	29	1	110	Tr	Tr	1	16	3
Guavas, common, raw, 1 cup	20	9	84	1	Tr	1	33	5
Honeydew, raw, ⅛ of melon	11	1	45	Tr	Tr	1	8	23
Kiwi fruit, fresh, raw, 1 fruit without skin	13	3	56	Tr	Tr	1	31	3
Kumquats, raw, 1 fruit	3	1	13	Tr	Tr	Tr	12	2
Lemon juice, canned or bottled, 1 fl oz	2	Tr	6	Tr	Tr	Tr	3	6
Lemons, raw, without peel, 1 fruit	8	2	24	Tr	Tr	1	22	2
Lime juice, raw, 1 fl oz	3	Tr	8	Tr	Tr	Tr	3	Tr
Limes, raw, 1 fruit	6	2	15	Tr	Tr	Tr	9	1
Mangos, raw, 1 fruit	35	4	135	1	Tr	1	21	4
Mulberries, raw, 1 cup	14	2	60	1	Tr	2	55	14
Nectarines, raw, 1 fruit	14	2	60	Tr	Tr	1	8	0
Olives, ripe, canned, 1 large	Tr	Tr	5	Tr	Tr	Tr	4	38
Orange juice, canned, unsweetened, 1 cup	25	Tr	105	Tr	Tr	1	20	5
Orange juice, frozen concentrate, unsweetened, prepared, 1 cup	27	Tr	112	Tr	Tr	2	22	2

FOOD, PORTION	TOTAL CARB (G)	FIBER (G)	CALORIES	TOTAL FAT (G)	SAT FAT (G)	PROTEIN (G)	CALCIUM (MG)	SODIUM (MG)
FRUITS AND FRUIT JUICES (CONT.)								
Orange-grapefruit juice, canned, unsweetened, 1 cup	25	Tr	106	Tr	Tr	1	20	7
Oranges, raw, 1 fruit	15	3	62	Tr	Tr	1	52	0
Papayas, raw, 1 medium	30	5	119	Tr	Tr	2	73	9
Passion-fruit (granadilla), raw, 1 fruit	4	2	17	Tr	Tr	Tr	2	5
Peach nectar, canned, 1 cup	35	1	134	Tr	Tr	1	12	17
Peaches, canned, heavy syrup pack, solids and liquids, 1 cup, halves or slices	68	3	252	Tr	Tr	1	8	21
Peaches, canned, juice pack, 1 cup, halves or slices	29	3	109	Tr	Tr	2	15	10
Peaches, frozen, sliced, sweetened, 1 cup, thawed	60	5	235	Tr	Tr	2	8	15
Peaches, raw, 1 medium fruit	9	1	38	Tr	Tr	1	6	0
Pears, canned, juice pack, solids and liquids, 1 cup, halves	32	4	124	Tr	Tr	1	22	10
Pears, raw, 1 medium fruit	26	5	96	Tr	Tr	1	15	2
Pineapple, canned, heavy syrup pack, solids and liquids, 1 cup, chunks	51	2	198	Tr	Tr	1	36	3
Pineapple, canned, juice pack, drained, 1 cup, chunks	28	2	109	Tr	Tr	1	29	2
Pineapple juice, canned, unsweetened, 1 cup	34	1	140	Tr	Tr	1	43	3
Pineapple, raw, 1 slice	7	1	27	Tr	Tr	Tr	7	1
Plantains, raw, 1 medium	57	4	218	1	Tr	2	5	7
Plums, canned, heavy syrup pack, solids and liquids, 1 plum	11	Tr	41	Tr	Tr	Tr	4	9
Plums, raw, 1 medium fruit	8	1	30	Tr	Tr	Tr	4	0
Prune juice, canned, 1 cup	45	3	182	Tr	Tr	2	31	10
Prunes, stewed, 1 cup, pitted	70	8	265	Tr	Tr	2	47	2

Food, portion	Total Carb (g)	Fiber (g)	Calories	Total Fat (g)	Sat Fat (g)	Protein (g)	Calcium (mg)	Sodium (mg)
Prunes, uncooked, 1 cup, pitted	109	12	408	1	Tr	4	73	3
Raisins, seedless, 1 small box, 1½ oz	34	2	129	Tr	Tr	1	22	5
Raspberries, canned, heavy syrup pack, solids and liquids, 1 cup	60	8	233	Tr	Tr	2	28	8
Raspberries, raw, 1 cup	15	8	64	1	Tr	1	31	1
Rhubarb, raw, 1 cup, diced	6	2	26	Tr	Tr	1	105	5
Strawberries, frozen, sweetened, whole, 1 cup	54	5	199	Tr	Tr	1	28	3
Strawberries, raw, 1 cup, whole	11	3	46	Tr	Tr	1	23	1
Tamarinds, raw, 1 medium fruit	1	Tr	5	Tr	Tr	Tr	1	1
Tangerines (mandarin oranges), canned, juice pack, 1 cup	24	2	92	Tr	Tr	2	27	12
Tangerines (mandarin oranges), raw, 1 medium	9	2	37	Tr	Tr	1	12	1
Watermelon, raw, 1/16 of melon	22	1	86	Tr	Tr	2	20	3
Lamb and Veal Products								
Lamb, ground, cooked, broiled, 3 oz	0	0	241	17	7	21	19	69
Lamb, leg, (shank and sirloin), cooked, roasted, 3 oz	0	NA	162	7	3	23	8	61
Lamb, loin, broiled, 3 oz	0	NA	163	7	3	23	18	68
Lamb, New Zealand, leg (shank and sirloin), roasted, 3 oz	0	0	209	13	6	21	9	37
Lamb, shoulder (arm and blade), cooked, 3 oz	0	NA	252	18	9	20	24	72
Veal, breast, boneless, cooked, braised, 3 oz	0	NA	240	16	6	22	7	54
Veal, ground, cooked, broiled, 3 oz	0	0	146	6	3	21	14	71
Veal, leg (top round), pan-fried, not breaded, 1 piece	0	0	529	13	4	96	20	223
Veal, loin, cooked, roasted, 3 oz	0	0	184	10	4	21	16	79

Food, portion	Total Carb (g)	Fiber (g)	Calories	Total Fat (g)	Sat Fat (g)	Protein (g)	Calcium (mg)	Sodium (mg)
Lamb and Veal Products (cont.)								
Veal, rib, cooked, braised, 3 oz	0	0	185	7	2	29	20	84
Veal, shoulder (arm and blade), roasted, 3 oz	0	0	156	7	3	22	23	82
Veal, sirloin, cooked, braised, 3 oz	0	0	214	11	4	27	14	67
Legumes and Legume Products								
Bacon bits, meatless, 1 tbsp	2	1	33	2	Tr	2	7	124
Bacon, meatless, 1 strip	Tr	Tr	16	1	Tr	1	1	73
Beans, adzuki, cooked, boiled, 1 cup	57	17	294	Tr	Tr	17	64	18
Beans, baked, canned, 1 cup	52	13	236	1	Tr	12	127	1008
Beans, baked, canned, with beef, 1 cup	45	NA	322	9	4	17	120	1264
Beans, baked, canned, with franks, 1 cup	40	18	368	17	6	17	124	1114
Beans, baked, canned, with pork and tomato sauce, 1 cup	49	12	248	3	1	13	142	1113
Beans, black, cooked, boiled, 1 cup	41	15	227	1	Tr	15	46	2
Beans, chili, barbeque, ranch style, cooked, 1 cup	43	11	245	3	Tr	13	78	1834
Beans, great northern, cooked, boiled, 1 cup	37	12	209	1	Tr	15	120	4
Beans, kidney, red, boiled, 1 cup	40	13	225	1	Tr	15	50	4
Beans, kidney, red, canned, 1 cup	40	16	218	1	Tr	13	61	873
Beans, navy, canned, 1 cup	54	13	296	1	Tr	20	123	1174
Beans, navy, cooked, boiled, 1 cup	48	12	258	1	Tr	16	127	2
Beans, pinto, cooked, boiled, 1 tbsp	3	1	15	Tr	Tr	1	4	1
Beans, white, cooked, boiled, 1 cup	45	11	249	1	Tr	17	161	11
Beans, yardlong, boiled, 1 cup	36	6	202	1	Tr	14	72	9
Beans, yellow, cooked, boiled, 1 cup	45	18	255	2	Tr	16	110	9
Broadbeans (fava beans), cooked, boiled, 1 cup	33	9	187	1	Tr	13	61	9

Food, portion	Total Carb (g)	Fiber (g)	Calories	Total Fat (g)	Sat Fat (g)	Protein (g)	Calcium (mg)	Sodium (mg)
Chickpeas (garbanzo beans), cooked, boiled, 1 cup	45	12	269	4	Tr	15	80	11
Chili with beans, canned, 1 cup	30	11	287	14	6	15	120	1336
Cowpeas (blackeyes, crowder, southern), cooked, boiled, 1 cup	36	11	200	1	Tr	13	41	7
Falafel, home-prepared, 1 patty	5	NA	57	3	Tr	2	9	50
Frankfurter, meatless, 1 frankfurter	5	3	163	10	1	14	23	330
GREEN GIANT, HARVEST BURGER, 1 patty	7	6	138	4	1	18	102	411
Hummus, commercial, 1 cup	36	15	415	24	4	20	95	948
Lentils, cooked, boiled, 1 cup	40	16	230	1	Tr	18	38	4
Lima beans (baby), cooked, boiled, 1 cup	42	14	229	1	Tr	15	53	5
Lima beans, cooked, boiled, 1 cup	39	13	216	1	Tr	15	32	4
Meat extender, 1 oz	11	5	89	1	Tr	11	58	3
MORI-NU, Tofu, silken, firm, 1 slice	2	Tr	52	2	Tr	6	27	30
MORI-NU, Tofu, silken, soft, 1 slice	2	Tr	46	2	Tr	4	26	4
Noodles, cellophane or long rice (mung beans), 1 cup	121	1	491	Tr	Tr	Tr	35	14
Peanut butter, chunk style, with salt, 2 tbsp	7	2	188	16	3	8	17	150
Peanut butter, smooth style, with salt, 2 tbsp	6	2	192	17	3	8	15	160
Peanuts, dry-roasted, without salt, 1 cup	31	12	854	73	10	35	79	9
Peanuts, oil-roasted, without salt, 1 cup, chopped	25	9	773	66	9	35	117	8
Peanuts, raw, 1 cup	24	12	828	72	10	38	134	26
Peas, split, cooked, boiled, 1 cup	41	16	231	1	Tr	16	27	4
Refried beans, canned, 1 cup	39	13	237	3	1	14	88	753
Sausage, meatless, 1 link	2	1	64	5	1	5	16	222
Soy flour, full-fat, raw, 1 cup, stirred	30	8	366	17	3	29	173	11

Food, portion	Total Carb (g)	Fiber (g)	Calories	Total Fat (g)	Sat Fat (g)	Protein (g)	Calcium (mg)	Sodium (mg)
Legumes and Legume Products (cont.)								
Soy milk, fluid, 1 cup	11	3	120	5	1	9	10	29
Soy sauce, soy and wheat (shoyu), 1 tbsp	1	Tr	8	Tr	Tr	1	3	914
Soy sauce, soy (tamari), 1 tbsp	1	Tr	11	Tr	Tr	2	4	1005
Soybeans, cooked, boiled, with salt, 1 cup	17	10	298	15	2	29	175	408
Soyburger, 1 patty	9	3	125	4	1	13	20	385
Tofu, fried, 1 piece	1	1	35	3	Tr	2	48	2
Tofu yogurt, 1 cup	42	1	246	5	1	9	309	92
Vegetarian fillets, 1 fillet	8	5	247	15	2	20	81	417
Vegetarian stew, 1 cup	17	3	304	7	1	42	77	988
Meals, Entrées, and Sidedishes								
BANQUET Chicken Pot Pie, frozen, 1 serving	36	1	382	22	9	10	28	948
BANQUET Salisbury Steak Meal, frozen meal, 1 serving	28	3	398	25	9	15	NA	0
BANQUET Turkey & Gravy with Dressing Meal, frozen meal, 1 serving	34	3	280	10	3	14	47	1061
Beef Pot Pie, frozen entrée, 1 serving	44	2	449	24	9	13	NA	737
Beef stew, canned entrée, 1 serving	16	3	218	12	5	11	28	947
Breakfast Burrito, Ham & Cheese, frozen entrée, 1 serving	28	1	212	7	2	10	NA	405
CHEF BOYARDEE Beef Ravioli in Tomato & Meat Sauce, 1 serving	37	4	229	5	2	8	20	1174
Chicken pot pie, frozen entrée, 1 serving	43	2	484	29	10	13	33	857
CHUN KING Sweet & Sour Vegetables & Sauce with Chicken, canned entrée, 1 serving	32	NA	165	2	0	6	NA	564
Cinnamon Swirl French Toast with Sausage, 1 serving	38	2	415	23	7	13	NA	502

Food, portion	Total Carb (g)	Fiber (g)	Calories	Total Fat (g)	Sat Fat (g)	Protein (g)	Calcium (mg)	Sodium (mg)
CROISSANT POCKETS Chicken, Broccoli, and Cheddar, frozen, 1 serving	39	1	301	11	3	11	NA	652
GREEN GIANT, Broccoli in Cheese Flavored Sauce, frozen, 1 serving	10	NA	75	3	1	3	NA	538
HAMBURGER HELPER, Cheeseburger Macaroni, dry mix, 1 serving	29	NA	178	5	1	5	NA	914
HEALTHY CHOICE, Cheddar Broccoli Potatoes with Cheese Sauce, frozen, 1 serving	53	6	327	7	3	13	241	549
HEALTHY CHOICE Chicken Teriyaki with Rice Medley, frozen meal, 1 serving	37	3	268	6	3	17	37	602
HEALTHY CHOICE Traditional Meat Loaf with Tomato Sauce, frozen meal, 1 serving	52	6	316	5	3	15	48	459
HORMEL Chili with Beans, 1 cup	34	8	240	4	2	17	69	1163
HORMEL Corned Beef Hash, canned entrée, 1 serving	22	3	387	24	10	21	45	1003
HORMEL, DINTY MOORE Beef Stew, 1 serving	16	3	222	13	6	11	19	984
HORMEL Turkey Chili with Beans, 1 serving	26	6	203	3	1	19	116	1198
HOT POCKETS, Beef & Cheddar Stuffed Sandwich, frozen, 1 serving	39	NA	403	20	9	16	337	906
KRAFT Macaroni and Cheese Dinner Original Flavor, unprepared, 1 serving	48	1	259	3	1	11	92	561
LEAN CUISINE Rice and Chicken Stir-Fry with Vegetables, frozen entrée, 1 serving	40	6	270	7	1	12	NA	632
LIPTON, Alfredo Egg Noodles in a Creamy Sauce, dry mix, 1 serving	39	NA	259	7	3	10	79	1097
Macaroni and Cheese, canned entrée, 1 serving	29	3	199	6	3	8	113	1058
MARIE CALLENDER'S Escalloped Noodles & Chicken, frozen entrée, 1 cup	38	NA	397	21	7	13	104	1007

Food, portion	Total Carb (g)	Fiber (g)	Calories	Total Fat (g)	Sat Fat (g)	Protein (g)	Calcium (mg)	Sodium (mg)
Meals, Entrées, and Sidedishes (cont.)								
OLD EL PASO Chili with Beans, 1 serving	22	10	249	10	2	18	NA	588
Scrambled Eggs & Sausage with Hashed Brown Potatoes, frozen breakfast, 1 serving	17	1	361	27	7	13	NA	772
STOUFFER'S, Creamed Spinach, frozen, 1 serving	9	2	169	13	4	4	141	335
STOUFFER'S Lasagna with Meat & Sauce, frozen entrée, 1 serving	26	3	277	11	5	19	230	735
STOUFFER'S LEAN CUISINE Spaghetti with Meat Sauce, frozen entrée, 1 serving	51	6	313	6	1	14	NA	610
SUNNY FRESH, Frozen Bagel French Toast with Maple Syrup, 1 serving	21	0	190	5	1	14	40	283
SWEET SUE Chicken & Dumplings, canned, 1 serving	23	3	218	7	2	15	NA	946
THE BUDGET GOURMET Italian Sausage Lasagna, frozen entrée, 1 serving	40	3	456	24	8	21	316	903
Tortellini, pasta with cheese filling, ¾ cup	38	2	249	6	3	11	123	279
Turkey Pot Pie, frozen entrée, 1 serving	70	4	699	35	11	26	NA	1390
TYSON Beef Stir Fry Kit, frozen entrée, 1 serving	71	NA	433	5	0	26	NA	1584
TYSON Chicken Fajita Kit, frozen entrée, 1 serving	17	NA	129	3	1	8	NA	350
WEIGHT WATCHERS Roast Turkey Medallions and Mushrooms, frozen meal, 1 serving	35	3	214	2	Tr	15	NA	504
Nut and Seed Products								
Almonds, dry roasted, with salt added, whole kernels, 1 cup	27	16	824	73	6	30	367	468
Almonds, whole, 1 cup	28	17	827	72	6	30	355	1
Cashew nuts, dry roasted, salt added, halves and whole, 1 cup	45	4	786	63	13	21	62	877

FOOD, PORTION	TOTAL CARB (G)	FIBER (G)	CALORIES	TOTAL FAT (G)	SAT FAT (G)	PROTEIN (G)	CALCIUM (MG)	SODIUM (MG)
Coconut cream, canned, 1 cup	25	7	568	52	47	8	3	148
Coconut meat, dried, sweetened, flaked, 1 cup	35	3	351	24	21	2	10	189
Coconut milk, canned, 1 cup	6	NA	445	48	43	5	41	29
Hazelnuts or filberts, whole, 1 cup	23	13	848	82	6	20	154	0
Macadamia nuts, dry roasted, whole or halves, 1 cup	18	11	962	102	16	10	94	5
Mixed nuts, peanuts, dry roasted, salt added, 1 cup	35	12	814	70	9	24	96	917
Pecans, halves, 1 cup	14	10	684	71	6	9	69	0
Pine nuts, pignolia, dried, 1 cup	18	5	909	92	7	18	22	3
Pistachio nuts, dry roasted, salt added, 1 cup	33	13	699	57	7	26	135	498
Pumpkin and squash kernels, dried, 1 cup	25	5	747	63	12	34	59	25
Sesame seeds, whole, dried, 1 tbsp	2	1	52	4	1	2	88	1
Sunflower seed kernels, dried, 1 cup	27	15	821	71	7	33	167	4
Sunflower seed kernels, dry roasted, hulled, 1 cup	31	14	745	64	7	25	90	4
Walnuts, English, chopped, 1 cup	16	8	765	76	7	18	115	2
PORK PRODUCTS								
Bacon, cured, pan-fried, 1 slice cooked	Tr	0	42	3	1	3	1	192
Breakfast strips, cooked, cured, 3 slices	Tr	0	156	12	4	10	5	714
Canadian-style bacon, cured, grilled, 2 slices	1	0	87	4	1	11	5	727
Ham, boneless, extra lean (5% fat), roasted, 3 oz	1	0	123	5	2	18	7	1023
Ham, boneless, regular (11% fat), roasted, 3 oz	0	0	151	8	3	19	7	1275
Ham, cured, boneless, extra lean, roasted, 3 oz	Tr	0	140	7	2	19	7	1177

Food, portion	Total Carb (g)	Fiber (g)	Calories	Total Fat (g)	Sat Fat (g)	Protein (g)	Calcium (mg)	Sodium (mg)
PORK PRODUCTS (CONT.)								
Ham, leg, shank half, roasted, 3 oz	0	0	246	17	6	22	13	50
Ham, patties, cured, grilled, 1 patty, cooked	1	0	205	19	7	8	5	638
Ham, regular (13% fat), canned, roasted, 3 oz	Tr	0	192	13	4	17	7	800
Pork, chops, bone-in, pan-fried, 3 oz	0	0	291	24	9	18	26	57
Pork, country-style ribs, roasted, 3 oz	0	0	279	22	8	20	21	44
Pork, fresh, ground, cooked, 3 oz	0	0	252	18	7	22	19	62
Pork, oriental style, dehydrated, 1 cup	Tr	0	135	14	5	3	2	151
Pork shoulder, roasted, 3 oz	0	0	238	18	7	17	9	911
Pork, sirloin (chops), boneless, braised, 3 oz	0	0	149	6	2	23	11	39
Pork, tenderloin, roasted, 3 oz	0	0	147	5	2	24	5	47
POULTRY PRODUCTS								
Chicken, breast, meat and skin, cooked, roasted, ½ breast, bone removed	0	0	193	8	2	29	14	70
Chicken, breast, meat and skin, fried, batter, ½ breast, bone removed	13	Tr	364	18	5	35	28	385
Chicken, dark meat and skin, cooked, fried, batter, ½ chicken, bone removed	26	NA	828	52	14	61	58	820
Chicken, dark meat and skin, cooked, roasted, ½ chicken, bone removed	0	0	423	26	7	43	25	145
Chicken, drumstick, meat and skin, cooked, roasted, 1 drumstick, bone removed	0	0	112	6	2	14	6	47
Chicken, drumstick, meat and skin, fried, batter, 1 drumstick, bone removed	6	Tr	193	11	3	16	12	194
Chicken, giblets, cooked, simmered, 1 cup, chopped or diced	1	0	229	7	2	39	20	97

Food, portion	Total Carb (g)	Fiber (g)	Calories	Total Fat (g)	Sat Fat (g)	Protein (g)	Calcium (mg)	Sodium (mg)
Chicken, leg, meat and skin, cooked, roasted, 1 leg, bone removed	0	0	264	15	4	30	14	99
Chicken, leg, meat and skin, fried, batter, 1 leg, bone removed	14	Tr	431	26	7	34	28	441
Chicken, light meat and skin, cooked, roasted, ½ chicken, bone removed	0	0	293	14	4	38	20	99
Chicken, light meat and skin, fried, batter, ½ chicken, bone removed	18	NA	521	29	8	44	38	540
Chicken, thigh, meat and skin, cooked, roasted, 1 thigh, bone removed	0	0	153	10	3	16	7	52
Chicken, thigh, meat and skin, fried, batter, 1 thigh, bone removed	8	Tr	238	14	4	19	15	248
Chicken, wing, meat and skin, cooked, roasted, 1 wing, bone removed	0	0	99	7	2	9	5	28
Chicken wing, meat and skin, fried, batter, 1 wing, bone removed	5	Tr	159	11	3	10	10	157
Cornish game hens, meat and skin, cooked, roasted, 1 bird	0	0	668	47	13	57	33	164
Duck, meat and skin, cooked, roasted, ½ duck	0	0	1287	108	37	73	42	225
Turkey and gravy, frozen, 1½-oz package	7	0	95	4	1	8	20	787
Turkey bacon, cooked, 1 cup pieces	3	0	313	23	7	24	7	1874
Turkey, breast, meat and skin, roasted, ½ breast, bone removed	0	0	1633	64	18	248	181	544
Turkey, ground, cooked, 1 patty (4 oz raw)	0	0	193	11	3	22	21	88
Turkey, leg, meat and skin, roasted, 1 leg	0	0	148	7	2	20	23	55
Turkey, wing, meat and skin, cooked, roasted, 1 wing, bone removed	0	0	426	23	6	51	45	113
SAUSAGES AND LUNCHEON MEATS								
Beef, cured, dried, 1 oz	1	0	43	1	Tr	9	2	791
Beef, cured, pastrami, 1 oz	1	0	98	8	3	5	3	344

☐ Good Carb Choice ☐ Better Carb Choice

Food, portion	Total Carb (g)	Fiber (g)	Calories	Total Fat (g)	Sat Fat (g)	Protein (g)	Calcium (mg)	Sodium (mg)
Sausages and Luncheon Meats (cont.)								
Beef, sausage, smoked, 1 sausage	1	0	134	12	5	6	3	486
Beerwurst, beer salami, pork and beef, 2 oz	2	1	155	13	5	8	15	410
Bologna, beef, 1 serving	1	0	87	8	3	3	9	302
Bologna, pork, 1 slice	Tr	0	57	5	2	4	3	272
Bologna, turkey, 1 serving	1	Tr	59	4	1	3	34	351
Bratwurst, chicken, cooked, 1 serving, 2.96 oz	0	0	148	9	9	16	9	60
CARL BUDDIG, Smoked Sliced Ham, 1 serving	1	0	93	5	2	11	9	787
CARL BUDDIG, Smoked Sliced Turkey, light and dark meat, 1 serving	1	0	91	5	2	10	34	625
Chicken breast, oven-roasted, fat-free, sliced, 1 serving	1	0	33	Tr	Tr	7	3	457
Corned beef, canned, 1 oz	0	0	71	4	2	8	3	285
Frankfurter, beef, 1 frankfurter	2	0	149	13	5	5	6	513
Frankfurter, chicken, 1 frankfurter	3	0	116	9	2	6	43	617
Frankfurter, turkey, 1 frankfurter	1	0	102	8	3	6	48	642
Ham, minced, 1 slice	Tr	0	55	4	2	3	2	261
Ham, sliced, extra lean, (5% fat), 1 slice	Tr	0	37	1	Tr	5	2	400
Ham, sliced, regular (11% fat), 1 slice	1	Tr	46	2	1	5	7	365
Kielbasa, Polish, turkey and beef, smoked, 1 serving	2	0	127	10	3	7	NA	672
Liver sausage, liverwurst, pork, 2½" dia×¼" thick	Tr	0	59	5	2	3	5	155
LOUIS RICH, Turkey Breast (oven roasted, portion fat-free), 1 serving	1	0	50	Tr	Tr	11	10	659
Pastrami, beef, 98% fat-free, 1 serving	1	0	54	1	0	11	5	576
Paté, chicken liver, canned, 1 tbsp	1	0	26	2	1	2	1	50

Food, portion	Total Carb (g)	Fiber (g)	Calories	Total Fat (g)	Sat Fat (g)	Protein (g)	Calcium (mg)	Sodium (mg)
Pepperoni, pork, beef, 1 oz	1	Tr	130	11	5	6	6	501
Polish sausage, pork, 10" long×1¼" dia	4	0	740	65	23	32	27	1989
Pork and beef sausage, fresh, cooked, 1 link	Tr	0	51	5	2	2	1	105
Salami, cooked, beef, 1 slice	Tr	0	67	6	3	3	2	296
Salami, dry or hard, pork, 1 slice	Tr	0	41	3	1	2	1	226
Sausage, chicken, beef, pork, skinless, smoked, 1 link	7	0	181	12	4	11	84	869
Sausage, Italian, pork, cooked, 1 link	1	0	268	21	8	17	20	765
Sausage, Polish, pork and beef, smoked, 1 serving	2	0	229	20	7	9	5	644
SPAM, Pork with ham, minced, 1 serving	2	0	174	15	6	7	8	767
Turkey sausage, reduced-fat, brown and serve, 1 cup	14	Tr	256	13	4	22	40	790
SNACKS								
Banana chips, 3 oz	50	7	441	29	25	2	15	5
Beef jerky, chopped and formed, 1 piece	2	Tr	82	5	2	7	4	443
Beef sticks, smoked, 1 stick	1	NA	110	10	4	4	14	296
BETTY CROCKER Fruit Roll Ups, berry flavored, 2 rolls	24	NA	104	1	Tr	Tr	NA	89
Cheese puffs and twists, low-fat, 1 oz	21	3	122	3	1	2	101	364
CHEX mix, 1 oz	18	2	120	5	2	3	10	288
Chips, corn-based, extruded, plain, 1 bag, 7 oz	113	10	1067	66	9	13	251	1247
Corn cakes, very low-sodium, 1 cake	8	NA	35	Tr	Tr	1	2	3
Granola bars, hard, chocolate chip, 1 bar	17	1	105	4	3	2	18	83
Granola bars, hard, plain, 1 bar	18	1	132	6	1	3	17	82
Granola bars, soft, uncoated, chocolate chip, 1 bar	19	1	118	5	3	2	26	76

Food, portion	Total Carb (g)	Fiber (g)	Calories	Total Fat (g)	Sat Fat (g)	Protein (g)	Calcium (mg)	Sodium (mg)
Snacks (cont.)								
Popcorn, air-popped, 1 cup	6	1	31	Tr	Tr	1	1	Tr
Popcorn, caramel-coated, with peanuts, 1 oz	23	1	113	2	Tr	2	19	84
Popcorn, cheese-flavor, 1 cup	6	1	58	4	1	1	12	98
Popcorn, oil-popped, 1 cup	6	1	55	3	1	1	1	97
Pork skins, barbecue-flavor, 1 oz	Tr	NA	153	9	3	16	12	756
Potato chips, barbecue-flavor, 1 bag, 7 oz	105	9	972	64	16	15	99	1485
Potato chips, fat-free, salted, 1 bag, 8 oz	190	17	860	1	Tr	22	79	1460
Potato chips, made from dried potatoes, plain, 1 can, 7 oz	101	7	1105	76	19	12	48	1299
Potato chips, plain, salted, 1 bag, 8 oz	120	10	1217	79	25	16	54	1348
Pretzels, hard, plain, unsalted, 10 twists	48	2	229	2	Tr	5	22	173
Pretzels, soft, 1 medium	80	2	389	4	1	9	26	1615
Puffs or twists, corn-based, extruded, cheese-flavor, 1 8 oz bag	122	2	1258	78	15	17	132	2384
Rice cakes, cracker, 1 cubic inch	3	Tr	16	Tr	Tr	Tr	Tr	3
Rice cakes, brown rice, corn, 1 cake	7	Tr	35	Tr	Tr	1	1	26
Sesame sticks, wheat-based, salted, 1 oz	13	1	153	10	2	3	48	422
Tortilla chips, plain, 1 oz	18	2	142	7	1	2	44	150
Trail mix, regular, 1 cup	67	NA	693	44	8	21	117	344
Trail mix, tropical, 1 cup	92	NA	570	24	12	9	80	14
Trail mix, with chocolate chips, salted nuts and seeds, 1 cup	66	NA	707	47	9	21	159	177
Soups, Sauces, and Gravies								
Barbecue sauce, 1 cup (8 fl oz)	32	3	188	5	1	5	48	2038
CHEF-MATE Basic Cheddar Cheese Sauce, 1 serving	8	0	82	5	2	2	46	471

FOOD, PORTION	TOTAL CARB (G)	FIBER (G)	CALORIES	TOTAL FAT (G)	SAT FAT (G)	PROTEIN (G)	CALCIUM (MG)	SODIUM (MG)
CHEF-MATE Hot Dog Chili Sauce, 1 serving	9	2	69	2	1	3	20	399
Gravy, au jus, canned, 1 cup	6	0	38	Tr	Tr	3	10	119
Gravy, beef, canned, 1 cup	11	1	123	5	3	9	14	1305
Gravy, brown instant, dry, 1 serving	4	Tr	25	1	Tr	1	8	339
Gravy, turkey, canned, 1 cup	12	1	121	5	1	6	10	1373
Hollandaise, dehydrated, prepared with water, 1 cup	14	1	238	20	12	5	124	1564
KRAFT Barbecue Sauce Original, 2 tbsp	9	Tr	39	Tr	0	Tr	5	424
LJ MINOR Italian Sauce, 1 serving	11	1	61	1	Tr	1	34	304
LJ MINOR Stir Fry Sauce, 1 serving	2	0	16	1	Tr	Tr	2	233
LJ MINOR Sweet N' Sour Sauce, 1 serving	8	Tr	40	1	Tr	Tr	6	116
LJ MINOR Teriyaki Sauce, 1 serving	4	0	21	1	Tr	Tr	1	159
ORTEGA Enchilada Sauce, 1 serving	2	Tr	15	1	Tr	Tr	7	77
ORTEGA Picante Sauce, 1 serving	2	0	10	Tr	Tr	Tr	13	252
Sauce, pasta, spaghetti/marinara, ready-to-serve, 1 cup	21	4	143	5	1	4	55	1030
Soup, bean with ham, canned, chunky, 1 cup	27	11	231	9	3	13	78	972
Soup, beef broth bouillon and consomme, canned, condensed, 1 cup	4	0	59	0	0	11	17	1279
Soup, beef mushroom, canned, prepared with equal volume water, 1 cup	6	Tr	73	3	1	6	5	942
Soup, beef stroganoff, canned, chunky style, 1 cup	22	1	235	11	6	12	48	1044
Soup, beef with vegetables and barley, canned, 1 serving	10	NA	77	2	1	5	NA	898
Soup, black bean, canned, prepared with equal volume water, 1 cup	20	4	116	2	Tr	6	44	1198

Food, portion	Total Carb (g)	Fiber (g)	Calories	Total Fat (g)	Sat Fat (g)	Protein (g)	Calcium (mg)	Sodium (mg)
Soups, Sauces, and Gravies (cont.)								
Soup, chicken broth, canned, prepared with equal volume water, 1 cup	1	0	38	1	Tr	5	10	763
Soup, chicken noodle, canned, prepared with equal volume water, 1 cup	9	1	75	2	1	4	17	1106
Soup, chicken vegetable, canned, prepared with equal volume water, 1 cup	9	1	75	3	1	4	17	945
Soup, chicken with rice, canned, prepared with equal volume water, 1 cup	7	1	60	2	Tr	4	17	815
Soup, chili beef, canned, prepared with equal volume water, 1 cup	21	10	170	7	3	7	43	1035
Soup, clam chowder, New England, canned, prepared with equal volume milk, 1 cup	17	1	164	7	3	9	186	992
Soup, cream of chicken, canned, prepared with equal volume water, 1 cup	9	Tr	117	7	2	3	34	986
Soup, cream of chicken, prepared with equal volume milk, 1 cup	15	Tr	191	11	5	7	181	1047
Soup, cream of mushroom, canned, prepared with equal volume milk, 1 cup	15	Tr	203	14	5	6	179	918
Soup, cream of potato, canned, prepared with equal volume milk, 1 cup	17	Tr	149	6	4	6	166	1061
Soup, lentil with ham, canned, 1 cup	20	NA	139	3	1	9	42	1319
Soup, minestrone, chunky, ready-to-serve, 1 cup	21	6	127	3	1	5	60	864
Soup, mushroom barley, canned, prepared with equal volume water, 1 cup	12	1	73	2	Tr	2	12	891
Soup, onion, canned, condensed, 1 cup	16	2	113	3	1	8	54	2116
Soup, pea, green, canned, prepared with equal volume milk, 1 cup	32	3	239	7	4	13	173	970
Soup, sirloin burger with vegetables, ready-to-serve, 1 serving	16	6	185	9	3	10	NA	866

Food, portion	Total Carb (g)	Fiber (g)	Calories	Total Fat (g)	Sat Fat (g)	Protein (g)	Calcium (mg)	Sodium (mg)
Soup, tomato, canned, prepared with equal volume milk, 1 cup	22	3	161	6	3	6	159	744
Soup, tomato, canned, prepared with equal volume water, 1 cup	17	Tr	85	2	Tr	2	12	695
Soup, turkey noodle, canned, condensed, 1 cup	17	2	138	4	1	8	23	1632
Soup, vegetable beef, prepared with equal volume water, 1 cup	10	Tr	78	2	1	6	17	791
Soup, vegetarian vegetable, canned, prepared with equal volume water, 1 cup	12	Tr	72	2	Tr	2	22	822
Sweets								
100 GRAND Bar, 1 bar, 1.5 oz	31	Tr	192	8	5	1	30	86
3 MUSKETEERS Bar, 1 bar, 1.81 oz	39	1	212	7	3	2	43	99
5TH AVENUE Candy Bar, 1 bar	35	2	270	13	4	5	41	126
AFTER EIGHT Mints, 1 serving	31	1	147	6	3	1	9	5
ALMOND JOY Candy Bar, 1 package, 1.76 oz	29	2	235	13	9	2	31	70
BABY RUTH Bar, 1 bar, 0.75 oz	13	1	97	5	3	1	9	45
BIT-O'-HONEY Candy Chews, 6 pieces	32	0	160	3	2	1	20	120
BUTTERFINGER Bar, 1 bar, fun size	15	Tr	100	4	2	1	7	45
Butterscotch, 3 pieces	14	0	63	1	Tr	Tr	Tr	63
CARAMELLO Candy Bar, 1 bar, 1.25 oz	22	Tr	162	7	4	2	75	43
Caramels, 1 piece	8	Tr	39	1	1	Tr	14	25
Chewing gum, 1 stick	2	Tr	7	Tr	Tr	0	0	Tr
CHUNKY Bar, 1 bar, 1.25 oz	20	2	173	10	8	3	50	19
Frostings, chocolate, creamy, ready-to-eat, 2 tbsp	26	Tr	163	7	2	Tr	3	75
Frostings, vanilla, creamy, ready-to-eat, package	26	Tr	160	6	1	0	1	70
Frozen yogurts, chocolate, 1 cup	38	4	221	6	4	5	174	110

Food, portion	Total Carb (g)	Fiber (g)	Calories	Total Fat (g)	Sat Fat (g)	Protein (g)	Calcium (mg)	Sodium (mg)
Sweets (cont.)								
Fruit and juice bars, 1 bar, 2.5 fl oz	16	1	63	Tr	0	1	4	3
Fudge, chocolate, prepared-from-recipe, 1 piece	13	Tr	70	2	1	Tr	8	8
GOOBERS Chocolate Covered Peanuts, 1 serving	20	3	210	14	5	6	52	17
Gumdrops, starch jelly, 10 gummy bears	22	Tr	87	0	0	0	1	10
Hard candies, 1 piece	6	0	24	Tr	0	0	Tr	2
HEATH BITES, 15 pieces	25	1	207	12	6	2	34	96
HERSHEY'S MILK CHOCOLATE WITH ALMOND BITES, 17 pieces	20	1	215	14	7	4	86	29
Honey, 1 tbsp	17	Tr	64	0	0	Tr	1	1
Ice creams, chocolate, ½ cup	19	1	143	7	4	3	72	50
Ice creams, strawberry, ½ cup	18	1	127	6	3	2	79	40
Ice creams, vanilla, ½ cup	17	1	145	8	5	3	92	58
Italian ice, restaurant-prepared, ½ cup	16	0	61	Tr	0	Tr	1	5
Jams and preserves, 1 tbsp	14	Tr	56	Tr	Tr	Tr	4	6
Jellies, 1 serving	15	Tr	56	Tr	Tr	Tr	1	6
Jelly beans, 10 large	26	Tr	105	Tr	0	0	1	14
KIT KAT BIG KAT Bar, 1 bar, 1.94 oz	35	1	286	15	10	3	76	35
KRACKEL Chocolate Bar, 1 bar, 1.45 oz	26	1	210	11	7	3	65	80
"M&M's" Milk Chocolate Candies, 1 package, 1.69 oz	34	1	236	10	6	2	50	29
"M&M's" Peanut Chocolate Candies, 1 package, 1.67 oz	28	2	243	12	5	4	47	23
MARS Almond Bar, 1 bar, 1.76 oz	31	1	234	12	4	4	84	85
Marshmallows, 1 regular	6	Tr	23	Tr	Tr	Tr	Tr	6
Milk chocolate, 10 kisses	27	2	246	14	7	4	87	36
MILKY WAY Bar, 1 bar, 1.9 oz	39	1	228	9	4	2	70	130

Food, portion	Total Carb (g)	Fiber (g)	Calories	Total Fat (g)	Sat Fat (g)	Protein (g)	Calcium (mg)	Sodium (mg)
Molasses, 1 tbsp	15	0	58	Tr	Tr	0	41	7
Molasses, blackstrap, 1 tbsp	12	0	47	0	0	0	172	11
MOUNDS Candy Bar, 1 package, 1.9 oz	31	2	258	14	11	2	11	77
MR. GOODBAR Chocolate Bar, 1 bar, 1.75 oz	27	2	264	16	7	5	54	20
OH HENRY! Bar, 1 bar	17	1	120	6	2	2	21	60
Pie fillings, apple, canned, 1 can	156	6	601	1	Tr	1	24	262
Pie fillings, canned, cherry, 1 can	167	4	684	Tr	Tr	2	65	107
POLANER ALL-FRUIT Strawberry Spread, 1 tbsp	10	NA	42	0	0	Tr	NA	4
Puddings, banana, ready-to-eat, 5 oz	30	Tr	180	5	1	3	121	278
Puddings, chocolate, ready-to-eat, 5 oz	33	1	197	6	1	4	128	183
Puddings, lemon, ready-to-eat, 5 oz	36	Tr	178	4	1	Tr	3	199
Puddings, rice, ready-to-eat, 5 oz	31	Tr	231	11	2	3	74	121
Puddings, tapioca, ready-to-eat, 5 oz	28	Tr	169	5	1	3	119	226
Puddings, vanilla, ready-to-eat, 4 oz	25	0	146	4	1	3	99	153
RAISINETS Chocolate Covered Raisins, 1 package	32	2	185	7	3	2	49	16
REESE'S CRUNCHY COOKIE CUPS, 1 package, ¾ oz	12	1	101	6	2	2	16	52
REESE'S NUTRAGEOUS Candy Bar, 2 bars	18	1	176	11	3	4	23	48
REESE'S PEANUT BUTTER CUPS, 1 package, 1.6 oz	25	2	232	14	5	5	35	141
REESE'S PIECES Candy, 1 package, 1.63 oz	28	1	229	11	8	6	32	89
ROLO Caramels in Milk Chocolate, 1 package, 1.91 oz	37	Tr	256	11	8	3	78	102
Sherbet, orange, 1 bar, 2.75 fl oz	20	2	95	1	1	1	36	30

☐ Good Carb Choice ☐ Better Carb Choice

Food, portion	Total Carb (g)	Fiber (g)	Calories	Total Fat (g)	Sat Fat (g)	Protein (g)	Calcium (mg)	Sodium (mg)
Sweets (cont.)								
SKITTLES Bite Size Candies, 1 package, 2 oz	52	0	231	2	Tr	Tr	0	9
SKOR Toffee Bar, 1 bar, 1.4 oz	24	1	209	13	7	1	NA	124
SNICKERS Bar, 1 bar, 2 oz	34	1	273	14	5	5	54	152
SPECIAL DARK Chocolate Bar, 1 bar, 1.45 oz	24	3	218	13	0	2	12	2
STARBURST Fruit Chews, 1 serving	34	0	158	3	Tr	Tr	2	22
Sugars, brown, 1 tsp, packed	4	0	17	0	0	0	4	2
Sugars, granulated, 1 tsp	4	0	16	0	0	0	Tr	0
Sugars, powdered, 1 tsp unsifted	2	0	10	0	0	0	0	0
SYMPHONY Milk Chocolate Bar, 1 bar, 1.5 oz	24	1	223	13	8	4	105	42
Syrups, chocolate, fudge-type, 2 tbsp	24	1	133	3	2	2	38	131
Syrups, corn, dark, 1 tbsp	16	0	57	0	0	0	4	31
Syrups, corn, light, 1 tbsp	16	0	59	Tr	0	0	1	24
Syrups, maple, 1 tbsp	13	0	52	Tr	Tr	0	13	2
Syrups, table blends, pancake, 1 tbsp	12	Tr	47	0	0	0	1	16
Toppings, butterscotch or caramel, 2 tbsp	27	Tr	103	Tr	Tr	1	22	143
Toppings, strawberry, 2 tbsp	28	Tr	107	Tr	Tr	Tr	3	9
TWIX Caramel Cookie Bars, 1 package, 2.06 oz	38	1	289	14	5	3	52	112
TWIZZLERS Strawberry Twists Candy, 4 pieces	30	0	133	1	0	1	0	109
YORK Peppermint Pattie, 1 patty, 1.5 oz	35	1	165	3	2	1	5	12
Vegetables and Vegetable Products								
Artichoke, cooked, boiled, with salt, 1 artichoke	13	6	60	Tr	Tr	4	54	397

FOOD, PORTION	TOTAL CARB (G)	FIBER (G)	CALORIES	TOTAL FAT (G)	SAT FAT (G)	PROTEIN (G)	CALCIUM (MG)	SODIUM (MG)
Artichoke hearts, cooked, boiled, without salt, ½ cup	9	5	42	Tr	Tr	3	38	80
Artichokes, raw, 1 artichoke	13	7	60	Tr	Tr	4	56	120
Asparagus, canned, solids and liquids, ½ cup	3	1	18	Tr	Tr	2	18	32
Asparagus, frozen, boiled, with salt, 1 cup	3	3	32	1	Tr	5	32	432
Asparagus, raw, 1 medium spear	1	Tr	3	Tr	Tr	Tr	4	0
Bamboo shoots, boiled, drained, 1 cup	2	1	14	Tr	Tr	2	14	5
Beans, fava, in pod, raw, 1 cup	22	NA	111	1	Tr	10	47	32
Beans, lima, canned, regular, solids and liquids, ½ cup	17	4	88	Tr	Tr	5	35	312
Beans, snap, green, boiled, drained, 1 cup	10	4	44	Tr	Tr	2	55	1
Beans, snap, green, canned, 1 cup	6	3	27	Tr	Tr	2	35	3
Beans, snap, green, raw, 1 cup	8	4	34	Tr	Tr	2	41	7
Beans, snap, yellow, boiled, drained, 1 cup	10	4	44	Tr	Tr	2	58	4
Beans, snap, yellow, raw, 1 cup	8	4	34	Tr	Tr	2	41	7
Beet greens, raw, 1 cup	2	1	8	Tr	Tr	1	44	86
Beets, raw, 1 cup	13	4	58	Tr	Tr	2	22	106
Beets, sliced, boiled, drained, ½ cup	8	2	37	Tr	Tr	1	14	65
Beets, sliced, canned, drained solids, 1 cup	12	3	53	Tr	Tr	2	26	330
Broccoli, chopped, boiled, drained, ½ cup	6	3	27	Tr	Tr	2	31	32
Broccoli, chopped, raw, 1 cup	6	2	30	Tr	Tr	2	41	29
Brussels sprouts, boiled, drained, 1 sprout	1	1	8	Tr	Tr	1	8	4
Brussels sprouts, raw, 1 sprout	2	1	8	Tr	Tr	1	8	5
Cabbage, napa, cooked, 1 cup	2	NA	13	Tr	0	1	32	12
Cabbage (pak-choi), boiled, drained, 1 cup	3	2	20	Tr	Tr	3	158	58

Food, portion	Total Carb (g)	Fiber (g)	Calories	Total Fat (g)	Sat Fat (g)	Protein (g)	Calcium (mg)	Sodium (mg)
Vegetables and Vegetable Products (cont.)								
Cabbage, raw, 1 cup, shredded	4	2	17	Tr	Tr	1	33	13
Carrot juice, canned, 1 cup	22	2	94	Tr	Tr	2	57	68
Carrots, baby, raw, 1 medium	1	Tr	4	Tr	Tr	Tr	3	8
Carrots, canned, regular pack, drained solids, 1 cup, sliced	8	2	36	Tr	Tr	Tr	36	353
Carrots, raw, 1 medium	6	2	25	Tr	Tr	1	20	42
Carrots, sliced, boiled, drained, ½ cup	6	2	27	Tr	Tr	1	23	45
Catsup, 1 tbsp	4	Tr	14	Tr	Tr	Tr	3	167
Cauliflower, boiled, drained, ½ cup	3	2	14	Tr	Tr	1	10	9
Cauliflower, raw, 1 floweret	1	Tr	3	Tr	Tr	Tr	3	4
Celery, diced, boiled, drained, 1 cup	6	2	27	Tr	Tr	1	63	137
Celery, diced, raw, 1 cup	4	2	17	Tr	Tr	1	48	96
Chard, Swiss, chopped, boiled, drained, 1 cup	7	4	35	Tr	Tr	3	102	313
Chard, Swiss, raw, 1 cup	1	1	7	Tr	Tr	1	18	77
Coleslaw, home-prepared, ½ cup	7	1	41	2	Tr	1	27	14
Collards, chopped, boiled, drained, 1 cup	9	5	49	1	Tr	4	266	30
Collards, raw, 1 cup	2	1	11	Tr	Tr	1	52	7
Coriander (cilantro), raw, 9 sprigs	1	1	5	Tr	Tr	Tr	13	9
Corn, sweet, white, boiled, drained, with salt, 1 ear	19	2	83	1	Tr	3	2	195
Corn, sweet, white, canned, cream style, regular pack, 1 cup	46	3	184	1	Tr	4	8	730
Corn, sweet, white, canned, whole kernel, drained solids, 1 cup	30	3	133	2	Tr	4	8	530
Corn, sweet, white, raw, 1 ear	27	4	123	2	Tr	5	3	21
Corn, sweet, yellow, boiled, drained, 1 ear	19	2	83	1	Tr	3	2	13

Food, portion	Total Carb (g)	Fiber (g)	Calories	Total Fat (g)	Sat Fat (g)	Protein (g)	Calcium (mg)	Sodium (mg)
Corn, sweet, yellow, canned, cream style, 1 cup	46	3	184	1	Tr	4	8	8
Corn, sweet, yellow, canned, whole kernel, drained solids, 1 cup	30	3	133	2	Tr	4	8	351
Corn, sweet, yellow, raw, 1 ear	27	4	123	2	Tr	5	3	21
Cowpeas (blackeyes), boiled, drained, 1 cup	40	11	224	1	Tr	14	39	9
Cowpeas, leafy tips, chopped, boiled, drained, 1 cup	1	NA	12	Tr	Tr	2	37	3
Cowpeas, leafy tips, raw, 1 leaf	Tr	NA	1	Tr	Tr	Tr	2	Tr
Cucumber, sliced, peeled, raw, 1 cup	3	1	14	Tr	Tr	1	17	2
Eggplant, boiled, drained, 1 cup	9	2	35	Tr	Tr	1	6	1
Gourd calabash, boiled, drained, with salt, 1 cup	5	NA	22	Tr	Tr	1	35	347
Grape leaves, canned, 1 leaf	Tr	NA	3	Tr	Tr	Tr	12	114
Kale, boiled, drained, 1 cup	7	3	36	1	Tr	2	94	30
Kale, raw, 1 cup	7	1	34	Tr	Tr	2	90	29
Leeks (bulb and lower leaf-portion), boiled, drained, 1 leek	9	1	38	Tr	Tr	1	37	12
Leeks (bulb and lower leaf-portion), raw, 1 leek	13	2	54	Tr	Tr	1	53	18
Lettuce, cos or romaine, raw, 1 inner leaf	Tr	Tr	2	Tr	Tr	Tr	3	1
Lettuce, green leaf, raw, 1 leaf	Tr	Tr	2	Tr	Tr	Tr	4	3
Lettuce, iceberg, raw, 1 leaf	Tr	Tr	2	Tr	Tr	Tr	3	1
Lettuce, red leaf, raw, 1 leaf, inner	Tr	Tr	Tr	Tr	0	Tr	1	1
Mountain yam, raw, 1 yam	69	NA	281	Tr	Tr	6	109	55
Mountain yam, steamed, 1 cup, cubed	29	NA	119	Tr	Tr	3	12	17
Mung beans, sprouted, stir-fried, 1 cup	13	2	62	Tr	Tr	5	16	11
Mushrooms, canned, drained solids, 1 medium	1	Tr	3	Tr	Tr	Tr	1	51

☐ Good Carb Choice ☐ Better Carb Choice

Food, portion	Total Carb (g)	Fiber (g)	Calories	Total Fat (g)	Sat Fat (g)	Protein (g)	Calcium (mg)	Sodium (mg)
Vegetables and Vegetable Products (cont.)								
Mushrooms, raw, 1 medium	1	Tr	4	Tr	Tr	1	1	1
Mushrooms, shiitake, dried, 1 mushroom	3	Tr	11	Tr	Tr	Tr	Tr	Tr
Mustard greens, boiled, drained, 1 cup	3	3	21	Tr	Tr	3	104	22
New Zealand spinach, chopped boiled, drained, 1 cup	4	NA	22	Tr	Tr	2	86	193
Okra, raw, 8 pods	7	3	29	Tr	Tr	2	77	8
Okra, sliced, boiled, drained, ½ cup	4	2	18	Tr	Tr	1	62	5
Onion rings, breaded, frozen, heated in oven, 10 rings	23	1	244	16	5	3	19	225
Onions, boiled, drained, 1 cup	21	3	92	Tr	Tr	3	46	6
Onions, raw, chopped, 1 tbsp	1	Tr	4	Tr	Tr	Tr	2	Tr
Onions, raw, 1 medium	11	2	46	Tr	Tr	1	24	3
Onions, raw, 1 thin slice	1	Tr	4	Tr	Tr	Tr	2	Tr
Parsley, raw, 10 sprigs	1	Tr	4	Tr	Tr	Tr	14	6
Peas and carrots, frozen, boiled, drained, ½ cup	8	2	38	Tr	Tr	2	18	54
Peas, boiled, drained, 1 cup	11	4	67	Tr	Tr	5	67	6
Peas, green, boiled, drained, 1 cup	25	9	134	Tr	Tr	9	43	5
Peas, green, canned, seasoned, solids and liquids, 1 cup	21	5	114	1	Tr	7	34	577
Peas, green, raw, 1 cup	21	7	117	1	Tr	8	36	7
Pepper, serrano, raw, 1 pepper	Tr	Tr	2	Tr	Tr	Tr	1	1
Peppers, hot chili, green, raw, 1 pepper	4	1	18	Tr	Tr	1	8	3
Peppers, hot chili, red, raw, 1 pepper	4	1	19	Tr	Tr	1	6	4
Peppers, jalapeno, raw, 1 pepper	1	Tr	4	Tr	Tr	Tr	1	Tr
Peppers, sweet, green, raw, 1 pepper	6	2	24	Tr	Tr	1	12	4
Peppers, sweet, red, raw, 1 pepper	7	2	31	Tr	Tr	1	8	2

FOOD, PORTION	TOTAL CARB (G)	FIBER (G)	CALORIES	TOTAL FAT (G)	SAT FAT (G)	PROTEIN (G)	CALCIUM (MG)	SODIUM (MG)
Peppers, sweet, yellow, raw, 1 pepper	12	2	50	Tr	Tr	2	20	4
Pickle, cucumber, sour, 1 slice	Tr	Tr	1	Tr	Tr	Tr	0	85
Pickle, cucumber, sweet, 1 midget gherkin	2	Tr	7	Tr	Tr	Tr	Tr	56
Pickle, cucumber, sweet, 1 slice	2	Tr	8	Tr	Tr	Tr	Tr	66
Pickle relish, hot dog, 1 tbsp	4	Tr	14	Tr	Tr	Tr	1	164
Pickle relish, sweet, 1 tbsp	5	Tr	20	Tr	Tr	Tr	Tr	122
Pickles, cucumber, dill, 1 slice	Tr	Tr	1	Tr	Tr	Tr	1	90
Poi, 1 cup	65	1	269	Tr	Tr	1	38	29
Potato, baked, flesh and skin, 1 medium	37	4	161	Tr	Tr	4	26	17
Potato flour, 1 cup	133	9	571	1	Tr	11	104	88
Potato pancakes, home-prepared, 1 pancake	22	2	207	12	2	5	18	386
Potato salad, home-prepared, 1 cup	28	3	358	21	4	7	48	1323
Potatoes, au gratin, home-prepared from recipe using butter, 1 cup	28	4	323	19	12	12	292	1061
Potatoes, boiled, cooked without skin, flesh, with salt, 1 medium	33	3	144	Tr	Tr	3	13	402
Potatoes, french fried, frozen, heated in oven, with salt, 10 strips	16	2	100	4	1	2	4	133
Potatoes, hashed brown, home-prepared, 1 cup	55	5	413	20	2	5	22	534
Potatoes, mashed, home-prepared, whole milk and margarine, 1 cup	36	3	237	9	2	4	42	699
Potatoes, mashed, prepared from flakes, whole milk and butter, 1 cup	23	2	204	11	6	4	61	344
Potatoes, red, flesh and skin, baked, 1 medium	34	3	154	Tr	Tr	4	16	14
Potatoes, russet, flesh and skin, baked, 1 medium	37	4	168	Tr	0	5	31	14

Food, portion	Total Carb (g)	Fiber (g)	Calories	Total Fat (g)	Sat Fat (g)	Protein (g)	Calcium (mg)	Sodium (mg)
Vegetables and Vegetable Products (cont.)								
Potatoes, scalloped, home-prepared with butter, 1 cup	26	5	211	9	6	7	140	821
Potatoes, white, flesh and skin, baked, 1 medium	36	4	163	Tr	Tr	4	17	12
Rutabagas, boiled, drained, 1 cup	15	3	66	Tr	Tr	2	82	34
Sauerkraut, canned, solids and liquids, 1 cup	6	4	27	Tr	Tr	1	43	939
Soybeans, sprouted, cooked, 1 cup	6	1	76	4	1	8	55	9
Spinach, canned, solids and liquids, 1 cup	7	5	44	1	Tr	5	194	176
Spinach, frozen, chopped or leaf, boiled, drained, ½ cup	5	4	30	Tr	Tr	4	145	92
Spinach, raw, 1 cup	1	1	7	Tr	Tr	1	30	24
Squash, butternut, cubed, baked, 1 cup	22	NA	82	Tr	Tr	2	84	8
Squash, summer, crookneck and straightneck, sliced, boiled, drained, 1 cup	11	3	48	Tr	Tr	2	38	12
Squash, summer, sliced, boiled, drained, 1 cup	8	3	36	1	Tr	2	49	2
Squash, winter, acorn, cubed, baked, 1 cup	30	9	115	Tr	Tr	2	90	8
Sweet potato, canned, vacuum pack, 1 cup	42	4	182	Tr	Tr	3	44	106
Sweet potato, cooked, baked in skin, 1 medium	24	4	103	Tr	Tr	2	43	41
Sweet potato, cooked, candied, home-prepared, 1 piece	29	3	144	3	1	1	27	74
Tomatillos, raw, 1 medium	2	1	11	Tr	Tr	Tr	2	Tr
Tomato juice, canned, 1 cup	10	1	41	Tr	Tr	2	24	24
Tomato products, canned, paste, with salt added, 6 oz can	32	8	139	1	Tr	7	61	1343
Tomato products, canned, sauce, 1 cup	18	4	78	1	Tr	3	32	1284

FOOD, PORTION	TOTAL CARB (G)	FIBER (G)	CALORIES	TOTAL FAT (G)	SAT FAT (G)	PROTEIN (G)	CALCIUM (MG)	SODIUM (MG)
Tomato products, canned, sauce, with mushrooms, 1 cup	21	4	86	Tr	Tr	4	32	1107
Tomato products, canned, sauce, with onions, green peppers, and celery, 1 cup	22	4	103	2	Tr	2	33	1365
Tomatoes, green, raw, 1 medium	6	1	28	Tr	Tr	1	16	16
Tomatoes, red, ripe, canned, stewed, 1 cup	16	3	66	Tr	Tr	2	87	564
Tomatoes, red, ripe, canned, whole, 1 medium	5	1	21	Tr	Tr	1	33	11
Tomatoes, red, ripe, cooked, 1 cup	10	2	43	Tr	Tr	2	26	26
Tomatoes, red, ripe, raw, 1 cup	8	2	38	1	Tr	2	9	16
Tomatoes, red, ripe, raw, 1 cherry	1	Tr	4	Tr	Tr	Tr	1	2
Tomatoes, sun-dried, 1 cup	30	7	139	2	Tr	8	59	1131
Turnip greens and turnips, frozen, boiled, drained, 1 cup	5	3	34	Tr	Tr	3	148	24
Turnips, raw, 1 cup	8	2	36	Tr	Tr	1	39	87
Vegetable juice cocktail, canned, 1 cup	11	2	46	Tr	Tr	2	27	653
Vegetables, mixed, canned, drained solids, 1 cup	15	5	80	Tr	Tr	4	44	243
Wasabi, root, raw, 1 cup, sliced	31	10	142	1	0	6	166	22
Waterchestnuts (matai), sliced, raw, ½ cup	15	2	60	Tr	Tr	1	7	9
Watercress, raw, 1 cup, chopped	Tr	Tr	4	Tr	Tr	1	41	14
Yam, cubed, boiled, drained, or baked, 1 cup	38	5	158	Tr	Tr	2	19	11
Yam, raw, 1 cup	42	6	177	Tr	Tr	2	26	14
Yardlong bean, sliced, boiled, drained, 1 cup	10	NA	49	Tr	Tr	3	46	4
Zucchini, baby, raw, 1 medium	Tr	Tr	2	Tr	Tr	Tr	2	Tr
Zucchini, includes skin, frozen boiled, drained, 1 cup	8	3	38	Tr	Tr	3	38	4

Enjoy Good Carb, Better Carb Recipes

The delectable recipes in this section will help you explore a whole new world of healthy eating. Choosing more good carbs will add color to your plate and flavor, as well as important nutrients and fiber, to your diet.

Nutritional information is provided with each recipe so you can make smart-carb choices. (Totals do not include optional ingredients or serving suggestions.) Preparation times are based on the approximate amount of time needed to assemble the recipe, including measuring, mixing, and chopping.

As you try these dishes, you'll see how easy it is to turn nutritious into simply delicious!

Go with Grains & Legumes

Thin-Crust Whole Wheat Veggie Pizza

Who doesn't love pizza? This healthy version contains whole grains, veggies and protein and tastes better than any pizza parlor version!

¾ to 1 cup all-purpose flour, divided
½ cup whole wheat flour
1 teaspoon quick-rise active dry yeast
1½ teaspoons dried basil leaves, crushed, divided
¼ teaspoon salt
1 tablespoon olive oil
1 large clove garlic, minced
½ cup very warm water (120° to 130°F)
1 teaspoon yellow cornmeal
½ cup no-salt-added tomato sauce
1 cup thinly sliced mushrooms
½ cup thinly sliced zucchini
⅓ cup chopped green onions
1 large roasted red bell pepper,* cut lengthwise into thin strips *or* ¾ cup sliced, drained, bottled roasted red peppers
1 cup (4 ounces) shredded part-skim mozzarella cheese
¼ teaspoon red pepper flakes

To roast pepper, cut pepper lengthwise into halves; remove stem, membrane and seeds. Broil 3 inches from heat, skin side up, until skin is blackened and blistered. Place halves in small resealable plastic food storage bag. Seal; set aside 15 minutes. Remove pepper from bag. Peel off skin; drain on paper towel.

Combine ½ cup all-purpose flour, whole wheat flour, yeast, 1 teaspoon basil and salt. Blend oil with garlic in small cup; stir into flour mixture with water. Stir in ¼ cup all-purpose flour until soft, slightly sticky dough forms, adding remaining ¼ cup all-purpose flour to prevent sticking if necessary. Knead dough on lightly floured surface about 5 minutes or until smooth and elastic. Shape dough into a ball. Cover with inverted bowl or clean towel; let rest 10 minutes.

Place oven rack in lowest position; preheat oven to 400°F. Spray 12-inch pizza pan or baking sheet with nonstick cooking spray; sprinkle with cornmeal and set aside. Roll dough into large circle on lightly floured surface. Transfer to prepared pan, stretching dough out to edge of pan. (Too much rolling makes crust heavy and dense; stretching dough to fit pan is best.)

Blend tomato sauce and remaining ½ teaspoon basil in small bowl; spread evenly over crust. Top with mushrooms, zucchini, green onions, roasted bell pepper and mozzarella; sprinkle crushed red pepper on top. Bake 20 to 25 minutes or until crust is golden brown and cheese melts.

Makes 4 servings

Thin-Crust Whole Wheat Veggie Pizza

Turkey Breast with Barley-Cranberry Stuffing

Thanks to a slow cooker, this meal cooks itself while you're away! You'll come home to a delicious, healthy dish of lean protein paired with grains and fruit.

Nutrients per serving:

Calories: 298
Carbohydrate: 33 g
Calories From Fat: 13%
Total Fat: 5 g
Saturated Fat: 1 g
Cholesterol: 55 mg
Sodium: 114 mg
Dietary Fiber: 6 g
Protein: 31 g

2 cups fat-free reduced-sodium chicken broth
1 cup uncooked quick-cooking barley
½ cup chopped onion
½ cup dried cranberries
2 tablespoons slivered almonds, toasted
½ teaspoon rubbed sage
½ teaspoon garlic-pepper seasoning
Nonstick cooking spray
1 fresh or frozen bone-in turkey breast half (about 2 pounds), thawed and skinned
⅓ cup finely chopped fresh parsley

Slow Cooker Directions

1. Combine broth, barley, onion, cranberries, almonds, sage and garlic-pepper seasoning in slow cooker.

2. Spray large nonstick skillet with cooking spray. Heat over medium heat until hot. Brown turkey breast on all sides; add to slow cooker. Cover; cook on LOW 3 to 4 hours or until internal temperature of turkey reaches 170°F when tested with meat thermometer inserted into thickest part of breast, not touching bone.

3. Transfer turkey to cutting board; cover with foil and let stand 10 to 15 minutes before carving. Internal temperature will rise 5° to 10°F during stand time. Stir parsley into sauce mixture in slow cooker. Serve sliced turkey with sauce and stuffing.

Makes 6 servings

Turkey Breast with Barley-Cranberry Stuffing

Bulgur Pilaf with Tomato & Zucchini

Bulgur is a light, nutty version of whole wheat that has been pre-cooked to cut preparation time down to practically zero. Paired with zucchini and tomato, bulgur makes this healthful dish a fast, easy way to enjoy whole-grain goodness.

Nutrients per serving:

Calories: 98
Carbohydrate: 18 g
Calories From Fat: 19%
Total Fat: 2 g
Saturated Fat: trace g
Cholesterol: 0 mg
Sodium: 92 mg
Dietary Fiber: 5 g
Protein: 3 g

1 cup uncooked bulgur wheat
1 tablespoon olive oil
¾ cup chopped onion
2 cloves garlic, minced
½ pound zucchini, thinly sliced
1 can (14½ ounces) no-salt-added whole tomatoes, drained and coarsely chopped
1 cup fat-free reduced-sodium chicken broth*
1 teaspoon dried basil leaves, crushed
⅛ teaspoon black pepper

1. Rinse bulgur thoroughly in colander under cold water, removing any debris. Drain well; set aside.

2. Heat oil in large saucepan over medium heat. Add onion and garlic; cook and stir 3 minutes or until onion is tender. Stir in zucchini and tomatoes; reduce heat to medium-low. Cook, covered, 15 minutes or until zucchini is almost tender, stirring occasionally.

3. Stir chicken broth, bulgur, basil and pepper into vegetable mixture. Bring to a boil over high heat. Reduce heat to low. Cook, covered, over low heat 15 minutes or until bulgur is tender and liquid is almost completely absorbed, stirring occasionally. Remove from heat; let stand, covered, 10 minutes. Stir gently before serving.

Makes 8 servings

Bulgur Pilaf with Tomato & Zucchini

Whole Wheat Popovers

Using whole wheat flour instead of all-purpose flour increases nutrients and adds flavor to these popovers. They're easy to make, and magical to watch pop up if your oven has a window.

1¼ cups whole wheat pastry flour
1¼ cups milk
 3 eggs
 2 tablespoons melted butter
 ¼ teaspoon salt
 1 tablespoon cold butter, cut into pieces

1. Position rack in lower third of oven. Preheat oven to 400°F. Spray popover pan with nonstick cooking spray. (If popover pan is not available, jumbo muffin tin or custard cups may be used.)

2. Place flour, milk, eggs, melted butter and salt in food processor or blender. Process until batter is smooth and the consistency of heavy cream. (Batter may also be blended in large bowl with electric mixer.) Meanwhile, place popover pan in oven for 2 minutes to preheat. Immediately place one piece of cold butter in each popover cup and return to oven 1 minute until butter melts.

3. Fill each cup halfway with batter. Bake 20 minutes.(Do not open oven or popovers may fall.) Reduce oven temperature to 350°F. Bake 20 minutes more. Remove from cups and cool slightly on wire rack. Serve warm.   *Makes 6 popovers*

Nutrients per serving:
Calories: 201
Carbohydrate: 21g
Calories From Fat: 44%
Total Fat: 10 g
Saturated Fat: 4 g
Cholesterol: 126 mg
Sodium: 200 mg
Dietary Fiber: 3 g
Protein: 8 g

Black Bean Mexicali Salad

 1 can (15 ounces) black beans, rinsed and drained
 1 cup fresh or thawed frozen corn
 6 ounces roasted red bell peppers, cut into thin strips or coarsely chopped
 ½ cup chopped red or yellow onion, divided
 ⅓ cup mild chipotle or regular salsa
 2 tablespoons cider vinegar
 2 ounces part-skim mozzarella cheese, cut into ¼-inch cubes

1. Place all ingredients except cheese and 1 tablespoon onion in medium bowl. Toss gently to blend well. Let stand 15 minutes to blend flavors.

2. Just before serving, gently fold in all but 2 tablespoons of cheese. Sprinkle remaining cheese and reserved tablespoon onion on top.   *Makes 7 servings*

Nutrients per serving:
Calories: 124
Carbohydrate: 22 g
Calories From Fat: 13%
Total Fat: 2 g
Saturated Fat: 1 g
Cholesterol: 5 mg
Sodium: 278 mg
Dietary Fiber: 5 g
Protein: 7 g

Whole Wheat Popovers

Hot Three-Bean Casserole

Chick-peas and kidney beans add soluble fiber to this spicy side-dish casserole.

  2 tablespoons olive oil
  1 cup coarsely chopped onion
  1 cup chopped celery
  2 cloves garlic, minced
  1 can (15 ounces) chick-peas (garbanzo beans), rinsed and drained
  1 can (15 ounces) kidney beans, rinsed and drained
  1 cup coarsely chopped tomato
  1 can (8 ounces) tomato sauce
  1 cup water
  1 to 2 jalapeño peppers,* minced
  1 tablespoon chili powder
  2 teaspoons sugar
  1½ teaspoons ground cumin
  1 teaspoon salt
  1 teaspoon dried oregano
  ¼ teaspoon black pepper
  2½ cups (10 ounces) frozen cut green beans

Jalapeño peppers can sting and irritate the skin; wear rubber gloves when handling peppers and do not touch your eyes. Wash hands after handling jalapeño peppers.

1. Heat olive oil in large skillet over medium heat until hot. Add onion, celery and garlic. Cook and stir 5 minutes or until onion is translucent.

2. Add remaining ingredients except green beans. Bring to a boil; reduce heat to low. Simmer, uncovered, 20 minutes. Add green beans. Simmer, uncovered, 10 minutes or until green beans are just tender.   *Makes 12 servings*

Hot Three-Bean Casserole

Nutrients per serving:

Calories: 210
Carbohydrate: 34 g
Calories From Fat: 30%
Total Fat: 8 g
Saturated Fat: 1 g
Cholesterol: 0 mg
Sodium: 15 mg
Dietary Fiber: 8 g
Protein: 6 g

Tabbouleh in Tomato Cups

4 large firm ripe tomatoes (about 8 ounces each)
2 tablespoons olive oil
4 green onions with tops, thinly sliced diagonally
1 cup bulgur wheat
1 cup water
2 tablespoons lemon juice
1 tablespoon chopped fresh mint leaves
Salt and pepper
Lemon peel and mint leaves for garnish

1. To prepare tomato cups, remove stems. Cut tomatoes in half crosswise. Scoop pulp and seeds out of tomatoes into medium bowl, leaving ¼-inch-thick shells.

2. Invert tomatoes on paper-towel-lined plate; let drain 20 minutes. Meanwhile, chop tomato pulp. Set aside.

3. Heat oil in 2-quart saucepan over medium-high heat. Cook and stir white parts of onions in hot oil 1 to 2 minutes until wilted. Add bulgur; cook 3 to 5 minutes until browned.

4. Add reserved tomato pulp, water, lemon juice and mint to bulgur mixture. Bring to a boil over high heat; reduce heat to medium-low. Cover; simmer gently 15 to 20 minutes until liquid is absorbed.

5. Set aside a few sliced green onion tops for garnish; stir remaining green onions into bulgur mixture. Add salt and pepper to taste. Spoon mixture into tomato cups.*

6. Preheat oven to 400°F. Place filled cups in 13×9-inch baking dish; bake 15 minutes or until heated through. Top with reserved onion tops. Garnish, if desired. Serve immediately.   *Makes 4 main-dish servings*

Tomato cups may be covered and refrigerated at this point up to 24 hours.

Tabbouleh in Tomato Cups

Nutrients per serving:

Calories: 264
Carbohydrate: 35 g
Calories From Fat: 22%
Total Fat: 7 g
Saturated Fat: <1 g
Cholesterol: 0 mg
Sodium: 667 mg
Dietary Fiber: 16 g
Protein: 19 g

Hearty Lentil Stew

1 cup dried lentils, sorted, rinsed and drained
1 package (16 ounces) frozen green beans
2 cups cauliflower florets
1 cup chopped onion
1 cup baby carrots, cut in half crosswise
3 cups fat-free reduced-sodium chicken broth
2 teaspoons ground cumin
¾ teaspoon ground ginger
1 can (15 ounces) chunky tomato sauce with garlic and herbs
½ cup dry-roasted peanuts

Slow Cooker Directions

1. Place lentils in slow cooker. Top with green beans, cauliflower, onion and carrots. Combine broth, cumin and ginger in large bowl; mix well. Pour mixture over vegetables. Cover; cook on LOW 9 to 11 hours.

2. Stir in tomato sauce. Cover; cook on LOW 10 minutes. Ladle stew into bowls. Sprinkle peanuts evenly over each serving. *Makes 6 servings*

Hearty Lentil Stew

Wild Rice & Lentil Pilaf

4½ cups water, divided
¾ cup dried brown lentils, sorted, rinsed and drained
1 box (6.2-ounce) quick-cooking white and wild rice with seasoning packet
1 tablespoon plus 2 teaspoons extra-virgin olive oil, divided
2 cups finely chopped yellow onions
1 medium red bell pepper, chopped
1 cup thinly sliced celery
4 cloves garlic, minced
½ teaspoon dried oregano leaves
½ teaspoon salt
Dash ground red pepper (optional)

1. Bring 4 cups water to a boil in medium saucepan. Stir in lentils and return to a boil. Reduce heat to low and simmer, uncovered, 10 minutes. Stir in rice and seasoning packet. Cover tightly and simmer 5 minutes. Remove from heat; set aside.

2. Meanwhile, heat large nonstick skillet over medium-high heat until hot. Add 2 teaspoons oil and tilt skillet to coat bottom evenly. Add onions, bell pepper, celery, garlic and oregano; cook 12 minutes or until celery is crisp-tender, stirring frequently. Stir in remaining ½ cup water, salt and ground red pepper, if desired.

3. Stir onion mixture and remaining 1 tablespoon oil into rice mixture; toss gently.

Makes 7 (1-cup) servings

Variation: For a more decorative dish, coat a 6-cup mold with cooking spray. Place rice mixture in mold and press down gently but firmly to allow rice mixture to stick together. Place a dinner plate on top of mold and invert mold onto plate. Tap gently on side and top of mold to release rice mixture and slowly remove mold. Garnish with red bell pepper cutouts or strips.

Wild Rice & Lentil Pilaf

Nutrients per
serving:

(1 slice bread)

Calories: 51
Carbohydrate: 6 g
Calories From Fat: 35%
Total Fat: 2 g
Saturated Fat: g
Cholesterol: 0 mg
Sodium: 79 mg
Dietary Fiber: 1 g
Protein: 2 g

No-Knead Sandwich Bread

There's no need to leave the bread off your sandwich—bake up a delicious, healthy loaf with this easy recipe. As a bonus, nothing beats the aroma of freshly baked bread!

2 packages (2¼ teaspoons) active dry yeast
¾ cup warm water (110° to 115°F)
3 tablespoons canola oil
1 cup all-purpose flour
⅔ cup uncooked old-fashioned oats
¼ cup soy flour*
¼ cup wheat gluten*
¼ cup sesame seeds*
2 teaspoons sugar substitute
1 teaspoon salt

* Soy flour, wheat gluten and sesame seeds are available in the natural foods sections of many supermarkets and at health food stores.

1. Stir yeast into water in small bowl; let stand 5 minutes. Add oil.

2. Combine all-purpose flour, oats, soy flour, gluten, sesame seeds, sugar substitute and salt in food processor fitted with plastic dough blade. Using on/off pulsing action, process until well blended.

3. With processor running, slowly pour yeast mixture through feed tube; then using on/off pulsing action, process until dough comes together and forms a mass. Unlock processor lid, but do not remove; let dough rise 1 hour or until doubled in bulk.

4. Spray 8×4×2-inch loaf pan with nonstick cooking spray. Using on/off pulsing action, process briefly until dough comes together and forms a ball. Turn dough onto floured work surface. Shape into disc. (Dough will be slightly sticky.) Roll dough on floured surface into 12×8-inch rectangle. Roll up from short side; fold under ends and place in prepared pan. Cover with towel; let rise in warm place 45 minutes or until doubled in bulk.

5. Preheat oven to 375°F. Bake 35 minutes or until bread is golden brown and sounds hollow when tapped. Remove from pan and cool completely on wire rack. Cut into 30 (¼-inch-thick) slices before serving. *Makes 30 servings*

No-Knead Sandwich Bread

Savory Lentil Casserole

1¼ cups dried brown or green lentils, sorted, rinsed and drained
2 tablespoons olive oil
1 large onion, chopped
3 cloves garlic, minced
8 ounces fresh shiitake or button mushrooms, sliced
2 tablespoons all-purpose flour
1½ cups beef broth
1 tablespoon Worcestershire sauce
1 tablespoon balsamic vinegar
4 ounces Canadian bacon, minced
½ teaspoon salt
½ teaspoon black pepper
½ cup grated Parmesan cheese
2 to 3 plum tomatoes, seeded and chopped

1. Preheat oven to 400°F. Place lentils in medium saucepan; cover with enough water to come 1 inch over lentils. Bring to a boil over high heat. Reduce heat to low. Simmer, covered, 20 to 25 minutes until lentils are barely tender; drain.

2. Meanwhile, heat oil in large skillet over medium heat. Add onion and garlic; cook and stir 3 minutes. Add mushrooms; cook and stir 10 minutes or until liquid is evaporated and mushrooms are tender. Sprinkle flour over mushroom mixture; stir well. Cook and stir 1 minute. Stir in beef broth, Worcestershire, vinegar, Canadian bacon, salt and pepper. Cook and stir until mixture is thick and bubbly.

3. Grease 1½-quart casserole. Stir lentils into mushroom mixture. Spread evenly in prepared casserole. Sprinkle with cheese. Bake 20 minutes.

4. Sprinkle tomatoes over casserole just before serving.   *Makes 4 servings*

Savory Lentil Casserole

Cannellini Parmesan Casserole

Nutrients per serving:

Calories: 302
Carbohydrate: 47 g
Calories From Fat: %
Total Fat: 10 g
Saturated Fat: g
Cholesterol: 10 mg
Sodium: 1440 mg
Dietary Fiber: 12 g
Protein: 21 g

A super-quick dish chock full of good-for-you beans and vegetables. All you need to add is a leafy green side salad and a slice of whole grain bread.

2 tablespoons olive oil
1 cup chopped onion
2 teaspoons minced garlic
1 teaspoon dried oregano leaves
¼ teaspoon black pepper
2 cans (14½ ounces each) onion- and garlic-flavored diced tomatoes, undrained
1 jar (14 ounces) roasted red peppers, drained and cut into ½-inch squares
2 cans (about 19 ounces each) white cannellini beans or Great Northern beans, rinsed and drained
1 teaspoon dried basil leaves *or* 1 tablespoon chopped fresh basil
¾ cup (3 ounces) grated Parmesan cheese

1. Heat oil in Dutch oven over medium heat until hot. Add onion, garlic, oregano and black pepper; cook and stir 5 minutes or until onion is tender.

2. Increase heat to high. Add tomatoes with juice and red peppers; cover and bring to a boil.

3. Reduce heat to medium. Stir in beans; cover and simmer 5 minutes, stirring occasionally. Stir in basil and sprinkle with cheese.   *Makes 6 servings*

Prep and Cook Time: 20 minutes

Cannellini Parmesan Casserole

Chive Whole Wheat Drop Biscuits

These healthy biscuits are a welcome accompaniment to soups, chicken, or meal-in-one salads. They also make a tasty afternoon snack.

1¼ cups whole wheat flour
¾ cup all-purpose flour
3 tablespoons toasted wheat germ, divided
1 tablespoon baking powder
1 tablespoon chopped fresh chives *or* 1 teaspoon dried chives
2 teaspoons sugar
3 tablespoons cold margarine
1 cup fat-free (skim) milk
½ cup shredded low-fat process American cheese

1. Preheat oven to 450°F. Spray baking sheet with nonstick cooking spray; set aside.

2. Combine whole wheat flour, all-purpose flour, 2 tablespoons wheat germ, baking powder, chives and sugar in medium bowl. Cut in margarine with pastry blender or two knives until mixture resembles coarse meal. Add milk and American cheese; stir until just combined.

3. Drop dough by rounded teaspoonfuls about 1 inch apart onto prepared baking sheet. Sprinkle with remaining 1 tablespoon wheat germ. Bake 10 to 12 minutes or until golden brown. Remove immediately from baking sheet. Serve warm.

Makes 12 servings

Nutrients per serving:

(1 biscuit)

Calories: 125
Carbohydrate: 18 g
Calories From Fat: 28%
Total Fat: 4 g
Saturated Fat: 2 g
Cholesterol: 3 mg
Sodium: 237 mg
Dietary Fiber: 2 g
Protein: 5 g

Chive Whole Wheat Drop Biscuits

Curried Walnut Grain Burgers

Here's a way to enjoy grains, nuts and veggies all rolled into one scrumptious burger. Make these burgers even healthier with whole wheat couscous, bread crumbs and burger buns.

Nutrients per serving:

Calories: 381
Carbohydrate: 49 g
Calories From Fat: 34%
Total Fat: 14 g
Saturated Fat: 2 g
Cholesterol: 106 mg
Sodium: 689 mg
Dietary Fiber: 4 g
Protein: 15 g

2 eggs
⅓ cup plain yogurt
2 teaspoons Worcestershire sauce
2 teaspoons curry powder
½ teaspoon salt
¼ teaspoon ground red pepper
1⅓ cups cooked couscous or brown rice
½ cup finely chopped walnuts
½ cup grated carrot
½ cup minced green onions
⅓ cup plain dry bread crumbs
4 sesame seed hamburger buns
  Honey mustard
  Thinly sliced cucumber or apple
  Alfalfa sprouts

1. Combine eggs, yogurt, Worcestershire sauce, curry, salt and red pepper in large bowl; beat until blended. Stir in couscous, walnuts, carrot, green onions and bread crumbs. Shape into 4 (1-inch-thick) patties.

2. Coat grill rack with nonstick cooking spray; place rack on grill over medium-hot coals (350° to 400°F). Place burgers on rack and grill 5 to 6 minutes per side or until done. Serve on buns with mustard, cucumber and sprouts. *Makes 4 servings*

Variation: Burgers can be broiled 4 inches from heat source for 5 to 6 minutes per side or until done.

Note: To lower the carb count serve on a bed of greens instead of a bun.

Prep and Cook Time: 25 minutes

Curried Walnut Grain Burger

Nutrients per serving:

Calories: 238
Carbohydrate: 37 g
Calories From Fat: 30%
Total Fat: 8 g
Saturated Fat: 1 g
Cholesterol: 1 mg
Sodium: 693 mg
Dietary Fiber: 4 g
Protein: 6 g

Mixed Grain Tabbouleh

Adding brown rice to this traditional Middle Eastern favorite adds a healthy twist. You get the benefit of two nutritious complex carb grains—bulgur and brown rice.

½ **cup uncooked bulgur wheat**
3 **cups canned chicken broth, divided**
1 **cup uncooked long grain brown rice**
1 **cup chopped tomatoes**
¼ **cup fresh mint leaves, chopped**
¼ **cup fresh basil, chopped**
¼ **cup fresh oregano, chopped**
½ **cup minced green onions, including green parts**
3 **tablespoons fresh lemon juice**
3 **tablespoons olive oil**
½ **teaspoon salt**
½ **teaspoon black pepper**

1. Combine bulgur and 1 cup chicken broth in 1-quart saucepan. Bring to a boil over medium-high heat. Reduce heat to low. Simmer, covered, 15 minutes or until broth is absorbed and bulgur is fluffy; set aside.

2. Meanwhile, combine brown rice and remaining 2 cups chicken broth in 2-quart saucepan. Bring to a boil over medium-high heat. Reduce heat to low. Simmer, covered, about 45 minutes or until broth is absorbed and rice is tender; set aside.

3. Combine tomatoes, chopped herbs, green onions, lemon juice, oil, salt and pepper in large bowl. Stir in bulgur and rice. Allow to cool to room temperature. Garnish with lemon wedges and mint leaves, if desired.

Makes 6 (1-cup) servings

Mixed Grain Tabbouleh

Ham, Barley and Almond Bake

This one-dish meal showcases barley in a delicious mixture of veggies and herbs. Pair with a side salad of mixed leafy greens.

½ **cup slivered almonds**
1 **tablespoon margarine or butter**
1 **cup uncooked barley**
1 **cup chopped carrots**
1 **bunch green onions, sliced**
2 **ribs celery, sliced**
3 **cloves garlic, minced**
1 **pound lean smoked ham, cubed**
2 **teaspoons dried basil leaves**
1 **teaspoon dried oregano leaves**
¼ **teaspoon black pepper**
2 **cans (14 ounces each) reduced-sodium beef broth**
½ **pound fresh green beans, cut into 1-inch pieces**

1. Preheat oven to 350°F. Spray 13×9-inch baking dish with nonstick cooking spray; set aside.

2. Spread almonds in single layer on baking sheet. Bake 5 minutes or until golden brown, stirring frequently. Set aside.

3. Melt margarine in large skillet over medium-high heat. Add barley, carrots, onions, celery and garlic; cook and stir 2 minutes or until onions are tender. Remove from heat. Stir in ham, toasted almonds, basil, oregano and pepper. Pour into prepared dish.

4. Add broth to medium saucepan; bring to a boil over high heat. Pour over barley mixture.

5. Cover tightly with foil and bake 20 minutes. Remove from oven; stir in green beans. Bake, covered, 30 minutes or until barley is tender.   *Makes 8 servings*

Ham, Barley and Almond Bake

Whole Wheat Herb Bread

Pass the bread basket and help yourself to this delicious whole-wheat treat. Enjoy it as an accompaniment to hearty soups and meal-in-one salads.

⅔ cup water
⅔ cup fat-free (skim) milk
2 teaspoons sugar
2 envelopes active dry yeast
3 egg whites, lightly beaten
3 tablespoons olive oil
1 teaspoon salt
½ teaspoon dried basil leaves
½ teaspoon dried oregano leaves
4 to 4½ cups whole wheat flour, divided

1. Bring water to a boil in small saucepan. Remove from heat; stir in milk and sugar. When mixture cools to warm (110° to 115°F), add yeast. Mix well; let stand 10 minutes or until bubbly.

2. Blend egg whites, oil, salt, basil and oregano in large bowl. Add yeast mixture; mix well. Add 4 cups flour, ½ cup at a time, mixing well after each addition, until dough is no longer sticky. Knead about 5 minutes or until smooth and elastic, adding enough of remaining flour to make a smooth and elastic dough. Form into a ball. Cover and let rise in warm place about 1 hour or until doubled in bulk.

3. Preheat oven to 350°F. Punch dough down and place on lightly floured surface. Divide into 4 pieces and roll each piece into a ball. Lightly spray baking sheet with nonstick cooking spray. Place dough balls on prepared baking sheet. Bake 30 to 35 minutes or until golden brown and loaves sound hollow when tapped with finger.

Makes 24 servings (4 round loaves, 6 slices per loaf)

Nutrients per serving:
(1 slice)

Calories: 90
Carbohydrate: 17 g
Calories From Fat: 20%
Total Fat: 2 g
Saturated Fat: <1 g
Cholesterol: <1 mg
Sodium: 109 mg
Dietary Fiber: 3 g
Protein: 4 g

Whole Wheat Herb Bread

Far East Tabbouleh

Nutrients per serving:

Calories: 73
Carbohydrate: 13 g
Calories From Fat: 23%
Total Fat: 2 g
Saturated Fat: <1 g
Cholesterol: 0 mg
Sodium: 156 mg
Dietary Fiber: 3 g
Protein: 2 g

1¾ cups boiling water
¾ cup bulgur wheat
2 tablespoons lemon juice
2 tablespoons reduced-sodium teriyaki sauce
1 tablespoon olive oil
¾ cup diced seeded cucumber
¾ cup diced seeded tomato
½ cup thinly sliced green onions
½ cup minced fresh cilantro or parsley
1 tablespoon minced fresh ginger
1 clove garlic, minced

1. Combine water and bulgur in small bowl. Cover with plastic wrap; let stand 45 minutes or until bulgur is puffed, stirring occasionally. Drain in wire mesh sieve; discard liquid.

2. Combine bulgur, lemon juice, teriyaki sauce and oil in large bowl. Stir in cucumber, tomato, onions, cilantro, ginger and garlic until well blended. Cover; refrigerate 4 hours, stirring occasionally. Garnish as desired.   *Makes 4 servings*

Far East Tabbouleh

French Lentil Salad

Nutrients per serving:

Calories: 264
Carbohydrate: 34 g
Calories From Fat: 28%
Total Fat: 8 g
Saturated Fat: 1 g
Cholesterol: 0 mg
Sodium: 406 mg
Dietary Fiber: 8 g
Protein: 16 g

Two healthy carb foods, lentils and walnuts, star in this fiber-packed, protein-rich salad. Tote this along for lunch, but let it sit at room temperature for about 30 minutes before you eat it—the flavors will be even more pronounced.

¼ **cup chopped walnuts**
1½ **cups dried lentils, sorted, rinsed and drained**
4 **green onions, finely chopped**
3 **tablespoons balsamic vinegar**
2 **tablespoons chopped fresh parsley**
1 **tablespoon olive oil**
¾ **teaspoon salt**
½ **teaspoon dried thyme leaves**
¼ **teaspoon black pepper**

1. Preheat oven to 375°F.

2. Spread walnuts in even layer on baking sheet. Bake 5 minutes or until lightly browned. Cool completely on baking sheet; set aside.

3. Combine 2 quarts water and lentils in large saucepan; bring to a boil over high heat. Cover; reduce heat to medium-low. Simmer 30 minutes or until lentils are tender, stirring occasionally. Drain lentils; discard liquid.

4. Combine lentils, onions, vinegar, parsley, oil, salt, thyme and pepper in large bowl. Cover; refrigerate 1 hour or until cool.

5. Serve on lettuce leaves, if desired. Top with toasted walnuts before serving.

Makes 4 servings

French Lentil Salad

Help Yourself to Vegetables

Nutrients per serving:

Calories: 225
Carbohydrate: 30 g
Calories From Fat: 22%
Total Fat: 6 g
Saturated Fat: 3 g
Cholesterol: 27 mg
Sodium: 729 mg
Dietary Fiber: 6 g
Protein: 15 g

Grilled Portobello Mushroom Sandwich

    1 large portobello mushroom, cleaned and stem removed
    ¼ medium green bell pepper, halved
    1 thin slice red onion
    1 whole wheat hamburger bun, split
    2 tablespoons fat-free Italian dressing
    1 (1 ounce) reduced-fat part-skim mozzarella cheese slice

1. Brush mushroom, bell pepper, onion and cut sides of bun with dressing; set bun aside. Place vegetables over medium-hot coals. Grill 2 minutes.

2. Turn vegetables over; brush with dressing. Grill 2 minutes or until vegetables are tender. Remove bell pepper and onion from grill.

3. Place bun halves on grill cut sides down. Turn mushroom top side up; brush with any remaining dressing and cover with cheese, if desired. Grill 1 minute or until cheese is melted and bun is lightly toasted.

4. Cut pepper into strips. Place mushroom on bottom half of bun; top with pepper strips and onion slice. Cover with top half of bun.

Note: To broil, brush mushroom, bell pepper, onion and cut sides of bun with dressing. Place vegetables on greased rack of broiler pan; set bun aside. Broil vegetables 4 to 6 inches from heat 3 minutes; turn over. Brush with dressing. Broil 3 minutes or until vegetables are tender. Place mushroom, top side up, on broiler pan; top with cheese. Place bun, cuts sides up, on broiler pan. Broil 1 minute or until cheese is melted and bun is toasted. Assemble sandwich as directed above.

Makes 1 serving

Grilled Portobello Mushroom Sandwich

Curried Eggplant, Squash & Chick-Pea Stew

Whether you call them chick-peas, or garbanzo beans, it's smart to enjoy more of these luscious legumes. Chick-peas provide more iron than most other beans and are high in fiber, too.

Nutrients per serving:

Calories: 216
Carbohydrate: 38 g
Calories From Fat: 14%
Total Fat: 4 g
Saturated Fat: <1 g
Cholesterol: 0 mg
Sodium: 477 mg
Dietary Fiber: 10 g
Protein: 7 g

   1 **teaspoon olive oil**
½ **cup diced red bell pepper**
¼ **cup diced onion**
1¼ **teaspoons curry powder**
   1 **clove garlic, minced**
½ **teaspoon salt**
1¼ **cups cubed peeled eggplant**
¾ **cup cubed peeled acorn or butternut squash**
⅔ **cup rinsed and drained canned chick-peas (garbanzo beans)**
½ **cup vegetable broth or water**
   3 **tablespoons white wine**
     Hot pepper sauce (optional)
¼ **cup lemon-flavored sugar-free yogurt**
   2 **tablespoons chopped fresh parsley**

1. Heat oil in medium saucepan over medium heat. Add bell pepper and onion; cook and stir 5 minutes. Stir in curry powder, garlic and salt. Add eggplant, squash, chick-peas, broth and wine to saucepan. Cover; bring to a boil. Reduce heat and simmer 20 to 25 minutes just until squash and eggplant are tender.

2. Season to taste with hot pepper sauce, if desired. Serve with yogurt and parsley.

Makes 2 servings

Curried Eggplant, Squash & Chick-Pea Stew

Caribbean Coleslaw

You've never tasted coleslaw like this! Mangoes and red and yellow bell peppers are good sources of vitamins C and A. Tossed with cabbage and onions, they make a nutrient-packed side dish.

Orange-Mango Dressing (recipe follows)
8 cups shredded green cabbage
1½ large mangoes, peeled, pitted and diced
½ medium red bell pepper, thinly sliced
½ medium yellow bell pepper, thinly sliced
6 green onions, thinly sliced
¼ cup chopped fresh cilantro

1. Prepare Orange-Mango Dressing.

2. Combine cabbage, mangoes, bell peppers, green onions and cilantro in large bowl; stir gently to mix. Add Orange-Mango Dressing; toss gently to coat. Serve, or store in refrigerator up to 1 day. *Makes 12 servings*

Orange-Mango Dressing

½ mango, peeled, pitted and cubed
1 carton (6 ounces) plain nonfat yogurt
¼ cup frozen orange juice concentrate
3 tablespoons lime juice
½ to 1 jalapeño pepper,* stemmed, seeded and minced
1 teaspoon finely minced fresh ginger

*Jalapeño peppers can sting and irritate the skin; wear rubber gloves when handling peppers and do not touch eyes. Wash hands after handling.

Place mango in food processor; process until smooth. Add remaining ingredients; process until smooth.

Nutrients per serving:
Calories: 57
Carbohydrate: 14 g
Calories From Fat: 4%
Total Fat: <1 g
Saturated Fat: <1 g
Cholesterol: <1 mg
Sodium: 26 mg
Dietary Fiber: 2 g
Protein: 2 g

Caribbean Coleslaw

Southwestern Omelet Wrap

Refried beans add a healthy source of protein and fiber to this tempting omelet. Look for brands of refried beans that contain no lard.

Nutrients per serving:

Calories: 286
Carbohydrate: 16 g
Calories From Fat: 53%
Total Fat: 17 g
Saturated Fat: g
Cholesterol: 243 mg
Sodium: 796 mg
Dietary Fiber: 4 g
Protein: 19 g

2 teaspoons cornstarch
1 tablespoon water
1 egg
  Nonstick cooking spray
3 tablespoons canned refried beans, warmed
½ cup finely shredded romaine or iceberg lettuce
¼ cup (1 ounce) shredded Monterey Jack or Cheddar cheese
2 tablespoons chunky salsa
1 tablespoon bacon bits

1. To make omelet, dissolve cornstarch in water in small bowl. Add egg; whisk until blended.

2. Spray large nonstick skillet lightly with cooking spray; heat over medium-high heat. Add egg mixture, tilting skillet to cover bottom of skillet. Cook 1 to 2 minutes or until set. Turn omelet over; cook 30 seconds. Turn out onto cutting board, browned side down.

3. To make wrap, spread beans to edge of omelet. Sprinkle evenly with lettuce, cheese, salsa and bacon bits.

4. Gently roll up, sealing with refried beans. Serve immediately or wrap in plastic wrap and refrigerate. *Makes 1 serving*

Southwestern Omelet Wrap

Salsa Salad Bowl

Nutrients per serving:

Calories: 282
Carbohydrate: 37 g
Calories From Fat: 30%
Total Fat: 10 g
Saturated Fat: 4 g
Cholesterol: 16 mg
Sodium: 140 mg
Dietary Fiber: 11 g
Protein: 17 g

1 can (15 ounces) low-sodium black beans, rinsed and drained
1 pint cherry tomatoes, preferably sweet grape, quartered
4 ounces Mozzarella cheese, cut into ¼-inch cubes
½ of a medium poblano pepper or green bell pepper, chopped
½ cup chopped red onion
⅓ cup chopped fresh cilantro
¼ cup lime juice (juice of 2 medium limes)
1 tablespoon extra-virgin olive oil
¼ teaspoon salt
⅛ teaspoon cayenne pepper

1. In medium mixing bowl, combine beans, tomatoes, cheese, poblano pepper, onion and cilantro. Cover and refrigerate until needed.

2. Combine lime juice, olive oil, salt and cayenne in small container. Cover and refrigerate until needed.

3. To transport individual servings, place equal amounts of salad in 4 quart-size resealable plastic food storage bags or lidded containers. Stir dressing and put about 1½ tablespoons of dressing in each of 4 small resealable plastic food storage bags. Place the smaller bags inside the larger bags.

4. To serve, pour dressing into quart-size bag with salad. Seal bag and toss to coat salad with dressing.   *Makes 4 servings*

Salsa Salad Bowl

Italian Eggplant with Millet & Pepper Stuffing

¼ **cup uncooked millet**
2 **small eggplants (about ¾ pound total)**
¼ **cup chopped red bell pepper, divided**
¼ **cup chopped green bell pepper, divided**
1 **teaspoon olive oil**
1 **clove garlic, minced**
1½ **cups fat-free reduced-sodium chicken broth***
½ **teaspoon ground cumin**
½ **teaspoon dried oregano leaves, crushed**
⅛ **teaspoon red pepper flakes**

1. Stir millet in large, heavy skillet over medium heat 5 minutes or until golden. Transfer to small bowl; set aside.

2. Cut eggplants lengthwise into halves. Scoop out flesh, leaving about ¼-inch thick shell. Reserve shells; chop eggplant flesh. Combine 1 teaspoon red bell pepper and 1 teaspoon green bell pepper in small bowl; set aside.

3. Heat oil in same skillet over medium heat. Add chopped eggplant, remaining red bell pepper, green bell pepper and garlic; cook and stir about 8 minutes or until eggplant is tender.

4. Stir in toasted millet, chicken broth, cumin, oregano and crushed red pepper. Bring to a boil over high heat. Reduce heat to medium-low. Cook, covered, 35 minutes or until all liquid has been absorbed and millet is tender. Remove from heat; let stand, covered, 10 minutes. Preheat oven to 350°F. Pour 1 cup water into 8-inch square baking pan.

5. Fill reserved eggplant shells with eggplant-millet mixture. Sprinkle shells with reserved chopped bell peppers, pressing in lightly. Carefully place filled shells in prepared pan. Bake 15 minutes or until heated through.   *Makes 4 servings*

Italian Eggplant with Millet & Pepper Stuffing

Lemon & Fennel Marinated Vegetables

Although most vegetables lose vitamins during cooking, carrots are an exception. Cooking breaks down the cell walls of carrots, releasing far more beta-carotene than raw carrots. Beta-carotene is an anti-oxidant that may help prevent cancer and other diseases.

Nutrients per serving:

Calories: 47
Carbohydrate: 9 g
Calories From Fat: 24%
Total Fat: 1 g
Saturated Fat: <1 g
Cholesterol: 0 mg
Sodium: 15 mg
Dietary Fiber: 2 g
Protein: 1 g

1 cup water
2 medium carrots, cut diagonally into ½-inch-thick slices
1 cup small whole fresh mushrooms
1 small red or green bell pepper, cut into ¾-inch pieces
3 tablespoons lemon juice
1 tablespoon sugar
1 tablespoon olive oil
1 clove garlic, minced
½ teaspoon fennel seeds, crushed
½ teaspoon dried basil leaves, crushed
¼ teaspoon black pepper

1. Bring water to a boil in small saucepan over high heat. Add carrots; return to a boil. Reduce heat to medium-low. Cover and simmer about 5 minutes or until carrots are crisp-tender. Drain and cool.

2. Place carrots, mushrooms and bell pepper in large resealable plastic food storage bag. Combine lemon juice, sugar, oil, garlic, fennel seeds, basil and black pepper in small bowl. Pour over vegetables. Close bag securely; turn to coat. Marinate in refrigerator 8 to 24 hours, turning occasionally.

3. Drain vegetables; discard marinade. Place vegetables in serving dish. Serve with toothpicks.

Makes 4 servings

Lemon & Fennel Marinated Vegetables

Santa Fe Grilled Vegetable Salad

Nothing beats the flavor of food off the grill, especially if the marinade is as robust as this citrus-enhanced Southwestern fare. You may want to peel the eggplant after grilling as the skin may be slightly bitter.

Nutrients per serving:

Calories: 63
Carbohydrate: 11 g
Calories From Fat: 27%
Total Fat: 2 g
Saturated Fat: <1 g
Cholesterol: <1 mg
Sodium: 70 mg
Dietary Fiber: 1 g
Protein: 2 g

2 baby eggplants (6 ounces each), cut in half lengthwise
1 medium yellow summer squash, cut in half lengthwise
1 medium zucchini, cut in half lengthwise
1 green bell pepper, quartered
1 red bell pepper, quartered
1 small onion, peeled and cut in half
½ cup orange juice
2 tablespoons lime juice
1 tablespoon olive oil
2 cloves garlic, minced
1 teaspoon dried oregano leaves
¼ teaspoon salt
¼ teaspoon ground red pepper
¼ teaspoon black pepper
2 tablespoons chopped fresh cilantro

1. Combine all ingredients except cilantro in large bowl; toss to coat.

2. To prevent sticking, spray grid with nonstick cooking spray. Prepare coals for direct grilling. Place vegetables on grill, 2 to 3 inches from hot coals; reserve marinade. Grill 3 to 4 minutes per side or until tender and lightly charred; cool 10 minutes. Or, place vegetables on rack of broiler pan coated with nonstick cooking spray; reserve marinade. Broil 2 to 3 inches from heat, 3 to 4 minutes per side or until tender; cool 10 minutes.

3. Remove peel from eggplant, if desired. Slice vegetables into bite-size pieces; return to marinade. Stir in cilantro; toss to coat. *Makes 8 servings*

Santa Fe Grilled Vegetable Salad

Spaghetti Squash with Black Beans & Zucchini

Not only is spaghetti squash a good-for-you food, it's also a fun-for-you food! Veggies, beans and flavorful seasonings combine for a delicious and beautiful dish.

Nutrients per serving:

Calories: 219
Carbohydrate: 34 g
Calories From Fat: 30%
Total Fat: 8 g
Saturated Fat: 1 g
Cholesterol: 0 mg
Sodium: 613 mg
Dietary Fiber: 8 g
Protein: 12 g

1 spaghetti squash (about 2 pounds)
2 zucchini, cut lengthwise into ¼-inch-thick slices
  Nonstick cooking spray
2 cups chopped seeded tomatoes
1 can (about 15 ounces) black beans, rinsed and drained
2 tablespoons chopped fresh basil
2 tablespoons olive oil
2 tablespoons red wine vinegar
1 large clove garlic, minced
½ teaspoon salt

1. Pierce spaghetti squash in several places with fork. Wrap in large piece of heavy-duty foil, using drugstore wrap technique.* Grill squash on covered grill over medium coals 45 minutes to 1 hour or until easily depressed with back of long-handled spoon, turning a quarter turn every 15 minutes. Remove squash from grill and let stand in foil 10 to 15 minutes.

2. Meanwhile, spray both sides of zucchini slices with cooking spray. Grill on uncovered grill over medium coals 4 minutes or until tender, turning once.

3. Remove spaghetti squash from foil and cut in half; scoop out seeds. With two forks, comb strands of pulp from each half and place in large salad bowl. Add tomatoes, beans, zucchini and basil. Combine olive oil, vinegar, garlic and salt in small bowl; mix thoroughly. Add to vegetables and toss gently to combine.

Makes 4 servings

*Place food in the center of an oblong piece of heavy-duty foil, leaving at least a two-inch border around the food. Bring the two long sides together above the food; fold down in a series of locked folds, allowing for heat circulation and expansion. Fold short ends up and over again. Press folds firmly to seal the foil packet.

Spaghetti Squash with Black Beans & Zucchini

Moroccan Lentil & Vegetable Soup

Not only do lentils taste good, but they are also high in soluble fiber, which may help lower blood cholesterol.

Nutrients per serving:

Calories: 131
Carbohydrate: 20 g
Calories From Fat: 20%
Total Fat: 3 g
Saturated Fat: <1 g
Cholesterol: 0 mg
Sodium: 264 mg
Dietary Fiber: 2 g
Protein: 8 g

- **1 tablespoon olive oil**
- **1 cup chopped onion**
- **4 medium cloves garlic, minced**
- **½ cup dried lentils, sorted, rinsed and drained**
- **1½ teaspoons ground coriander**
- **1½ teaspoons ground cumin**
- **½ teaspoon black pepper**
- **½ teaspoon ground cinnamon**
- **3¾ cups fat-free reduced-sodium chicken broth**
- **½ cup chopped celery**
- **½ cup chopped sun-dried tomatoes (not packed in oil)**
- **1 medium yellow summer squash, chopped**
- **½ cup chopped green bell pepper**
- **½ cup chopped fresh parsley**
- **1 cup chopped plum tomatoes**
- **¼ cup chopped fresh cilantro or basil**

1. Heat oil in medium saucepan over medium heat. Add onion and garlic; cook 4 to 5 minutes or until onion is tender, stirring occasionally. Stir in lentils, coriander, cumin, black pepper and cinnamon; cook 2 minutes. Add chicken broth, celery and sun-dried tomatoes; bring to a boil over high heat. Reduce heat to low; simmer, covered, 25 minutes.

2. Stir in squash, bell pepper and parsley. Continue cooking, covered, 10 minutes or until lentils are tender.

3. Top with plum tomatoes and cilantro just before serving.   *Makes 6 servings*

Moroccan Lentil & Vegetable Soup

Sweet-Sour Turnip Green Salad

Nutrients per serving:

Calories: 49
Carbohydrate: 11 g
Calories From Fat: 7%
Total Fat: <1 g
Saturated Fat: <1 g
Cholesterol: 0 mg
Sodium: 41 mg
Dietary Fiber: 3 g
Protein: 2 g

Common in the southern United States, turnip greens are an excellent source of vitamins A and C, and are also a good source of calcium.

2 cups shredded stemmed washed turnip greens
2 cups washed mixed salad greens
1 cup sliced plum tomatoes or quartered cherry tomatoes
½ cup shredded carrot
⅓ cup sliced green onions
8 tablespoons water, divided
2 teaspoons all-purpose flour
1 tablespoon packed brown sugar
½ teaspoon celery seeds
   Dash pepper
1 tablespoon white wine vinegar

1. Combine turnip greens, salad greens, tomatoes and carrot in salad bowl; set aside. Combine green onions and 2 tablespoons water in small saucepan. Bring to a boil over high heat. Reduce heat to medium. Cook, covered, 2 to 3 minutes or until onions are tender.

2. Mix remaining 6 tablespoons water and flour in small bowl until smooth. Stir into green onions in saucepan. Add brown sugar, celery seeds and pepper; cook and stir until mixture boils and thickens. Cook and stir 1 minute more. Stir in vinegar. Pour hot dressing over salad; toss to coat. Serve immediately.   *Makes 4 servings*

Sweet-Sour Turnip Green Salad

Nutrients per serving:

Calories: 234
Carbohydrate: 41 g
Calories From Fat: 21%
Total Fat: 6 g
Saturated Fat: 1 g
Cholesterol: 0 mg
Sodium: 340 mg
Dietary Fiber: 14 g
Protein: 8 g

Middle Eastern Grilled Vegetable Wraps

Eating a variety of vegetables not only brings interesting new flavors to the table, it's a delicious and colorful way to get a wide range of nutrients in your diet.

  1 large eggplant (about 1 pound), cut crosswise into ⅜-inch slices
    Nonstick cooking spray
¾ pound large mushrooms
  1 red bell pepper, quartered
  1 green bell pepper, quartered
  2 green onions, sliced
¼ cup fresh lemon juice
⅛ teaspoon black pepper
  4 large (10-inch) fat-free flour tortillas
½ cup (4 ounces) hummus (chickpea spread)*
⅓ cup lightly packed fresh cilantro
12 large fresh basil leaves
12 large fresh mint leaves

Four ounces crumbled reduced-fat feta cheese can be substituted for hummus.

1. Prepare grill for direct cooking.

2. Lightly spray eggplant with cooking spray. If mushrooms are small, thread onto skewers.

3. Grill peppers, skin-side down, over hot coals until blackened. Place in paper bag; seal. Steam 5 minutes; remove skin. Grill eggplant and mushrooms, covered, over medium coals about 2 minutes on each side or until tender and lightly browned. Cut eggplant and peppers into ½-inch strips; cut mushrooms into quarters. Combine grilled vegetables, onions, lemon juice and black pepper in medium bowl.

4. Grill tortillas on both sides about 1 minute or until warmed. Spoon ¼ of hummus, ¼ of herbs, and ¼ of vegetables down center of each tortilla. Roll to enclose filling; serve immediately.   *Makes 4 servings*

Middle Eastern Grilled Vegetable Wrap

Broccoli & Cauliflower Stir-Fry

2 dry-pack sun-dried tomatoes
1 tablespoon plus 1 teaspoon reduced-sodium soy sauce
1 tablespoon rice wine vinegar
1 teaspoon brown sugar
1 teaspoon dark sesame oil
⅛ teaspoon red pepper flakes
2¼ teaspoons canola oil
1 clove garlic, finely chopped
2 cups cauliflower florets
2 cups broccoli florets
⅓ cup thinly sliced red or green bell pepper

1. Place tomatoes in small bowl; cover with boiling water. Let stand 5 minutes. Drain; coarsely chop. Meanwhile, blend soy sauce, vinegar, brown sugar, sesame oil and red pepper flakes in small bowl.

2. Heat vegetable oil in wok or large nonstick skillet over medium-high heat until hot. Add garlic; stir-fry 30 seconds. Add cauliflower and broccoli; stir-fry 4 minutes. Add tomatoes and bell pepper; stir-fry 1 minute or until vegetables are crisp-tender. Add soy sauce mixture; cook and stir until heated through. Serve immediately.

Makes 2 servings

Broccoli & Cauliflower Stir-Fry

Layered Southwest Salad

Nutrients per serving:

Calories: 311
Carbohydrate: 31 g
Calories From Fat: 37%
Total Fat: 14 g
Saturated Fat: 7 g
Cholesterol: 174 mg
Sodium: 1142 mg
Dietary Fiber: 10 g
Protein: 23 g

Creamy Ranch-Style Dressing (recipe follows)
1 **jicama (¾ pound), peeled and cut into 8 wedges**
1 **can (15 ounces) black beans, drained and rinsed**
⅔ **cup salsa**
½ **cup diced red onion**
10 **ounces spinach, washed, stemmed and chopped**
1 **package (10 ounces) frozen corn, cooked, drained and cooled**
4 **large hard-cooked eggs, peeled and sliced**
1½ **cups (6 ounces) shredded Cheddar cheese**
Fresh oregano for garnish

Prepare Creamy Ranch-Style Dressing. Cut jicama wedges crosswise into ⅛-inch-thick slices. Combine beans, salsa and onion in medium bowl. Layer half of spinach, jicama, bean mixture, corn, eggs and Creamy Ranch-Style Dressing in large salad bowl. Repeat first 5 layers beginning with spinach and ending with eggs; sprinkle with cheese. Drizzle with remaining dressing. Cover and refrigerate 1 to 2 hours before serving. Garnish, if desired. *Makes 6 servings*

Creamy Ranch-Style Dressing

⅔ **cup cottage cheese**
½ **cup buttermilk**
1 **tablespoon white wine vinegar**
1 **clove garlic**
½ **teaspoon salt**
½ **teaspoon black pepper**
½ **teaspoon ground cumin**
½ **teaspoon dried oregano**

Combine all ingredients in blender; cover and process until smooth. Cover and refrigerate 1 hour. *Makes 1¹/₂ cups dressing*

Layered Southwest Salad

Marinated Black-Eyed Pea & Tomato Salad

What could be easier or healthier? Perfect on a hot summer day when no one feels like cooking, this refreshing dish boasts five grams of fiber per serving.

Nutrients per serving:

Calories: 145
Carbohydrate: 22 g
Calories From Fat: 25%
Total Fat: 4 g
Saturated Fat: 1 g
Cholesterol: 0 mg
Sodium: 478 mg
Dietary Fiber: 5 g
Protein: 6 g

1 cup diced tomatoes
1 can (15 ounces) black-eyed peas, rinsed and drained
½ cup finely chopped Anaheim or green bell pepper
½ cup chopped fresh parsley
¼ cup finely chopped red onion
2 tablespoons cider vinegar
1 tablespoon extra-virgin olive oil
½ teaspoon dried thyme leaves
¼ teaspoon salt
¼ teaspoon hot pepper sauce

Combine all ingredients in serving bowl; mix well.

Makes 4 servings

Italian-Style Collard Greens

We could all use more greens in our diet—they're packed with vitamin A and phytochemicals. This garlicky Italian specialty pairs collard greens with high-fiber, protein-rich white beans.

Nutrients per serving:

Calories: 148
Carbohydrate: 32 g
Calories From Fat: 12%
Total Fat: 2 g
Saturated Fat: <1 g
Cholesterol: 0 mg
Sodium: 233 mg
Dietary Fiber: 10 g
Protein: 10 g

½ pound collard greens, stemmed and washed
1 teaspoon olive oil
1 cup coarsely chopped celery
¾ cup coarsely chopped onion
2 large cloves garlic, minced
1 can (14½ ounces) no-salt-added stewed tomatoes, undrained
2 teaspoons dried Italian seasoning
1 can (15 ounces) white beans (such as cannellini, Great Northern or navy), rinsed and drained

1. Pat collard greens dry and coarsely chop.

2. Heat oil in large saucepan over medium heat. Add celery, onion and garlic; cook and stir 5 minutes. Add chopped greens, stewed tomatoes with juice and seasoning. Cook and stir, breaking up tomatoes, until greens wilt. Bring to a boil over high heat. Reduce heat to low. Simmer, covered, 15 minutes. Add beans; simmer, covered, 5 minutes more.

Makes 4 servings

Marinated Black-Eyed Pea & Tomato Salad

Eggplant Squash Bake

Eggplant is low in carbohydrate, calories, sodium and fat. No wonder it's such a big part of the Mediterranean diet many nutritionists and doctors consider so healthy. Layered with low-fat cheeses as it is here, eggplant lets you enjoy the flavor of lasagna with a lot less fat and carbs.

½ **cup chopped onion**
1 **clove garlic, minced**
  Nonstick olive oil cooking spray
1 **cup part-skim ricotta cheese**
1 **jar (4 ounces) diced pimientos, drained**
¼ **cup grated Parmesan cheese**
2 **tablespoons fat-free (skim) milk**
1½ **teaspoons dried marjoram**
¾ **teaspoon dried tarragon**
¼ **teaspoon salt**
¼ **teaspoon ground nutmeg**
¼ **teaspoon black pepper**
1 **cup no-sugar-added meatless spaghetti sauce, divided**
½ **pound eggplant, peeled and cut into thin crosswise slices**
2 **medium zucchini, cut in half then lengthwise into thin slices**
2 **medium yellow summer squash, cut in half then lengthwise into thin slices**
2 **tablespoons shredded part-skim mozzarella cheese**

Microwave Directions

1. Combine onion and garlic in medium microwavable bowl. Spray lightly with cooking spray. Microwave at HIGH 1 minute.

2. Add ricotta, pimientos, Parmesan, milk, marjoram, tarragon, salt, nutmeg and pepper; mix well. Spray 9- or 10-inch round microwavable baking dish with cooking spray. Spread ⅓ cup spaghetti sauce in bottom of dish.

3. Layer half of eggplant, zucchini and summer squash in dish; top with ricotta mixture. Layer remaining eggplant, zucchini and summer squash over ricotta mixture. Top with remaining ⅔ cup spaghetti sauce.

4. Cover with vented plastic wrap. Microwave at HIGH 17 to 19 minutes or until vegetables are tender, rotating dish every 6 minutes. Top with mozzarella cheese. Let stand 10 minutes before serving. *Makes 4 servings*

Eggplant Squash Bake

Nutrients per serving:

Calories: 208
Carbohydrate: 39 g
Calories From Fat: 13%
Total Fat: 3 g
Saturated Fat: <1 g
Cholesterol: 0 mg
Sodium: 945 mg
Dietary Fiber: 10 g
Protein: 10 g

Veggie Tostadas

Kidney and Great Northern beans star in these nutritious veggie tostadas. Beans are high in protein and with this peppy Tex-Mex seasoning, you'll never miss the meat in this vegetarian main course.

1 tablespoon olive oil
1 cup chopped onion
1 cup chopped celery
2 large cloves garlic, chopped
1 can (15½ ounces) red kidney beans, rinsed and drained
1 can (15½ ounces) Great Northern beans, rinsed and drained
1 can (14½ ounces) salsa-style diced tomatoes
2 teaspoons mild chili powder
1 teaspoon cumin
2 tablespoons chopped fresh cilantro
6 small corn tortillas
 Optional toppings: shredded lettuce, chopped tomatoes, shredded Cheddar cheese and sour cream

1. Heat oil in large skillet over medium heat. Add onion, celery and garlic. Cook and stir 8 minutes or until softened. Add beans and tomatoes. Stir to blend. Add chili powder and cumin; stir. Reduce heat to medium-low. Simmer 30 minutes, stirring occasionally until thickened.

2. Meanwhile, preheat oven to 400°F. Place tortillas in single layer directly on oven rack. Bake 10 to 12 minutes or until crisp. Place one tortilla on each plate. Spoon bean mixture evenly over each one. Top with lettuce, tomatoes, Cheddar cheese and sour cream to taste. *Makes 6 servings*

Veggie Tostadas

Pick Poultry for Protein

Nutrients per serving:

Calories: 244
Carbohydrate: 15 g
Calories From Fat: 23%
Total Fat: 6 g
Saturated Fat: 1 g
Cholesterol: 76 mg
Sodium: 175 mg
Dietary Fiber: 3 g
Protein: 30 g

Chicken with Kale Stuffing

Kale is a member of the cabbage family. This cruciferous veggie is a nutrition powerhouse packed with vitamins A and C, folic acid (a B vitamin), calcium and iron.

4 boneless skinless chicken breast halves
1 cup sliced mushrooms
½ cup chopped onion
2 tablespoons dry white wine
1 teaspoon chopped fresh oregano *or* **¼ teaspoon dried oregano leaves, crushed**
1 clove garlic, minced
½ teaspoon black pepper
2 cups chopped stemmed washed kale
2 tablespoons light mayonnaise
½ cup seasoned bread crumbs

1. Preheat oven to 400°F. Coat shallow baking dish with nonstick cooking spray; set aside. Remove fat from chicken. Pound chicken with meat mallet to ½-inch thickness; set aside.

2. Heat skillet over medium-high heat. Add mushrooms, onion, wine, oregano, garlic and pepper; cook and stir about 5 minutes or until onion is softened. Add kale; cook and stir until kale is wilted.

3. Spread kale mixture evenly over flattened chicken breasts. Roll up chicken; secure with toothpicks or metal skewers. Brush chicken with mayonnaise; coat with bread crumbs. Place chicken, seam side down, in prepared baking dish. Bake 25 minutes or until chicken is golden brown and no longer pink near centers. Remove toothpicks before serving.

Makes 4 servings

Chicken with Kale Stuffing

Nutrients per serving:

Calories: 182
Carbohydrate: 19 g
Calories From Fat: 10%
Total Fat: 2 g
Saturated Fat: 1 g
Cholesterol: 38 mg
Sodium: 140 mg
Dietary Fiber: 4 g
Protein: 22 g

Mandarin Turkey Salad with Buttermilk-Herb Dressing

This colorful salad combines fruit, vegetables and protein for a balanced main course. Choose in-season vegetables in a variety of colors for maximum nutrition, freshness and taste appeal.

> **Buttermilk-Herb Dressing (recipe follows)**
> **1 can (about 14 ounces) fat-free reduced-sodium chicken broth**
> **1¼ pounds turkey tenderloin, cut in half lengthwise**
> **½ teaspoon dried basil leaves**
> **½ pound (about 8 cups) mesclun salad greens, washed and dried**
> **2 pounds (about 10 cups) raw cut-up vegetables such as broccoli florets, red or yellow bell peppers, carrots and red onion**
> **1 can (11 ounces) mandarin orange segments, drained**

1. Prepare Buttermilk-Herb Dressing; set aside.

2. Place broth in medium saucepan; bring to a boil over high heat. Add turkey and basil. Return to a boil; reduce heat. Simmer, covered, 12 to 14 minutes or until turkey is no longer pink in centers.

3. Remove turkey from broth. When cool enough to handle, shred turkey into strips.

4. Divide salad greens among 6 individual plates. Divide turkey evenly over salad greens. Arrange vegetables and orange segments around turkey. Drizzle each serving with 2 tablespoons Buttermilk-Herb Dressing. *Makes 6 servings*

Buttermilk-Herb Dressing

> **½ cup plus 1 tablespoon nonfat buttermilk**
> **3 tablespoons raspberry-flavored vinegar**
> **1 tablespoon chopped fresh basil leaves**
> **1½ teaspoons snipped fresh chives**
> **¼ teaspoon minced garlic**

Place all ingredients in small bowl; stir to combine. Store, covered in refrigerator up to 2 days. *Makes about ¾ cup*

Mandarin Turkey Salad with Buttermilk-Herb Dressing

Chicken & Wild Rice with Indian Flavors

Did you know that wild rice isn't rice at all? It's actually a long-grain marsh grass? No matter, it's still considered a healthy carbohydrate and it complements the complex flavors of this delicious Indian dish perfectly.

Nutrients per serving:

Calories: 444
Carbohydrate: 33 g
Calories From Fat: 28%
Total Fat: 14 g
Saturated Fat: 2 g
Cholesterol: 99 mg
Sodium: 865 mg
Dietary Fiber: 5g
Protein: 47 g

¾ **teaspoon salt**
¾ **teaspoon ground cumin**
½ **teaspoon black pepper**
½ **teaspoon ground cinnamon**
½ **teaspoon ground turmeric**
4 **boneless skinless chicken breast halves (about 1½ pounds)**
1¼ **cups chicken broth**
1 **cup water**
¾ **cup wild rice**
2 **tablespoons olive oil, divided**
1 **onion, chopped**
2 **carrots sliced**
1 **red bell pepper, chopped**
1 **rib celery, chopped**
2 **cloves garlic, minced**
¼ **cup sliced almonds**

1. Combine salt, cumin, black pepper, cinnamon and turmeric in small bowl. Rub spice mixture on both sides of chicken. Place chicken on plate; cover and refrigerate at least 30 minutes and up to 3 hours.

2. Meanwhile, bring chicken broth and water to a boil in large saucepan. Stir in wild rice, cover and reduce heat to low. Cook about 45 minutes until rice is almost tender.

3. When rice is almost done, preheat oven to 350°F and spray 13×9-inch baking dish with nonstick cooking spray. Heat 1 tablespoon oil in large skillet over medium heat. Add chicken and brown both sides over medium high heat; set aside.

4. Add remaining 1 tablespoon oil to same skillet. Cook and stir onions, bell pepper, celery and garlic for 5 to 10 minutes or until crisp-tender.

5. Add vegetables to cooked rice in saucepan; stir to combine. Spread rice-vegetable mixture in prepared pan. Top with chicken breasts and sprinkle with almonds. Cover tightly with foil and bake 30 minutes or until chicken is no longer pink in center and rice is tender. *Makes 4 servings*

Chicken & Wild Rice with Indian Flavors

Pesto-Coated Baked Chicken

Pesto is Italian for "pounded." It's an uncooked sauce made from fresh basil, pine nuts, olive oil and Parmesan cheese. Slice any leftover chicken and toss it with whole wheat pasta, fresh veggies and olive oil for a yummy pasta salad.

    1 pound boneless skinless chicken breasts cut into ½-inch thick cutlets
    5 tablespoons prepared pesto
1½ teaspoons reduced-fat sour cream
1½ teaspoons reduced-fat mayonnaise
    1 tablespoon shredded Parmesan cheese
    1 tablespoon pine nuts

1. Preheat oven to 450°F. Arrange chicken in single layer in shallow baking pan. Combine pesto, sour cream and mayonnaise in small cup. Brush over chicken. Sprinkle with cheese and pine nuts.

2. Bake 8 to 10 minutes or until cooked through. *Makes 4 servings*

Variation: Chicken can be cooked on an oiled grid over a preheated grill.

Sunburst Chicken Salad

If you've been searching for a unique, delicious chicken salad recipe, look no further. The vitamin C in the kiwi and mandarin oranges boost absorption of iron from the chicken.

    1 tablespoon fat-free mayonnaise
    1 tablespoon fat-free sour cream
    2 teaspoons frozen orange juice concentrate, thawed
    ¼ teaspoon grated orange peel
    1 boneless skinless chicken breast (about ½ pound, cooked and chopped
    1 large kiwi, thinly sliced
    ⅓ cup mandarin oranges
    ¼ cup finely chopped celery
    4 lettuce leaves, washed
    2 tablespoons coarsely chopped cashews

Combine mayonnaise, sour cream, orange juice concentrate and orange peel in small bowl. Add chicken, kiwi, oranges and celery; toss to coat. Cover; refrigerate 2 hours. Serve on lettuce leaves. Sprinkle with cashews. *Makes 2 servings*

Pesto-Coated Baked Chicken

Chicken & Vegetable Tortilla Roll-Ups

Nutrients per serving:

Calories: 284
Carbohydrate: 33 g
Calories From Fat: 14%
Total Fat: 5 g
Saturated Fat: 2 g
Cholesterol: 52 mg
Sodium: 733 mg
Dietary Fiber: 11 g
Protein: 26 g

1 pound boneless skinless chicken breasts, cooked
1 cup chopped broccoli
1 cup diced carrots
1 can (10¾ ounces) 98% fat-free condensed cream of celery soup, undiluted
¼ cup reduced-fat (2%) milk
1 tablespoon dry sherry
½ cup grated Parmesan cheese
6 (10-inch) fat-free flour tortillas

1. Preheat oven to 350°F. Spray 13×9-inch baking dish with nonstick cooking spray; set aside. Cut chicken into 1-inch pieces; set aside.

2. Combine broccoli and carrots in 1-quart microwavable dish. Cover and microwave at HIGH 2 to 3 minutes or until vegetables are crisp-tender; set aside.

3. Combine soup, milk and sherry in small saucepan over medium heat; cook and stir 5 minutes. Stir in Parmesan cheese, chicken, broccoli and carrots. Cook 2 minutes or until cheese is melted. Remove from heat.

4. Spoon ¼ cup chicken mixture onto each tortilla. Roll up and place, seam side down, in prepared baking dish. Bake, covered, 20 minutes or until heated through.

Makes 6 servings

Chicken & Vegetable Tortilla Roll-Ups

Tuscan Chicken with White Beans

This hearty Italian stew will take the chill out of any blustery day. Fresh fennel adds a sweet and slightly licorice flavor to the savory rosemary-scented broth, and beans provide fiber.

1 large fresh fennel bulb (about ¾ pound)
1 teaspoon olive oil
8 ounces boneless skinless chicken thighs, cut into ¾-inch pieces
1 teaspoon dried rosemary leaves, crushed
½ teaspoon black pepper
1 can (14½ ounces) no-salt-added stewed tomatoes, undrained
1 can (14½ ounces) fat-free reduced-sodium chicken broth
1 can (about 15 ounces) cannellini beans, rinsed and drained
   Hot pepper sauce (optional)

1. Cut off and reserve ¼ cup chopped feathery fennel tops. Chop bulb into ½-inch pieces. Heat oil in large saucepan over medium heat. Add chopped fennel bulb; cook 5 minutes, stirring occasionally.

2. Sprinkle chicken with rosemary and pepper; add to saucepan. Cook and stir 2 minutes. Add tomatoes with juice and chicken broth; bring to a boil. Cover; simmer 10 minutes. Stir in beans; simmer, uncovered, 15 minutes or until chicken is cooked through and sauce thickens. Season to taste with hot sauce, if desired. Ladle into 4 shallow bowls; top with reserved fennel tops. *Makes 4 servings*

Prep Time: 15 minutes
Cook Time: 35 minutes

Tuscan Chicken with White Beans

Chicken Saltimbocca

Nutrients per serving:

Calories: 195
Carbohydrate: 10 g
Calories From Fat: 18%
Total Fat: 4 g
Saturated Fat: 1 g
Cholesterol: 72 mg
Sodium: 676 mg
Dietary Fiber: 2 g
Protein: 30 g

¼ **cup fresh basil leaves, coarsely chopped**
2 **tablespoons chopped fresh chives**
2 **teaspoons olive oil**
1 **clove garlic, minced**
½ **teaspoon dried oregano**
½ **teaspoon dried sage**
4 **boneless skinless chicken breast halves (about 4 ounces each)**
2 **slices (1 ounce *each*) smoked ham, cut in half**
   Nonstick cooking spray
½ **cup chicken broth**
1 **cup spaghetti sauce**
2 **cups cooked spaghetti squash, warmed (see tip)**

1. Blend basil, chives, oil, garlic, oregano and sage in small bowl. Lightly pound chicken breasts between 2 pieces of plastic wrap with flat side of meat mallet to ½- to ¾-inch thickness. Spread ¼ of herb mixture over each chicken breast. Place 1 ham slice over herb mixture; roll up to enclose filling. Secure with toothpicks.

2. Spray medium nonstick skillet with cooking spray. Heat skillet over medium-high heat. Cook chicken breasts seam side up 2 to 3 minutes or until browned. Turn chicken; cook 2 to 3 minutes or until browned. Add chicken broth, reduce heat and simmer, covered, 20 to 25 minutes or until chicken is cooked through.

3. Remove chicken to cutting board, leaving liquid in skillet. Let chicken cool 5 minutes. Add spaghetti sauce to skillet; cook over medium-low heat 2 to 3 minutes or until heated through, stirring occasionally.

4. Remove toothpicks from chicken and cut crosswise into slices. To serve, place spaghetti squash on serving platter or individual plates; arrange chicken slices over squash and top with spaghetti sauce. *Makes 4 servings*

Tip: To quickly cook spaghetti squash, cut a 2½-pound squash in half with a sturdy sharp knife. Remove seeds from each half. Place halves cut sides down in a microwavable baking dish. Add ½ cup water, cover with plastic wrap and cook at HIGH 10 to 15 minutes or until squash is soft. Let cool 10 to 15 minutes. Scrape out squash "strands" with a fork. A 2½-pound spaghetti squash yields about 4 cups.

Chicken Saltimbocca

California Turkey Chili

Nutrients per serving:

Calories: 388
Carbohydrate: 37 g
Calories From Fat: 27%
Total Fat: 11 g
Saturated Fat: 2 g
Cholesterol: 53 mg
Sodium: 952 mg
Dietary Fiber: 11 g
Protein: 29 g

1¼ cups chopped onion
1 cup chopped green bell pepper
2 cloves garlic, minced
3 tablespoons vegetable oil
1 can (28 ounces) kidney beans, drained
1 can (28 ounces) stewed tomatoes, undrained
1 cup red wine or water
3 cups cubed cooked California-grown turkey
1 tablespoon chili powder
1 tablespoon chopped fresh cilantro *or* 1 teaspoon dried coriander
1 teaspoon crushed red pepper
½ teaspoon salt
  Shredded Cheddar cheese (optional)
  Additional chopped onion (optional)
  Additional chopped fresh cilantro (optional)

Cook and stir onion, green pepper and garlic in oil in large saucepan over high heat until tender. Add beans, tomatoes with liquid, wine, turkey, chili powder, cilantro, red pepper and salt. Cover; simmer 25 minutes or until heated through. Top with cheese, onion or cilantro, if desired.   *Makes 6 servings*

Favorite recipe from **California Poultry Federation**

California Turkey Chili

Nutrients per serving:

Calories: 387
Carbohydrate: 11 g
Calories From Fat: 53%
Total Fat: 23 g
Saturated Fat: 2 g
Cholesterol: 101 mg
Sodium: 222 mg
Dietary Fiber: 4 g
Protein: 35 g

Orange-Almond Chicken

Calcium-rich almonds create a crunchy coating for low-fat chicken breasts. Add a heaping helping of your favorite green vegetable on the side for a nutritious, easy-to-make meal.

    1½ pounds boneless skinless chicken breasts
        Salt and black pepper
    1½ cups sliced almonds
     2 tablespoons flour
        Grated peel of 1 medium orange (about 2 teaspoons)
     1 egg
     2 tablespoons water
     2 to 4 tablespoons olive oil
        Juice of 2 medium oranges (about ½ cup)
    ¾ cup chicken broth
     1 tablespoon Dijon mustard
        Additional grated orange peel and almonds for garnish (optional)

1. Cover chicken breasts with plastic wrap and pound to ¼-inch thickness; season with salt and pepper. Place almonds and flour in bowl of food processor and pulse until coarse crumbs are formed; add orange zest and pulse to combine.

2. Lightly beat egg and water in shallow bowl. Place almond mixture on plate. Dredge chicken breasts in egg and then in almond mixture, pressing to make coating stick.

3. Heat 2 tablespoons oil in large skillet over medium-high heat. Cook chicken in batches without crowding the skillet until lightly browned and no longer pink in center, about 5 minutes a side. Remove and keep warm.

4. Add orange juice to same skillet; cook and stir scraping up browned bits until reduced by about half. Add chicken broth and mustard; cook and stir 2 or 3 minutes. Pour over chicken. Garnish with additional orange zest and almonds, if desired.

Makes 6 servings

Orange-Almond Chicken

Nutrients per serving:

Calories: 224
Carbohydrate: 11 g
Calories From Fat: 31%
Total Fat: 8 g
Saturated Fat: 1 g
Cholesterol: 69 mg
Sodium: 813 mg
Dietary Fiber: 3 g
Protein: 27 g

Sassy Chicken & Peppers

This dish couldn't be easier to prepare. If you're in a real time crunch, use frozen bell pepper strips—they're just as nutritious and flavorful as fresh.

2 teaspoons Mexican seasoning*
2 (4-ounce) boneless skinless chicken breast halves
2 teaspoons canola oil
1 small red onion, sliced
½ red bell pepper, cut into long, thin strips
½ yellow or green bell pepper, cut into long, thin strips
¼ cup chunky salsa or chipotle salsa
1 tablespoon lime juice
Lime wedges (optional)

*If Mexican seasoning is not available, substitute 1 teaspoon chili powder, ½ teaspoon ground cumin, ½ teaspoon salt and ⅛ teaspoon ground red pepper.

1. Sprinkle seasoning over both sides of chicken.

2. Heat oil in large nonstick skillet over medium heat. Add onion; cook 3 minutes, stirring occasionally.

3. Add bell pepper strips; cook 3 minutes, stirring occasionally. Stir salsa and lime into vegetables.

4. Push vegetables to edges of skillet; add chicken to skillet. Cook 5 minutes; turn. Continue to cook 4 minutes or until chicken is no longer pink in the center and vegetables are tender.

5. Transfer chicken to serving plates; top with vegetable mixture and garnish with lime wedges, if desired.   *Makes 2 servings*

Sassy Chicken & Peppers

Roast Turkey with Cranberry Stuffing

A New England twist enlivens this quintessential holiday dish. Taking off the turkey skin after roasting eliminates loads of fat without removing any of the succulence.

    1 loaf (12 ounces) Italian or French bread, cut into ½-inch cubes
    2 tablespoons margarine
  1½ cups chopped onions
  1½ cups chopped celery
    2 teaspoons poultry seasoning
    1 teaspoon dried thyme leaves
    ½ teaspoon dried rosemary, crushed
    ¼ teaspoon salt
    ¼ teaspoon black pepper
    1 cup coarsely chopped fresh cranberries
    1 tablespoon sugar
    ¾ cup fat-free reduced-sodium chicken broth
    1 turkey (8 to 10 pounds)

1. Preheat oven to 375°F.

2. Arrange bread on two 15×10-inch jelly roll pans. Bake 12 minutes or until lightly toasted. *Reduce oven temperature to 350°F.*

3. Melt margarine in large saucepan over medium heat. Add onions and celery; cook and stir 8 minutes or until vegetables are tender; remove from heat. Add bread cubes, poultry seasoning, thyme, rosemary, salt and pepper; mix well. Combine cranberries and sugar in small bowl; mix well. Add to bread mixture; toss well. Drizzle chicken broth evenly over mixture; toss well.

4. Spray roasting pan and rack with nonstick cooking spray. Remove giblets from turkey. Rinse turkey and cavity in cold water; pat dry with paper towels. Fill turkey cavity loosely with stuffing. Place turkey, breast side up, on prepared rack in roasting pan. Bake 3 hours or until thermometer inserted in thickest part of thigh registers 180°F and juices run clear.

5. Meanwhile, place remaining stuffing in casserole sprayed with nonstick cooking spray. Cover casserole; refrigerate until baking time.

6. Transfer turkey to serving platter. Cover loosely with foil; let stand 20 minutes. Place covered casserole of stuffing in oven; increase temperature to 375°F. Bake 25 to 30 minutes or until hot.

7. Remove and discard turkey skin. Slice turkey and serve with cranberry stuffing.

Makes 20 servings

Roast Turkey with Cranberry Stuffing

Nutrients per serving:

Calories: 157
Carbohydrate: 8 g
Calories From Fat: 8%
Total Fat: 1 g
Saturated Fat: <1 g
Cholesterol: 66 mg
Sodium: 234 mg
Dietary Fiber: 1 g
Protein: 27 g

Quick Orange Chicken

2 tablespoons frozen orange juice concentrate
1 tablespoon no-sugar-added orange marmalade
1 teaspoon Dijon mustard
¼ teaspoon salt
4 boneless skinless chicken breast halves (about 1 pound)
½ cup fresh orange sections
2 tablespoons chopped fresh parsley

Microwave Directions

1. For sauce, combine juice concentrate, marmalade, mustard and salt in 8-inch shallow round microwavable dish until juice concentrate is thawed.

2. Add chicken, coating both sides with sauce. Arrange chicken around edge of dish without overlapping. Cover with vented plastic wrap. Microwave at HIGH (100% power) 3 minutes; turn chicken over. Microwave at MEDIUM-HIGH (70% power) 4 minutes or until chicken is no longer pink in center.

3. Remove chicken to serving plate. Microwave remaining sauce at HIGH (100% power) 2 to 3 minutes or until slightly thickened.

4. To serve, spoon sauce over chicken; top with orange sections and parsley.

Makes 4 servings

Quick Orange Chicken

Thai Curry Stir-Fry

Nutrients per serving:

Calories: 273
Carbohydrate: 27 g
Calories From Fat: 20%
Total Fat: 6 g
Saturated Fat: 1 g
Cholesterol: 57 mg
Sodium: 308 mg
Dietary Fiber: 5 g
Protein: 28 g

Thai food is easy to love. Full of fresh vegetables, lean protein and complex carbohydrates, it also tastes fabulous! Use brown rice in this recipe for extra nutrition and flavor.

½ cup fat-free reduced-sodium chicken broth
2 teaspoons cornstarch
1½ teaspoons curry powder
2 teaspoons reduced-sodium soy sauce
⅛ teaspoon red pepper flakes
   Nonstick olive oil cooking spray
3 green onions, sliced
2 cloves garlic, minced
2 cups broccoli florets
⅔ cup sliced carrot
1½ teaspoons olive oil
6 ounces boneless skinless chicken breast, cut into bite-size pieces
⅔ cup hot cooked rice, prepared without salt

1. Stir together broth, cornstarch, curry powder, soy sauce and red pepper. Set aside.

2. Spray nonstick wok or large nonstick skillet with cooking spray. Heat over medium-high heat. Add onions and garlic; stir-fry 1 minute. Remove from wok.

3. Add broccoli and carrot to wok; stir-fry 2 to 3 minutes or until crisp-tender. Remove from wok.

4. Add oil to hot wok. Add chicken and stir-fry 2 to 3 minutes or until no longer pink. Stir broth mixture. Add to wok. Cook and stir until broth mixture comes to a boil and thickens slightly. Return all vegetables to wok. Heat through.

Makes 2 servings

Thai Curry Stir-Fry

Southwest Turkey Tenderloin Stew

This low-fat, high-fiber recipe is an alternative to an old favorite—beef stew! And not only is white-meat turkey lower in fat, it's a good source of iron, zinc and B vitamins.

Nutrients per serving:

Calories: 203
Carbohydrate: 23 g
Calories From Fat: 13%
Total Fat: 3 g
Saturated Fat: 1 g
Cholesterol: 45 mg
Sodium: 827 mg
Dietary Fiber: 6 g
Protein: 25 g

1½ **pounds turkey tenderloin, cut into ¾-inch pieces**
1 **tablespoon chili powder**
1 **teaspoon ground cumin**
¼ **teaspoon salt**
1 **red bell pepper, cut into ¾-inch pieces**
1 **green bell pepper, cut into ¾-inch pieces**
¾ **cup chopped red or yellow onion**
3 **cloves garlic, minced**
1 **can (15½ ounces) chili beans in spicy sauce, undrained**
1 **can (14½ ounces) chili-style stewed tomatoes, undrained**
¾ **cup prepared salsa or picante sauce**
  Fresh cilantro (optional)

Slow Cooker Directions

1. Place turkey in slow cooker. Sprinkle chili powder, cumin and salt over turkey; toss to coat.

2. Add red bell pepper, green bell pepper, onion, garlic, beans with sauce, tomatoes with juice and salsa; mix well. Cover and cook on LOW 5 hours or until turkey is no longer pink in center and vegetables are crisp-tender.

3. To serve, ladle into 6 bowls. Garnish with cilantro, if desired.

Makes 6 servings

Southwest Turkey Tenderloin Stew

Tandoori-Spiced Game Hens

Nutrients per serving:

Calories: 179
Carbohydrate: 6 g
Calories From Fat: 23%
Total Fat: 4 g
Saturated Fat: 1 g
Cholesterol: 110 mg
Sodium: 130 mg
Dietary Fiber: <1 g
Protein: 28 g

4 cups (32 ounces) plain nonfat yogurt
1 tablespoon curry powder
1 tablespoon sweet paprika
1 teaspoon bottled puréed ginger
1 teaspoon bottled puréed garlic
4 fresh Cornish game hens, all visible fat removed

1. Combine yogurt with curry powder, paprika, ginger and garlic in large bowl; mix well.

2. Cut game hens in half by cutting through breast bone. Remove triangular breast bone; discard. Rinse hens.

3. Place hens in resealable plastic food storage bags. Divide yogurt mixture among bags; seal bags. Marinate in refrigerator 2 to 3 hours or overnight, turning bags once or twice.

4. Preheat oven to 500°F. Remove hens from bags; discard marinade. Brush off excess marinade. Place hens on racks lightly sprayed with nonstick cooking spray. Place racks in shallow baking pans. Bake 30 to 35 minutes or until no longer pink in center and juices run clear. Remove skin before serving. *Makes 8 servings*

Note: To keep the hens moist, cook them with the skin on. Remove the skin before serving to keep the fat at 4 grams per serving. With skin, the fat is 24 grams per serving, 7 of it saturated.

Tandoori-Spiced Game Hen

Nutrients per serving:

Calories: 295
Carbohydrate: 21 g
Calories From Fat: 26%
Total Fat: 8 g
Saturated Fat: 1 g
Cholesterol: 66 mg
Sodium: 1339 mg
Dietary Fiber: 5 g
Protein: 32 g

Chicken and Black Bean Salad

Tomatoes and peppers add vitamin C, not to mention flavor, to this protein-rich salad. Serve it with crusty, whole-grain bread for lunch or dinner. Wrap any leftovers in whole-wheat tortillas for tasty burritos.

2 tablespoons vegetable oil, divided
1 medium red onion, diced
1 pound boneless skinless chicken breasts, cut into ¾-inch pieces
1 can (16 ounces) black beans, drained and rinsed
1 medium tomato, diced
½ cup pepperoncini peppers, seeded and diced
3 tablespoons chopped fresh parsley
2 tablespoons cider vinegar
1 teaspoon salt
1 teaspoon TABASCO® brand Pepper Sauce
Lettuce leaves
Whole pickled peppers for garnish

Heat 1 tablespoon oil in 10-inch skillet over medium heat until hot. Add red onion; cook until tender, about 5 minutes, stirring occasionally. Remove to large bowl. In same skillet add remaining 1 tablespoon oil. Over medium-high heat cook chicken pieces until well browned on all sides, about 5 minutes, stirring occasionally.

In large bowl toss red onion with chicken, beans, tomato, diced pepperoncini peppers, parsley, vinegar, salt and TABASCO® Sauce to mix well.

To serve, line large platter with lettuce leaves; top with chicken salad. Garnish with pickled peppers.   *Makes 4 servings*

Chicken and Black Bean Salad

Nutrients per serving:

Calories: 122
Carbohydrate: 2 g
Calories From Fat: 19%
Total Fat: 3 g
Saturated Fat: 1 g
Cholesterol: 58 mg
Sodium: 80 mg
Dietary Fiber: 1 g
Protein: 22 g

Broiled Chicken Breast with Cilantro Salsa

Quick and easy to prepare, low in fat and high in flavor, this dish is a great summer staple. Add any leftover chicken to a leafy green salad and use the salsa as dressing.

4 boneless skinless chicken breast halves (4 ounces each)
4 tablespoons lime juice, divided
Black pepper
½ cup lightly packed fresh cilantro, chopped
⅓ cup thinly sliced or minced green onions
¼ to ½ jalapeño pepper,* seeded and minced
2 tablespoons pine nuts, toasted (optional)

*Jalapeño peppers can sting and irritate the skin. Wear rubber gloves when handling peppers and do not touch eyes. Wash hands after handling.

1. Spray broiler pan or baking sheet with nonstick cooking spray.

2. Brush chicken with 2 tablespoons lime juice. Place on prepared pan. Sprinkle generously with pepper; set aside.

3. Combine remaining 2 tablespoons lime juice, cilantro, onions, jalapeño pepper and pine nuts, if desired, in small bowl; stir to combine. Set aside.

4. Broil chicken 1 to 2 inches from heat 8 to 10 minutes or until chicken is no longer pink in center. Serve with cilantro salsa. Garnish with lime slices, if desired.

Makes 4 servings

Broiled Chicken Breasts with Cilantro Salsa

Treat Yourself to Lean Meat

Nutrients per serving:

Calories: 245
Carbohydrate: 28 g
Calories From Fat: 16%
Total Fat: 4 g
Saturated Fat: 1 g
Cholesterol: 35 mg
Sodium: 679 mg
Dietary Fiber: 8 g
Protein: 24 g

Chipotle Chili con Carne

Rich with nutrient-dense beans and vegetables, this is a Southwestern version of comfort food. Serve this flavorful dish with warm homemade corn bread.

  1 tablespoon chili powder
  1 tablespoon ground cumin
  ¾ pound beef for stew, cut into 1-inch pieces
    Nonstick cooking spray
  1 can (about 14 ounces) fat-free reduced-sodium beef broth
  1 tablespoon minced canned chipotle chilies in adobo sauce, or to taste
  1 can (14½ ounces) diced tomatoes, undrained
  1 large green bell pepper *or* 2 poblano chili peppers, cut into ½-inch pieces
  2 cans (16 ounces each) pinto or red beans, rinsed and drained
    Chopped fresh cilantro (optional)

1. Combine chili powder and cumin in medium bowl. Add beef and toss to coat. Coat large saucepan or Dutch oven with cooking spray; heat over medium heat. Add beef; cook 5 minutes, stirring occasionally. Add beef broth and chipotle chilies with sauce; bring to a boil. Reduce heat; cover and simmer 1 hour 15 minutes or until beef is very tender.

2. With slotted spoon, transfer beef to carving board, leaving juices in saucepan. Using two forks, shred beef. Return beef to saucepan; add tomatoes with juice and bell pepper. Bring to a boil; stir in beans. Simmer, uncovered, 20 minutes or until bell pepper is tender. Garnish with cilantro, if desired.   *Makes 6 servings*

Prep Time: 15 minutes
Cook Time: 1 hour 40 minutes

Chipotle Chili con Carne

Pork & Plum Kabobs

Nutrients per serving:

Calories: 264
Carbohydrate: 19 g
Calories From Fat: 32%
Total Fat: 9 g
Saturated Fat: 3 g
Cholesterol: 69 mg
Sodium: 205 mg
Dietary Fiber: 2 g
Protein: 26 g

Plums are a natural source of potassium. They add sweetness and flavor to the lean pork in this light summertime entrée.

¾ pound boneless pork loin chops (1 inch thick), trimmed of fat and cut into 1-inch pieces
1½ teaspoons ground cumin
½ teaspoon ground cinnamon
¼ teaspoon salt
¼ teaspoon garlic powder
¼ teaspoon ground red pepper
¼ cup no-sugar-added red raspberry spread
¼ cup sliced green onions
1 tablespoon orange juice
3 plums, seeded and cut into wedges

1. Place pork in large resealable plastic food storage bag. Combine cumin, cinnamon, salt, garlic powder and red pepper in small bowl. Sprinkle over meat in bag. Shake to coat meat with spices.

2. Prepare grill for direct grilling. Combine raspberry spread, green onions and orange juice in small bowl; set aside.

3. Alternately thread pork and plum wedges onto 8 skewers. Grill kabobs directly over medium heat 12 to 14 minutes or until meat is barely pink in center, turning once during grilling. Brush frequently with reserved raspberry mixture during last 5 minutes of grilling. *Makes 4 servings*

Serving Suggestion: A crisp, cool salad makes a great accompaniment to these sweet grilled kabobs.

Prep Time: 10 minutes
Grill Time: 12 to 14 minutes

Pork & Plum Kabobs

Stuffed Flank Steak

Discover a delightful new way to eat your spinach in this elegant entrée. This dish is easy to prepare and smells wonderful while cooking. Add a whole-grain pilaf and a vegetable side to round out the meal.

Nutrients per serving:

Calories: 288
Carbohydrate: 7 g
Calories From Fat: 40%
Total Fat: 13 g
Saturated Fat: 6 g
Cholesterol: 56 mg
Sodium: 990 mg
Dietary Fiber: 1 g
Protein: 28 g

1 cup dry red wine
¼ cup soy sauce
2 garlic cloves, minced
1 large flank steak, 1½ to 2 pounds
1 cup thawed frozen chopped spinach, squeezed dry
1 jar (7 ounces) roasted red bell peppers, drained and chopped
½ cup crumbled blue cheese
   Salt and pepper

1. Combine wine, soy sauce and garlic in small bowl. Place steak in large resealable plastic food storage bag; pour marinade over steak. Seal bag and marinate in refrigerator 2 hours.

2. Preheat oven to 350°F. Combine spinach, peppers and cheese in medium bowl. Remove steak from marinade, pat dry and lay on flat surface. Reserve marinade.

3. Spoon spinach and pepper mixture across the length of the steak, covering bottom ⅔ of steak. Roll steak tightly around vegetables, securing with toothpicks or string.

4. Season with salt and pepper and place in roasting pan, seam side down. Bake 30 to 40 minutes for medium-rare, or until desired degree of doneness is reached, basting twice with reserved marinade. Do not baste during last 10 minutes of cooking time. Allow steak to rest about 10 minutes and slice. *Makes 6 servings*

Stuffed Flank Steak

Nutrients per serving:

Calories: 271
Carbohydrate: 9 g
Calories From Fat: 55%
Total Fat: 17 g
Saturated Fat: 6 g
Cholesterol: 63 mg
Sodium: 98 mg
Dietary Fiber: 3 g
Protein: 22 g

Pork & Peppers Mexican-Style

Bell peppers are wonderful vegetables for those who are counting carbs. They add natural sweetness, yet are low in carbohydrate. Always select firm glossy peppers. The riper the pepper, the better its flavor and nutritional content.

  2 tablespoons olive oil
½ cup chopped green onions
¾ pound lean pork, cut into ¼-inch pieces
3 bell peppers, preferably red, green and yellow, diced (about 2 cups)
1 teaspoon chopped garlic
   Salt and pepper
1 cup sliced fresh mushrooms
1 teaspoon cumin
1 teaspoon chili powder
½ teaspoon ground dried chipotle pepper (optional)
¼ cup shredded Cheddar cheese
¼ cup sour cream

1. Heat oil in large skillet over medium high heat. Add green onions; cook and stir 2 minutes. Add pork; cook and stir 5 minutes or until browned. Add peppers and garlic. Cook and stir 5 minutes or until peppers begin to soften.

2. Season with salt and pepper. Add mushrooms, cumin, chili powder and chipotle pepper, if desired. Cook and stir 10 to 15 minutes until pork is cooked through and vegetables have softened.

3. Serve topped with shredded cheese and sour cream. *Makes 4 servings*

Tip: Those not restricting carbohydrates can enjoy this dish rolled-up in tortillas, burrito-style.

Pork & Peppers Mexican-Style

Beef & Blue Cheese Salad

Nutrients per serving:

Calories: 288
Carbohydrate: 11 g
Calories From Fat: 70%
Total Fat: 23 g
Saturated Fat: 5 g
Cholesterol: 21 mg
Sodium: 872 mg
Dietary Fiber: 2 g
Protein: 11 g

1 package (10 ounces) mixed green lettuce leaves
4 ounces sliced rare deli roast beef, cut into thin strips
1 large tomato, seeded and coarsely chopped *or* 8 large cherry tomatoes, halved
2 ounces (½ cup) crumbed blue or Gorgonzola cheese
1 cup croutons
½ cup prepared Caesar or Italian salad dressing

1. In large bowl, combine lettuce, roast beef, tomato, cheese and croutons.

2. Drizzle with dressing; toss well. Serve immediately.   *Makes 4 servings*

Cook's Notes: Gorgonzola is one of Italy's great cheeses. It has an ivory-colored interior that is streaked with bluish-green veins. Gorgonzola is made from cow's milk and has a creamy savory flavor. It can be found cut into wedges and wrapped in foil in most supermarkets.

Prep Time: 10 minutes

Beef & Blue Cheese Salad

One Pan Pork Fu Yung

This Chinese-American version of the omelet uses bean sprouts to add texture and nutrients. Choose fresh-looking sprouts with no brown patches or off odors.

- **1 cup fat-free reduced-sodium chicken broth**
- **1 tablespoon cornstarch**
- **½ teaspoon sesame oil, divided**
- **2 teaspoons canola oil**
- **½ pound boneless pork tenderloin, minced**
- **5 green onions, thinly sliced, divided**
- **1 cup sliced mushrooms**
- **¼ teaspoon white pepper**
- **¼ teaspoon salt (optional)**
- **1 cup bean sprouts**
- **2 eggs**
- **2 egg whites**

1. In small pan, combine broth, cornstarch and ¼ teaspoon sesame oil. Cook over medium heat, stirring, until sauce thickens, about 5 to 6 minutes; set aside.

2. Heat canola oil in 12-inch nonstick skillet over high heat. Add pork; stir-fry about 4 minutes or until no longer pink.

3. Reserve 2 tablespoons green onion. Add remaining ¼ teaspoon sesame oil, mushrooms, remaining green onions, pepper and salt, if desired, to skillet. Cook and stir about 4 to 5 minutes or until lightly browned. Add sprouts to skillet; stir-fry about 1 minute. With spatula, flatten mixture in skillet.

4. Combine eggs and egg whites in medium bowl; pour over pork mixture in skillet. Reduce heat to low. Cover; cook about 3 minutes or until eggs are set.

5. Cut into 4 wedges before serving. Top each wedge with ¼ cup sauce and sprinkle with reserved green onion.   *Makes 4 servings*

To round it out: Serve with Lettuce Wrap Salad: Separate Boston lettuce leaves and arrange on a platter with grated carrot, radish slices, seedless cucumber rounds, red bell pepper strips and bean sprouts. Serve with a dipping sauce made by whisking together 1 cup fat-free, reduced-sodium chicken broth, 1 tablespoon rice vinegar, ¼ teaspoon sesame oil, ¼ teaspoon puréed ginger and ¼ teaspoon prepared garlic. Serve dressing in small dishes for dipping.

One Pan Pork Fu Yung

Joe's Special

Nonstick cooking spray
1 pound lean ground beef
2 cups sliced mushrooms
1 small onion, chopped
2 teaspoons Worcestershire sauce
1 teaspoon dried oregano leaves
1 teaspoon ground nutmeg
½ teaspoon garlic powder
½ teaspoon salt
1 package (10 ounces) frozen chopped spinach, thawed
4 large eggs, lightly beaten
⅓ cup grated Parmesan cheese

1. Spray large skillet with cooking spray. Add ground beef, mushrooms and onion; cook over medium-high heat 6 to 8 minutes or until onion is tender, breaking beef apart with wooden spoon. Add Worcestershire, oregano, nutmeg, garlic powder and salt. Cook until meat is no longer pink.

2. Drain spinach (do not squeeze dry); stir into meat mixture. Push mixture to one side of pan. Reduce heat to medium. Pour eggs into other side of pan; cook, without stirring, 1 to 2 minutes or until set on bottom. Lift eggs to allow uncooked portion to flow underneath. Repeat until softly set. Gently stir into meat mixture and heat through. Stir in cheese. *Makes 4 to 6 servings*

Prep and Cook Time: 20 minutes

Joe's Special

Panama Pork Stew

Sweet potatoes are the star of this stew and they are nutritional superstars, too. One sweet potato provides about two and a half times the RDA for healthy adults of vitamin A, plus fiber, potassium and vitamin C.

Nutrients per serving:

Calories: 282
Carbohydrate: 30 g
Calories From Fat: 21%
Total Fat: 7 g
Saturated Fat: 2 g
Cholesterol: 54 mg
Sodium: 459 mg
Dietary Fiber: 6 g
Protein: 27 g

2 small sweet potatoes (about 12 ounces total), peeled and cut into 2-inch pieces
1 package (10 ounces) frozen corn
1 package (9 ounces) frozen cut green beans
1 cup chopped onion
1¼ pounds lean pork stew meat, cut into 1-inch cubes
1 can (14½ ounces) diced tomatoes, undrained
¼ cup water
1 to 2 tablespoons chili powder
½ teaspoon salt
½ teaspoon ground coriander

Slow Cooker Directions

Place potatoes, corn, green beans and onion in slow cooker. Top with pork. Combine tomatoes with juice, water, chili powder, salt and coriander in medium bowl. Pour over pork in slow cooker. Cover; cook on LOW 7 to 9 hours.   *Makes 6 servings*

Panama Pork Stew

Nutrients per serving:

Calories: 141
Carbohydrate: 14 g
Calories From Fat: 26%
Total Fat: 4 g
Saturated Fat: 2 g
Cholesterol: 27 mg
Sodium: 238 mg
Dietary Fiber: 3 g
Protein: 13 g

Thai Beef Salad

The fresh, intense flavors used to create this unique dish eliminate the need for any added fat. Be sure to use deeply colored varieties of lettuce (green, red); they have the most vitamins.

½ **beef flank steak (about 8 ounces)**
¼ **cup reduced-sodium soy sauce**
2 **jalapeño peppers,* finely chopped**
2 **tablespoons packed brown sugar**
1 **clove garlic, minced**
½ **cup lime juice**
6 **green onions, thinly sliced**
4 **carrots, diagonally cut into thin slices**
½ **cup finely chopped fresh cilantro**
4 **romaine lettuce leaves**

Jalapeño peppers can sting and irritate the skin; wear rubber gloves when handling peppers and do not touch eyes. Wash hands after handling peppers.

1. Place flank steak in resealable plastic food storage bag. Combine soy sauce, jalapeños, brown sugar and garlic in small bowl; mix well. Pour mixture over flank steak.

2. Close bag securely; turn to coat steak. Marinate in refrigerator 2 hours.

3. Preheat broiler. Drain steak; discard marinade. Place steak on rack of broiler pan. Broil 4 inches from heat 13 to 18 minutes for medium rare to medium or until desired doneness, turning once. Remove from heat; let stand 15 minutes.

4. Thinly slice steak across grain. Toss with lime juice, green onions, carrots and cilantro in large bowl. Serve salad immediately on lettuce leaves.

Makes 4 servings

Thai Beef Salad

Turkey Meat Loaf

Bulgur, a carbohydrate power-food, adds B vitamins and fiber to this classic dish. Using ground turkey breast in place of ground beef keeps the fat content low, and the unique spices make this dish anything but ordinary.

Nutrients per serving:

Calories: 197
Carbohydrate: 18 g
Calories From Fat: 22%
Total Fat: 5 g
Saturated Fat: <1 g
Cholesterol: 36 mg
Sodium: 437 mg
Dietary Fiber: 4 g
Protein: 20 g

    1 tablespoon vegetable oil
    ¾ cup chopped onion
    ½ cup chopped celery
    1 clove garlic, minced
    ⅔ cup fat-free reduced-sodium chicken broth or water
    ½ cup uncooked bulgur wheat
    ½ cup cholesterol-free egg substitute
    1 tablespoon reduced-sodium soy sauce
    ¼ teaspoon ground cumin
    ¼ teaspoon paprika
    ¼ teaspoon black pepper
    8 tablespoons chili sauce, divided
    1 pound 93% lean ground turkey

1. Heat oil in medium skillet over low. Add onion, celery and garlic. Cook and stir 3 minutes; add broth and bulgur. Bring to a boil. Reduce heat to low. Cover and simmer 10 to 15 minutes or until bulgur is tender and all liquid is absorbed. Transfer to large bowl; cool to lukewarm.

2. Preheat oven to 375°F. Stir egg substitute, soy sauce, cumin, paprika and pepper into bulgur. Add 6 tablespoons chili sauce and ground turkey. Stir well until blended.

3. Pat turkey mixture into greased 8½×4½-inch loaf pan. Top with remaining 2 tablespoons chili sauce.

4. Bake meat loaf about 45 minutes or until browned and juices run clear. Let stand 10 minutes. Remove from pan; cut into 10 slices.

Makes 5 servings (2 slices each)

Turkey Meat Loaf

Jamaican Pork & Mango Stir-Fry

This is a quick-to-prepare dish with Caribbean flair. Sensuous mango adds a refreshing, exotic flavor and contributes a generous helping of both vitamins A and C.

Nutrients per serving:

Calories: 264
Carbohydrate: 17 g
Calories From Fat: 38%
Total Fat: 11 g
Saturated Fat: 2 g
Cholesterol: 66 mg
Sodium: 349 mg
Dietary Fiber: 1 g
Protein: 24 g

1 pork tenderloin (about 1 pound)
2 tablespoons olive oil
1 tablespoon Caribbean jerk seasoning blend
1 medium mango, peeled and chopped, *or* ½ (26-ounce) jar mango slices in light syrup, chopped
1 red bell pepper, chopped
⅔ cup orange juice
2 teaspoons cornstarch
½ teaspoon jalapeño pepper sauce *or* ¼ teaspoon hot pepper sauce
¼ cup sliced green onions

1. Trim fat from pork and cut into thin strips.

2. Heat oil in large skillet or wok over medium-high heat until hot. Add pork and seasoning blend; stir-fry 2 minutes. Add mango and bell pepper; stir-fry 2 minutes or just until pork is no longer pink.

3. Blend orange juice, cornstarch and pepper sauce until smooth; add to skillet. Cook and stir 2 minutes or until sauce is clear and thickened. Stir in green onions.

Makes 4 servings

Serving Suggestion: Create an easy island side salad by adding canned pineapple tidbits and raisins to prepared coleslaw.

Tip: Look for firm but not hard mangoes with a yellow or red blush. Unripe fruit can be ripened in a paper bag for 1 to 3 days. Ripe mangoes have a sweet, fruity aroma.

Prep and Cook Time: 17 minutes

Jamaican Pork & Mango Stir-Fry

Yankee Pot Roast & Vegetables

Nutrients per serving:

Calories: 270
Carbohydrate: 15 g
Calories From Fat: 33%
Total Fat: 10 g
Saturated Fat: 4 g
Cholesterol: 75 mg
Sodium: 99 mg
Dietary Fiber: 3 g
Protein: 28 g

Potatoes are often labeled "bad carbs." Like most other foods, they are bad or good depending on how they are processed or prepared. Leave the skins on to keep more of the vitamins intact.

1 beef chuck pot roast (2½ pounds)
   Salt and black pepper
3 medium baking potatoes (about 1 pound), unpeeled and cut into quarters
2 large carrots, cut into ¾-inch slices
2 ribs celery, cut into ¾-inch slices
1 medium onion, sliced
1 large parsnip, cut into ¾-inch slices
2 bay leaves
1 teaspoon dried rosemary
½ teaspoon dried thyme leaves
½ cup reduced-sodium beef broth

Slow Cooker Directions

1. Trim excess fat from meat and discard. Cut meat into serving-size pieces; sprinkle with salt and pepper.

2. Combine vegetables, bay leaves, rosemary and thyme in slow cooker. Place beef over vegetables. Pour broth over beef. Cover; cook on LOW 8½ to 9 hours or until beef is fork-tender. Remove beef to serving platter. Arrange vegetables around beef. Remove and discard bay leaves. *Makes 10 to 12 servings*

Tip: To make gravy, ladle the juices into a 2-cup measure; let stand 5 minutes. Skim off and discard fat. Measure remaining juices and heat to a boil in small saucepan. For each cup of juice, mix 2 tablespoons of flour with ¼ cup of cold water until smooth. Stir flour mixture into boiling juices, stirring constantly 1 minute or until thickened.

Prep Time: 10 minutes
Cook Time: 8½ hours (in the slow cooker)

Yankee Pot Roast & Vegetables

Pork Chops with Jalapeño-Pecan Cornbread Stuffing

Using a slow cooker makes preparing this delightful dinner fast work. Adding nuts to the stuffing contributes taste, texture and a helping of good fat in the form of essential fatty acids.

> **6 boneless loin pork chops, 1 inch thick (1½ pounds)**
> **Nonstick cooking spray**
> **¾ cup chopped onion**
> **¾ cup chopped celery**
> **½ cup coarsely chopped pecans**
> **½ medium jalapeño pepper,* seeded and chopped**
> **1 teaspoon rubbed sage**
> **½ teaspoon dried rosemary**
> **⅛ teaspoon black pepper**
> **4 cups unseasoned cornbread stuffing mix**
> **1¼ cups reduced-sodium chicken broth**
> **1 egg, lightly beaten**

*Jalapeño peppers can sting and irritate the skin; wear rubber gloves when handling peppers and do not touch eyes. Wash hands after handling.

Slow Cooker Directions

1. Trim excess fat from pork and discard. Spray large skillet with nonstick cooking spray; heat over medium heat. Add pork; cook 10 minutes or until browned on both sides. Remove; set aside. Add onion, celery, pecans, jalapeño pepper, sage, rosemary and pepper to skillet. Cook 5 minutes or until onion and celery are tender; set aside.

2. Combine cornbread stuffing mix, vegetable mixture and broth in medium bowl. Stir in egg. Spoon stuffing mixture into slow cooker. Arrange pork on top. Cover and cook on LOW about 5 hours or until pork is tender and barely pink in center. Serve with vegetable salad, if desired. *Makes 6 servings*

Note: If you prefer a more moist stuffing, increase the chicken broth to 1½ cups.

Pork Chop with Jalapeño-Pecan Cornbread Stuffing

Roast Leg of Lamb

Nutrients per serving:

Calories: 172
Carbohydrate: 1 g
Calories From Fat: 37%
Total Fat: 7 g
Saturated Fat: 2 g
Cholesterol: 78 mg
Sodium: 121 mg
Dietary Fiber: <1 g
Protein: 25 g

3 tablespoons coarse-grained mustard
2 cloves garlic, minced*
1½ teaspoons dried rosemary, crushed
½ teaspoon black pepper
1 leg of lamb, well trimmed, boned, rolled and tied (about 4 pounds)
Mint jelly (optional)

For more intense garlic flavor inside the meat, cut garlic into slivers. Cut small pockets at random intervals throughout roast with tip of sharp knife; insert garlic slivers.

1. Preheat oven to 400°F. Combine mustard, garlic, rosemary and pepper. Rub mustard mixture over lamb.** Place roast on meat rack in shallow, foil-lined roasting pan. Roast 15 minutes. *Reduce oven temperature to 325°F;* roast about 20 minutes per pound for medium or until internal temperature reaches 145°F when tested with meat thermometer inserted into thickest part of roast.

2. Transfer roast to cutting board; cover with foil. Let stand 10 to 15 minutes before carving. Internal temperature will continue to rise 5° to 10°F during stand time.

3. Cut strings from roast; discard. Carve into 20 slices. Serve with mint jelly, if desired. *Makes 10 servings*

**At this point lamb may be covered and refrigerated up to 24 hours before roasting.*

Roast Leg of Lamb

Beef Caesar Salad

Nutrients per serving:

Calories: 303
Carbohydrate: 14 g
Calories From Fat: 48%
Total Fat: 16 g
Saturated Fat: 6 g
Cholesterol: 73 mg
Sodium: 235 mg
Dietary Fiber: 3 g
Protein: 25 g

1 bag (10 ounces) ready-to-use chopped romaine lettuce
2 tablespoons prepared fat-free Caesar salad dressing
1 boneless beef top sirloin steak (about 1 pound)
   Nonstick cooking spray
   Black pepper
2 slices whole-wheat bread, toasted, cut into 32 croutons

1. In large salad bowl, toss lettuce with the dressing. Divide salad greens evenly among 4 plates.

2. Cut steak lengthwise in half, then crosswise into ⅛-inch-thick strips. Spray 12-inch nonstick skillet with cooking spray and heat over high heat. Add beef; stir-fry 2 minutes or until beef is barely pink in center.

3. Top each plate with ¼ portion of steak strips. Season with pepper and top with 8 croutons.   *Makes 4 servings*

Serving Suggestion: Serve with tomato soup or a meatless vegetable soup such as minestrone.

Beef Caesar Salad

Nutrients per serving:

Calories: 182
Carbohydrate: 8 g
Calories From Fat: 23%
Total Fat: 5 g
Saturated Fat: 2 g
Cholesterol: 65 mg
Sodium: 304 mg
Dietary Fiber: 1 g
Protein: 27 g

Mustard-Crusted Roast Pork Tenderloin & Vegetables

Pork tenderloins are low in fat and cook quickly. Asparagus, a low-calorie, low-carbohydrate favorite, roasts alongside and provides a generous helping of vitamin A and potassium.

    3 tablespoons Dijon mustard
    4 teaspoons minced garlic, divided
    2 whole well-trimmed pork tenderloins (about 1 pound each)
    2 tablespoons dried thyme leaves
    1 teaspoon black pepper
    ½ teaspoon salt
    1 pound asparagus spears, ends trimmed
    2 red or yellow bell peppers (or one of each), cut lengthwise into ½-inch-wide strips
    1 cup fat-free reduced-sodium chicken broth, divided

1. Preheat oven to 375°F. Combine mustard and 3 teaspoons garlic in small bowl. Spread mustard mixture evenly over top and sides of both tenderloins. Combine thyme, black pepper and salt in small bowl; reserve 1 teaspoon mixture. Sprinkle remaining mixture evenly over tenderloins, patting so that seasoning adheres to mustard. Place tenderloins on rack in shallow roasting pan. Roast 25 minutes.

2. Arrange asparagus and bell peppers in single layer in shallow casserole or 13×9-inch baking pan. Add ¼ cup broth, reserved thyme mixture and remaining 1 teaspoon garlic; toss to coat.

3. Roast vegetables in oven, alongside pork tenderloins,15 to 20 minutes or until thermometer inserted into center of pork registers 160°F and vegetables are tender. Transfer tenderloins to carving board; tent with foil and let stand 5 minutes. Arrange vegetables on serving platter, reserving juices in dish; cover and keep warm. Add remaining ¾ cup broth and vegetable juices to roasting pan. Place over range-top burners; simmer 3 to 4 minutes over medium-high heat or until juices are reduced to ¾ cup, stirring frequently. Carve tenderloin crosswise into ¼-inch-thick slices; arrange on serving platter. Spoon juices over tenderloin and vegetables.

Makes 8 servings

Mustard-Crusted Roast Pork Tenderloin & Vegetables

Beefy Bean & Walnut Stir-Fry

1 teaspoon vegetable oil
3 cloves garlic, minced
1 pound lean ground beef or ground turkey
1 bag (16 ounces) BIRDS EYE® frozen Cut Green Beans, thawed
1 teaspoon salt
½ cup walnut pieces

- In large skillet, heat oil and garlic over medium heat about 30 seconds.
- Add beef and beans; sprinkle with salt. Mix well.
- Cook 5 minutes or until beef is well browned, stirring occasionally.
- Stir in walnuts; cook 2 minutes more.

Makes 4 servings

Serving Suggestion: Serve over hot cooked egg noodles or rice.

Birds Eye® Idea: When you add California walnuts to Birds Eye® vegetables, you not only add texture and a great nutty taste, but nutrition too.

Prep Time: 5 minutes
Cook Time: 7 to 10 minutes

Beefy Bean & Walnut Stir-Fry

Savor More Seafood

Orange Scallops with Spinach & Walnuts

Spinach, orange juice and walnuts provide vitamins A and C and omega-3 fatty acids. Scallops cook quickly, making this a great dish to serve when you're in a hurry.

12 sea scallops (approximately ¾ pound)
½ cup freshly squeezed orange juice
2 tablespoons olive oil
2 packages (8 ounces each) fresh baby spinach, stems removed
2 tablespoons toasted walnuts
   Salt and white pepper to taste
½ (11-ounce) can mandarin oranges in juice, drained

1. Rinse sea scallops and slice in half. Place in nonreactive dish and add orange juice. Stir well and set aside.

2. Place a 12-inch skillet over medium heat and add oil. Add spinach and cook until heated through and just wilted, stirring often.

3. Push spinach to edges of pan, forming a ring. Increase heat to medium high. Place scallops in the center of pan, and cook scallops, turning once, 1 to 2 minutes or until opaque.

4. Add walnuts, and season with salt and white pepper. To serve, make a bed of spinach on plate, top with scallops, pan juices and mandarin orange segments.

Makes 4 servings

Nutrients per serving:

Calories: 199
Carbohydrate: 6 g
Calories From Fat: 54%
Total Fat: 12 g
Saturated Fat: 1 g
Cholesterol: 27 mg
Sodium: 501 mg
Dietary Fiber: 10 g
Protein: 18 g

Orange Scallops with Spinach & Walnuts

Nutrients per serving:

Calories: 196
Carbohydrate: 13 g
Calories From Fat: 27%
Total Fat: 6 g
Saturated Fat: 1 g
Cholesterol: 32 mg
Sodium: 185 mg
Dietary Fiber: 4 g
Protein: 23 g

Warm Blackened Tuna Salad

Heart-healthy tuna served on a bed of fresh, raw vegetables is a nutritional combo that's hard to beat. All cabbage is good for you, but red cabbage has additional antioxidant properties.

5 cups torn romaine lettuce
2 cups coarsely shredded red cabbage
2 medium yellow or green bell peppers, cut into strips
1½ cups sliced zucchini
1 teaspoon onion powder
½ teaspoon garlic powder
½ teaspoon black pepper
½ teaspoon ground red pepper
½ teaspoon dried thyme leaves
12 ounces fresh or thawed frozen tuna steaks, cut 1 inch thick
⅓ cup water
¾ cup onion slices
2 tablespoons balsamic vinegar
1½ teaspoons Dijon-style mustard
1 teaspoon canola or vegetable oil
½ teaspoon chicken bouillon granules

1. Preheat broiler. Combine romaine, cabbage, bell peppers and zucchini in large bowl; set aside.

2. Combine onion powder, garlic powder, black pepper, ground red pepper and thyme in small bowl. Rub spice mixture onto both sides of tuna. Place tuna on broiler pan. Broil 4 inches below heat, turing once, for about 10 minutes or until desired degree of doneness. Cover and set aside.

3. For dressing, bring water to a boil in small saucepan over high heat. Add onion slices; reduce heat to medium-low. Simmer, covered, 4 to 5 minutes or until onion is tender. Add vinegar, mustard, oil and bouillon granules; cook and stir until heated through.

4. Place romaine mixture on four salad plates; slice tuna and arrange on top. Drizzle with dressing. Serve warm.   *Makes 4 servings*

Warm Blackened Tuna Salad

Grilled Salmon Fillets, Asparagus & Onions

Nutrients per serving:

Calories: 255
Carbohydrate: 8 g
Calories From Fat: 30%
Total Fat: 8 g
Saturated Fat: 1 g
Cholesterol: 86 mg
Sodium: 483 mg
Dietary Fiber: 2 g
Protein: 35 g

½ teaspoon paprika
6 salmon fillets (6 to 8 ounces each)
⅓ cup bottled honey-Dijon marinade or barbecue sauce
1 bunch (about 1 pound) fresh asparagus spears, ends trimmed
1 large red or sweet onion, cut into ¼-inch slices
1 tablespoon olive oil
Salt and black pepper

1. Prepare grill for direct grilling. Sprinkle paprika over salmon fillets. Brush marinade over salmon; let stand at room temperature 15 minutes.

2. Brush asparagus and onion slices with olive oil; season to taste with salt and pepper.

3. Place salmon, skin side down, in center of grid over medium coals. Arrange asparagus spears and onion slices around salmon. Grill salmon and vegetables on covered grill 5 minutes. Turn salmon, asparagus and onion slices. Grill 5 to 6 minutes more or until salmon flakes when tested with a fork and vegetables are crisp-tender. Separate onion slices into rings; arrange over asparagus. *Makes 6 servings*

Prep and Cook Time: 26 minutes

Grilled Salmon Fillet, Asparagus & Onions

Nutrients per serving:

(1 catfish fillet and ½ cup compote)

Calories: 305
Carbohydrate: 16 g
Calories From Fat: 59%
Total Fat: 21 g
Saturated Fat: 4 g
Cholesterol: 101 mg
Sodium: 97 mg
Dietary Fiber: 4 g
Protein: 16 g

Pecan Catfish with Cranberry Compote

Pecans add a crunchy coating rich with monounsaturated fats (heart-protective fats).

Cranberry Compote (recipe follows)
1½ cup pecans
2 tablespoons flour
1 egg
2 tablespoons water
Salt and pepper
4 catfish fillets (about 1¼ pounds)
2 tablespoons butter, divided

1. Prepare and refrigerate Cranberry Compote at least 3 hours and up to several days ahead.

2. Preheat oven to 425°F. Place pecans and flour in bowl of food processor; pulse just until finely chopped. *Do not overprocess.*

3. Place pecan mixture in shallow dish or plate. Whisk eggs and water in another shallow dish. Sprinkle salt and pepper on both sides of each fillet; dip first in egg, then in pecan mixture, pressing to make coating stick.

4. Melt 1 tablespoon butter in baking dish large enough to hold fillets in single layer. Place fillets in prepared pan. Dot with remaining 1 tablespoon butter. Bake 15 to 20 minutes or until fish begins to flake when tested with fork.   *Makes 4 servings*

Cranberry Compote

1 bag (12 ounces) cranberries
¾ cup water
½ cup sucralose-based sugar substitute
¼ cup orange juice
2 tablespoons dark brown sugar
2 teaspoons grated fresh ginger
¼ teaspoon five-spice powder
⅛ teaspoon salt
1 teaspoon butter

Wash and pick over cranberries. Combine cranberries and all remaining ingredients except butter in large saucepan. Heat over medium high heat, stirring occasionally about 15 minutes or until saucy consistency is reached. Remove from heat; stir in butter. Allow to cool; refrigerate until cold.   *Makes 8 servings (½-cup each)*

Pecan Catfish with Cranberry Compote

Coconut Shrimp with Pear Chutney

Pear Chutney (recipe follows)
3 tablespoons unsalted butter
1 pound large raw shrimp, peeled and deveined
½ cup shredded unsweetened coconut flakes
¾ teaspoon curry powder
½ teaspoon salt

1. Preheat oven to 425°F. Spray baking sheet with nonstick cooking spray. Prepare Pear Chutney.

2. Meanwhile, melt butter in skillet. Remove from heat. Add shrimp and coat with butter. Mix coconut with curry powder and salt in small bowl; spread mixture on dinner plate. Press shrimp into coconut mixture to coat all sides. Place shrimp on prepared baking sheet.

3. Roast shrimp 4 minutes. Turn and roast another 2 minutes or until almost cooked through. Serve with Pear Chutney. *Makes 4 servings*

Pear Chutney

1 tablespoon vegetable oil
1 jalapeño pepper, seeded and minced*
1½ teaspoons grated fresh ginger
1 small shallot, minced
1 medium unpeeled ripe pear, cored and diced into ½-inch pieces
1 tablespoon cider vinegar
1 teaspoon brown sugar
⅛ teaspoon salt
1 tablespoon water
1 tablespoon chopped green onion

1. Heat oil in medium saucepan. Add jalapeño, ginger and shallot. Cook over low heat 5 minutes or until shallot is tender. Add pear, vinegar, brown sugar and salt. Stir in 1 tablespoon water.

2. Cover and cook over low heat 15 minutes or until pear is tender. Check pear occasionally; if mixture is getting dry add 1 tablespoon water. Stir in scallion and cook 1 minute just to soften. *Makes 4 servings*

Nutrients per serving:
Calories: 301
Carbohydrate: 11 g
Calories From Fat: 54%
Total Fat: 18 g
Saturated Fat: 9 g
Cholesterol: 197 mg
Sodium: 536 mg
Dietary Fiber: 2 g
Protein: 24 g

Coconut Shrimp with Pear Chutney

Grilled Five-Spice Fish with Garlic Spinach

Chinese five-spice powder is available in Asian markets and many supermarkets. Use prepackaged and washed baby spinach to save time.

Nutrients per serving:

Calories: 133
Carbohydrate: 4 g
Calories From Fat: 22%
Total Fat: 3 g
Saturated Fat: <1 g
Cholesterol: 49 mg
Sodium: 405 mg
Dietary Fiber: 2 g
Protein: 22 g

1½ **teaspoons grated lime peel**
3 **tablespoons fresh lime juice**
4 **teaspoons minced fresh ginger**
½ **to 1 teaspoon Chinese five-spice powder**
½ **teaspoon sugar**
½ **teaspoon salt**
⅛ **teaspoon black pepper**
2 **teaspoons vegetable oil, divided**
1 **pound salmon steaks**
½ **pound fresh baby spinach leaves (about 8 cups lightly packed), washed**
2 **large cloves garlic, pressed through garlic press**

1. Combine lime peel, lime juice, ginger, 5-spice powder, sugar, salt, pepper and 1 teaspoon oil in 2-quart dish. Add salmon; turn to coat. Cover; refrigerate 2 to 3 hours.

2. Combine spinach, garlic and remaining 1 teaspoon oil in 3-quart microwavable dish; toss. Cover; microwave at HIGH (100% power) 2 minutes or until spinach is wilted. Drain; keep warm.

3. Meanwhile, prepare grill for direct cooking.

4. Remove salmon from marinade and place on oiled grid. Brush salmon with marinade. Grill salmon, covered, over medium-hot coals 4 minutes. Turn salmon; brush with marinade and grill 4 minutes or until salmon begins to flake with fork. Discard remaining marinade.

5. Serve fish over bed of spinach.

Makes 4 servings

Grilled Five-Spice Fish with Garlic Spinach

Broiled Caribbean Sea Bass

This dish provides the health benefits of fish plus added protein from beans and rice. Together, beans and grains provide the essential amino acids needed to form a complete protein.

Nutrients per serving:

Calories: 291
Carbohydrate: 25 g
Calories From Fat: 23%
Total Fat: 7 g
Saturated Fat: 1 g
Cholesterol: 58 mg
Sodium: 684 mg
Dietary Fiber: 2 g
Protein: 31 g

6 skinless sea bass or striped bass fillets (5 to 6 ounces each), about ½ inch thick
⅓ cup chopped fresh cilantro
2 tablespoons olive oil
2 tablespoons fresh lime juice
2 teaspoons hot pepper sauce
2 cloves garlic, minced
1 package (7 ounces) black beans and rice mix
Lime wedges

1. Place fish in shallow dish. Combine cilantro, oil, lime juice, pepper sauce and garlic in small bowl; pour over fish. Cover; marinate in refrigerator 30 minutes, but no longer than 2 hours.

2. Prepare black beans and rice mix according to package directions; keep warm.

3. Preheat broiler. Remove fish from marinade. Place fish on rack of broiler pan; drizzle with any remaining marinade. Broil, 4 to 5 inches from heat, 8 to 10 minutes or until fish is opaque. Serve fish with black beans and rice and lime wedges.

Makes 6 servings

Broiled Caribbean Sea Bass

Seafood Tacos with Fruit Salsa

Naturally low in fat, seafood adds a delicious touch to these tacos.

Nutrients per serving:

(2 tacos with 4 tablespoons fruit salsa)

Calories: 294
Carbohydrate: 43 g
Calories From Fat: 14%
Total Fat: 5 g
Saturated Fat: 1 g
Cholesterol: 24 mg
Sodium: 296 mg
Dietary Fiber: 6 g
Protein: 21 g

    1 to 2 teaspoons grated lemon peel
    2 tablespoons lemon juice
    1 teaspoon chili powder
    1 teaspoon ground allspice
    1 teaspoon olive oil
    1 teaspoon minced garlic
    ½ teaspoon ground cloves
    1 pound halibut or snapper fillets
    12 (6-inch) corn tortillas *or* 6 (7- to 8-inch) flour tortillas
    3 cups shredded romaine lettuce
    1 small red onion, halved and thinly sliced
       Fruit Salsa (recipe follows)

1. Combine lemon peel, lemon juice, chili powder, allspice, oil, garlic and cloves in small bowl. Rub fish with spice mixture; cover and refrigerate while grill heats. (Fish may be cut into smaller pieces for easier handling.)

2. Prepare Fruit Salsa. Spray grid with nonstick cooking spray. Adjust grid 4 to 6 inches above heat. Preheat grill to medium-high heat. Grill fish, covered, 3 minutes or until fish is lightly browned on bottom. Carefully turn fish over; grill 2 minutes or until fish is opaque in center and flakes when tested with fork. Remove from heat and cut into 12 pieces, removing bones if necessary. Cover to keep warm.

3. Place tortillas on grill in single layer and heat 5 to 10 seconds; turn and cook 5 to 10 seconds or until hot and pliable. Stack; cover to keep warm.

4. Top each tortilla with ¼ cup lettuce and red onion. Add 1 piece of fish and about 2 tablespoons Fruit Salsa. *Makes 6 servings*

Fruit Salsa: Combine 1 diced ripe papaya, 1 diced banana, 2 minced green onions, 3 tablespoons chopped fresh cilantro, 3 tablespoons lime juice and 2 seeded, diced jalapeño peppers* in small bowl. Serve at room temperature. Makes 12 servings.

*Jalapeño peppers can sting and irritate the skin; wear rubber gloves when handling peppers and do not touch eyes. Wash hands after handling.

Seafood Tacos with Fruit Salsa

Shrimp Scampi over Hot Tomato Relish

This version of shrimp scampi is prepared in heart-healthy olive oil with only a touch of butter. Add a green vegetable or mixed green salad for a quick, healthy dinner.

Nutrients per serving:

Calories: 327
Carbohydrate: 9 g
Calories From Fat: 61%
Total Fat: 22 g
Saturated Fat: 5 g
Cholesterol: 181 mg
Sodium: 470 mg
Dietary Fiber: 2 g
Protein: 24 g

  Hot Tomato Relish (recipe follows)
  ¼ cup olive oil
  1 tablespoon unsalted butter
  1 large clove garlic, minced
  1 pound large raw shrimp, peeled and deveined
  2 tablespoons minced Italian parsley
  1 tablespoon lemon juice
  ¼ teaspoon salt
  ¼ teaspoon black pepper
  4 lemon wedges

1. Prepare Hot Tomato Relish and set aside. Heat oil and butter in a large skillet over very low heat. Add garlic and cook 5 minutes; do not burn.

2. Add shrimp. Cook over low heat 5 minutes, turning once, or until shrimp are pink and cooked through. Stir in parsley, lemon juice, salt and pepper. Serve over Hot Tomato Relish with lemon wedges.   *Makes 4 servings*

Hot Tomato Relish

  1 tablespoon olive oil
  2 cups halved grape tomatoes
  ¼ teaspoon salt
  ¼ teaspoon black pepper
  1 tablespoon balsamic vinegar
  1 tablespoon minced fresh basil

Heat olive oil in large skillet. Add tomatoes and heat on high 1 to 2 minutes or until tomatoes are hot, but not cooked through. Season with salt and pepper. Sprinkle with balsamic vinegar and basil before serving.   *Makes 4 servings*

Shrimp Scampi over Hot Tomato Relish

Grilled Salmon Salad with Orange-Basil Vinaigrette

This beautiful dish is nutrient-rich with vitamins C and A. The salmon also provides a healthy dose of the fish oils that have been found likely to protect against heart disease.

Nutrients per serving:

Calories: 283
Carbohydrate: 23 g
Calories From Fat: 35%
Total Fat: 11 g
Saturated Fat: 2 g
Cholesterol: 60 mg
Sodium: 70 mg
Dietary Fiber: 3 g
Protein: 24 g

¼ cup frozen orange juice concentrate, thawed
1 tablespoon plus 1½ teaspoons white wine vinegar or cider vinegar
1 tablespoon chopped fresh basil *or* 1 teaspoon dried basil leaves
1½ teaspoons olive oil
1 (8-ounce) salmon fillet (about 1 inch thick)
4 cups torn mixed greens
¾ cup sliced strawberries
10 to 12 thin cucumber slices, cut into halves
⅛ teaspoon coarsely ground black pepper

1. Whisk together juice concentrate, vinegar, basil and olive oil. Set aside 2 tablespoons juice concentrate mixture. Reserve remaining mixture to use as salad dressing.

2. Prepare grill for direct grilling. Grill salmon, skin side down, over medium coals 5 minutes. Turn and grill 5 minutes or until fish flakes with fork, brushing frequently with 2 tablespoons juice concentrate mixture. Cool slightly.

3. Toss together greens, strawberries and cucumber in large bowl. Place on two serving plates.

4. Remove skin from salmon. Break salmon into chunks; arrange on greens mixture. Drizzle with reserved juice concentrate mixture. Sprinkle with pepper.

Makes 2 servings

Grilled Salmon Salad with Orange-Basil Vinaigrette

Nutrients per
serving:

Calories: 146
Carbohydrate: 9 g
Calories From Fat: 15%
Total Fat: 3 g
Saturated Fat: 1 g
Cholesterol: 47 mg
Sodium: 189 mg
Dietary Fiber: 1 g
Protein: 21 g

Caribbean Sea Bass with Mango Salsa

4 skinless sea bass fillets (4 ounces each), about 1 inch thick
1 teaspoon Caribbean jerk seasoning
   Nonstick cooking spray
1 ripe mango, peeled, pitted and diced, *or* 1 cup diced drained bottled
   mango
2 tablespoons chopped fresh cilantro
2 teaspoons fresh lime juice
1 teaspoon minced fresh or bottled jalapeño pepper*

*Jalapeño peppers can sting and irritate the skin; wear rubber gloves when handling peppers and do not touch eyes. Wash hands after handling.

1. Prepare grill or preheat broiler. Sprinkle fish with seasoning; coat lightly with cooking spray. Grill fish over medium coals or broil 5 inches from heat 4 to 5 minutes per side or until fish flakes when tested with fork.

2. Meanwhile, combine mango, cilantro, lime juice and jalapeño pepper in small bowl; mix well. Serve salsa over fish.   *Makes 4 servings*

Prep Time: 10 minutes
Cook Time: 8 minutes

Caribbean Sea Bass with Mango Salsa

Mahimahi with Fresh Pineapple Salsa

This fresh-tasting, low-fat, ultra-healthy salsa adds zing to broiled mahimahi. What a delicious way to get one of your two to three servings of fish a week that many nutrition experts recommend.

1½ cups diced fresh pineapple
¼ cup finely chopped red bell pepper
¼ cup finely chopped green bell pepper
2 tablespoons chopped fresh cilantro
2 tablespoons fresh lime juice, divided
½ teaspoon red pepper flakes
½ teaspoon grated lime peel
   Nonstick cooking spray
4 mahimahi fillets (4 ounces each)
1 tablespoon olive oil
½ teaspoon white pepper

1. To prepare salsa, combine pineapple, red and green peppers, cilantro, 1 tablespoon lime juice, red pepper flakes and lime peel in medium bowl. Set aside.

2. Preheat broiler. Spray rack of broiler pan with cooking spray. Rinse mahimahi and pat dry with paper towels. Place mahimahi-mahimahi on rack. Combine remaining 1 tablespoon lime juice and olive oil; brush on mahimahi-mahimahi.

3. Broil, 4 inches from heat, 2 minutes. Turn and brush second side with olive oil mixture; sprinkle with white pepper. Continue to broil 2 minutes or until mahimahi flakes when tested with fork. Serve with pineapple salsa.   *Makes 4 servings*

Note: Pineapple Salsa can be prepared 1 to 2 days ahead and refrigerated.

Prep and Cook Time: 25 minutes

Mahimahi with Fresh Pineapple Salsa

Teriyaki Salmon with Asian Slaw

Nutrients per
serving:

Calories: 354

Carbohydrate: 32 g

Calories From Fat: 28%

Total Fat: 11 g

Saturated Fat: 2 g

Cholesterol: 75 mg

Sodium: 730 mg

Dietary Fiber: 5 g

Protein: 32 g

4 tablespoons reduced-sodium teriyaki sauce, divided
2 (5- to 6-ounce) boneless salmon fillets with skin (1 inch thick)
2½ cups packaged coleslaw mix
1 cup fresh or frozen snow peas, cut lengthwise into thin strips
½ cup thinly sliced radishes
2 tablespoons orange marmalade
1 teaspoon dark sesame oil

1. Preheat broiler or prepare grill for direct cooking. Spoon 2 tablespoons teriyaki sauce over meaty sides of salmon. Let stand while preparing vegetable mixture.

2. Combine coleslaw mix, snow peas and radishes in large bowl. Combine remaining 2 tablespoons teriyaki sauce, marmalade and sesame oil in small bowl. Add to coleslaw mixture; toss well.

3. Broil salmon 4 to 5 inches from heat source or grill, flesh side down, over medium coals without turning 6 to 10 minutes until center is opaque.

4. Transfer coleslaw mixture to serving plates; top with salmon.

Makes 2 servings

Teriyaki Salmon with Asian Slaw

Lemon-Poached Halibut with Carrots

Nutrients per serving:

Calories: 224
Carbohydrate: 8 g
Calories From Fat: 17%
Total Fat: 4 g
Saturated Fat: 1 g
Cholesterol: 55 mg
Sodium: 338 mg
Dietary Fiber: 2 g
Protein: 36 g

3 medium carrots, cut into matchstick-size strips
¾ cup water
¼ cup dry white wine
2 tablespoons lemon juice
1 teaspoon dried rosemary
1 teaspoon dried marjoram leaves
1 teaspoon chicken or fish bouillon granules
¼ teaspoon black pepper
4 fresh or frozen halibut steaks, cut 1 inch thick (about 1½ pounds)
½ cup sliced green onions
Lemon slices for garnish (optional)

Combine carrots, water, wine, lemon juice, rosemary, marjoram, bouillon granules and pepper in large skillet. Bring to a boil over high heat. Carefully place fish and onions in skillet. Return just to a boil. Reduce heat to medium-low. Cover; simmer 8 to 10 minutes or until fish flakes when tested with fork.

Carefully transfer fish to serving platter with slotted spatula. Spoon vegetables over fish. Garnish with lemon slices, if desired. *Makes 4 servings*

Lemon-Poached Halibut with Carrots

Oven-Roasted Boston Scrod

Scrod is young cod. The firm, lean white flesh is versatile and easy to love. Like all seafood, it's a source of the essential omega-3 fatty acids.

½ **cup seasoned dry bread crumbs**
1 **teaspoon paprika**
1 **teaspoon grated fresh lemon peel**
1 **teaspoon dried dill weed**
3 **tablespoons all-purpose flour**
2 **egg whites**
1 **tablespoon water**
1½ **pounds Boston scrod or orange roughy fillets, cut into 6 (4-ounce) pieces**
2 **tablespoons margarine, melted**
  Tartar Sauce (recipe follows)
  Lemon wedges

1. Preheat oven to 400°F. Spray 15×10-inch jelly-roll pan with nonstick cooking spray. Combine bread crumbs, paprika, lemon peel and dill in shallow bowl or pie plate. Place flour in resealable plastic food storage bag. Beat egg whites and water together in another shallow bowl or pie plate.

2. Add fish, one fillet at a time, to bag. Seal bag; turn to coat fish lightly. Dip fish into egg white mixture, letting excess drip off. Roll fish in bread crumb mixture. Place in prepared jelly-roll pan. Repeat with remaining fish fillets. Drizzle margarine evenly over fish. Bake 15 to 18 minutes or until fish begins to flake when tested with fork.

3. Prepare Tartar Sauce while fish is baking. Serve fish with lemon wedges and Tartar Sauce. *Makes 6 servings*

Tartar Sauce

½ **cup fat-free or reduced-fat mayonnaise**
¼ **cup sweet pickle relish**
2 **teaspoons Dijon mustard**
¼ **teaspoon hot pepper sauce (optional)**

Combine all ingredients in small bowl; mix well. *Makes ⅔ cup sauce*

Oven-Roasted Boston Scrod

Hot Shrimp with Cool Salsa

Shrimp is low in saturated fat and a good source of niacin, iron and zinc. The melon and cucumber salsa makes a refreshing counterpoint to the spicy shrimp.

¼ **cup prepared salsa**
4 **tablespoons fresh lime juice, divided**
1 **teaspoon honey**
1 **clove garlic, minced**
2 **to 4 drops hot pepper sauce**
1 **pound large shrimp, peeled and deveined, with tails intact**
1 **cup finely diced honeydew melon**
½ **cup finely diced unpeeled cucumber**
2 **tablespoons minced parsley**
1 **green onion, finely chopped**
1½ **teaspoons sugar**
1 **teaspoon olive oil**
¼ **teaspoon salt**

1. To make marinade, combine prepared salsa, 2 tablespoons lime juice, honey, garlic and hot pepper sauce in small bowl. Thread shrimp onto skewers. Brush shrimp with marinade; set aside.

2. To make salsa, combine remaining 2 tablespoons lime juice, melon, cucumber, parsley, onion, sugar, oil and salt in medium bowl; mix well.

3. Grill shrimp over medium coals 4 to 5 minutes or until shrimp are opaque, turning once. Serve with salsa.

Makes 4 servings

Hot Shrimp with Cool Salsa

Southwest Roasted Salmon & Corn

Salmon is one of the best sources of omega-3 fatty acids. While corn is a starchy vegetable that is relatively high in carbohydrate, it is also provides vitamins A and some fiber.

2 medium ears fresh corn, unhusked
1 salmon fillet (6 ounces), cut into 2 equal pieces
1 tablespoon plus 1 teaspoon fresh lime juice, divided
1 clove garlic, minced
½ teaspoon chili powder
¼ teaspoon ground cumin
¼ teaspoon dried oregano leaves
⅛ teaspoon salt, divided
⅛ teaspoon black pepper
2 teaspoons margarine, melted
2 teaspoons minced fresh cilantro

1. Preheat oven to 400°F. Spray shallow 1-quart baking dish with nonstick cooking spray. Pull back husks from each ear of corn, leaving husks attached. Discard silk. Bring husks back up over each ear. Soak corn in cold water 20 minutes.

2. Place salmon, skin side down, in prepared dish. Pour 1 tablespoon lime juice over fillets. Marinate at room temperature 15 minutes.

3. Combine garlic, chili powder, cumin, oregano, half of salt and the pepper in small bowl. Pat salmon lightly with paper towel. Rub garlic mixture on tops and sides of salmon.

4. Remove corn from water. Place corn on one side of oven rack. Roast 10 minutes; turn.

5. Place salmon in baking dish on other side of oven rack. Roast 15 minutes or until salmon is opaque and flakes when tested with fork, and corn is tender.

6. Combine margarine, cilantro, remaining 1 teaspoon lime juice and remaining salt in small bowl. Remove husks from corn. Brush over corn. Serve corn with salmon.

Makes 2 servings

Recipe Tip: Roasting corn gives it a special flavor. However, it can also be cooked in boiling water. Omit steps 1 and 4. Husk the corn and place in a large pot of boiling water. Cover; remove from heat and let stand for 10 minutes. Drain and brush with cilantro butter as directed.

Southwest Roasted Salmon & Corn

Snack Wisely and Well

Leek Strudels

Nutrients per serving:

Calories: 52
Carbohydrate: 11 g
Calories From Fat: 9%
Total Fat: 1 g
Saturated Fat: <1 g
Cholesterol: 0 mg
Sodium: 107 mg
Dietary Fiber: 1 g
Protein: 1 g

Nonstick cooking spray
2 pounds leeks, cleaned and sliced (white parts only)
¼ teaspoon caraway seeds
¼ teaspoon salt
⅛ teaspoon white pepper
¼ cup fat-free reduced-sodium chicken broth
3 sheets thawed frozen phyllo dough, thawed
Butter-flavored nonstick cooking spray

1. Coat large skillet with nonstick cooking spray; heat over medium heat. Add leeks; cook and stir about 5 minutes or until tender. Stir in caraway seeds, salt and pepper. Add chicken broth; bring to a boil over high heat. Reduce heat to low. Simmer, covered, about 5 minutes or until broth is absorbed. Let cool to room temperature.

2. Preheat oven to 400°F. Cut each sheet of phyllo lengthwise into thirds. Spray 1 piece phyllo dough with nonstick cooking spray; spoon 2 tablespoons leek mixture onto bottom of piece. Fold 1 corner over filling to make triangle. Continue folding, as you would fold a flag, to make triangular packet.

3. Repeat with remaining phyllo dough and leek mixture. Place packets on cookie sheet; lightly coat tops of packets with butter-flavored cooking spray. Bake about 20 minutes or until golden brown. Serve warm. *Makes 9 servings*

Leek Strudels

Smoked Salmon Roses

This beautiful appetizer doesn't look or taste like health food, but salmon is an excellent source of the omega-3 fatty acids that experts believe are so important to heart health.

Nutrients per serving:

Calories: 40
Carbohydrate: 1 g
Calories From Fat: 67%
Total Fat: 3 g
Saturated Fat: 2 g
Cholesterol: 10 mg
Sodium: 106 mg
Dietary Fiber: <1 g
Protein: 3 g

  1 package (8 ounces) cream cheese, softened
  1 tablespoon prepared horseradish
  1 tablespoon minced fresh dill plus whole sprigs for garnish
  1 tablespoon half-and-half
  16 slices (12 to 16 ounces) smoked salmon
  1 red bell pepper, cut into thin strips

1. Combine cream cheese, horseradish, minced dill and half-and-half in a bowl. Beat until light.

2. Spread 1 tablespoon cream cheese mixture over each salmon slice. Roll up jelly-roll fashion. Slice each roll in half widthwise. Stand salmon rolls, cut side down, on a serving dish to resemble roses. Garnish each "rose" by tucking 1 pepper strip and 1 dill sprig in center.   *Makes 32 servings*

Garlic Bean Dip

This savory bean dip will satisfy even the most ardent garlic lover and beats store-bought versions both in flavor and nutrients.

Nutrients per serving:

Calories: 42
Carbohydrate: 7 g
Calories From Fat: 21%
Total Fat: 1 g
Saturated Fat: <1 g
Cholesterol: 0 mg
Sodium: 207 mg
Dietary Fiber: 1 g
Protein: 3 g

  4 cloves garlic
  1 can (15½ ounces) pinto or black beans, rinsed and drained
  ¼ cup pimiento-stuffed green olives
  4½ teaspoons lemon juice
  ½ teaspoon ground cumin
    Assorted fresh vegetables and crackers

1. Place garlic in food processor; process until minced. Add beans, olives, lemon juice and cumin; process until well blended but not entirely smooth.

2. Serve with vegetables and crackers.   *Makes 12 servings (about 1½ cups)*

Tip: To save time, buy fresh vegetables, such as carrots and celery, already cut up from the produce section of the supermarket.

Smoked Salmon Roses

Roasted Garlic Hummus

High-fiber chick-peas make this dip creamy and satisfying. Served with whole wheat pita, this is a snack that's nourishing, low in fat and delicious.

2 tablespoons Roasted Garlic (recipe follows)
1 can (15 ounces) chick-peas (garbanzo beans), rinsed and drained
¼ cup fresh parsley, stems removed
2 tablespoons lemon juice
2 tablespoons water
½ teaspoon curry powder
3 drops dark sesame oil
Dash hot pepper sauce
Whole-wheat pita bread (optional)

Prepare Roasted Garlic. Place chick-peas, parsley, 2 tablespoons Roasted Garlic, lemon juice, water, curry powder, sesame oil and hot pepper sauce in food processor or blender; process until smooth, scraping down side of bowl once. Serve with pita bread triangles, if desired. *Makes 6 (¼-cup) servings*

Roasted Garlic: Cut off top third of 1 large garlic head (not the root end) to expose cloves; discard top. Place head of garlic, trimmed end up, on 10-inch square of foil. Rub garlic generously with olive oil and sprinkle with salt. Gather foil ends together and close tightly. Roast in preheated 350°F oven 45 minutes or until cloves are golden and soft. When cool enough to handle, squeeze roasted garlic cloves from skins; discard skins.

Nutrients per serving:

Calories: 85
Carbohydrate: 15 g
Calories From Fat: 15%
Total Fat: 1 g
Saturated Fat: <1 g
Cholesterol: 0 mg
Sodium: 303 mg
Dietary Fiber: 4 g
Protein: 4 g

Roasted Garlic Hummus

Quick Pickled Green Beans

Nutrients per serving:

Calories: 21
Carbohydrate: 4 g
Calories From Fat: 6%
Total Fat: <1 g
Saturated Fat: <1 g
Cholesterol: 0 mg
Sodium: 119 mg
Dietary Fiber: 2 g
Protein: 1 g

½ pound (3½ cups loosely packed) whole green beans
½ red bell pepper, cut into strips (optional)
1 jalapeño or other hot pepper, cut into strips
1 large clove garlic, cut in half
1 bay leaf
1 cup white wine vinegar
1 cup water
½ cup white wine
1 tablespoon sugar
1 tablespoon salt
1 tablespoon whole coriander seed
1 tablespoon mustard seed
1 tablespoon whole peppercorns

1. Wash green beans and remove stem ends. Place in a glass dish just large enough to hold green beans and 2½ cups liquid. Add bell pepper strips, if desired. Tuck jalapeño, garlic and bay leaf between beans.

2. Place remaining ingredients in medium saucepan. Heat to a boil; stir to dissolve sugar and salt. Reduce heat and simmer 5 minutes. Pour mixture over green beans. They should be submerged in liquid. If not, add additional hot water to cover.

3. Cover and refrigerate at least 24 hours. Remove and discard bay leaf before serving. Flavor improves in 48 hours and beans may be kept refrigerated for up to 5 days.

Makes 6 appetizer servings

Quick Pickled Green Beans

Fast Guacamole & "Chips"

Avocado provides heart-healthy fat and folate. Crisp cucumbers stand in for high-fat taco chips and the taste combination is unbeatable.

2 ripe avocados
½ cup restaurant-style chunky salsa
¼ teaspoon hot pepper sauce (optional)
½ seedless cucumber, sliced into ⅛-inch rounds

1. Cut avocados in half; remove and discard pits. Scoop flesh into medium bowl. Mash with fork.

2. Add salsa and hot pepper sauce, if desired; mix well.

3. Transfer guacamole to serving bowl; surround with cucumber "chips".

Makes 8 servings, about 1¾ cups

Nutrients per serving:

Calories: 85
Carbohydrate: 5 g
Calories From Fat: 72%
Total Fat: 7 g
Saturated Fat: 1 g
Cholesterol: 0 mg
Sodium: 120 mg
Dietary Fiber: 2 g
Protein: 2 g

Fresh Cranberry-Pineapple Congeal

1 medium orange
1 cup fresh or thawed frozen cranberries
⅔ cup water
1 package (4-serving size) raspberry sugar-free gelatin
1 cup ice cubes
½ (8-ounce) can crushed pineapple in juice, drained

1. Grate orange peel into small bowl; set aside. Coarsely chop cranberries in blender or food processor; set aside.

2. Squeeze juice from orange into small saucepan. Add water; stir to combine. Bring to a boil over high heat. Remove from heat. Stir in gelatin until completely dissolved. Add ice cubes; stir until gelatin is slightly thickened. Remove any unmelted pieces of ice.

3. Stir in cranberries, pineapple and reserved orange peel. Pour mixture into 4 (6-ounce) glass dishes or 9-inch glass pie pan. Cover with plastic wrap; refrigerate until firm.

Makes 4 servings

Prep Time: 10 minutes
Chill Time: 1 hour

Nutrients per serving:

Calories: 50
Carbohydrate: 11 g
Calories From Fat: 0%
Total Fat: 0 g
Saturated Fat: 0 g
Cholesterol: 0 mg
Sodium: 60 mg
Dietary Fiber: 2 g
Protein: 2 g

Fast Guacamole & "Chips"

Honey Granola with Yogurt

Rich in calcium, whole grains and fruit, this homemade yogurt and granola parfait is luscious to look at as well as eat!

Nutrients per serving:

Calories: 162
Carbohydrate: 22 g
Calories From Fat: 28%
Total Fat: 5 g
Saturated Fat: 1 g
Cholesterol: 10 mg
Sodium: 96 mg
Dietary Fiber: 2 g
Protein: 9 g

½ cup uncooked old-fashioned rolled oats
¼ cup sliced almonds
2 tablespoons toasted wheat germ
1 tablespoon orange juice
1 tablespoon honey
½ teaspoon ground cinnamon
1½ cups strawberries
4 containers (6 ounces each) plain nonfat yogurt
1 teaspoon vanilla

1. Preheat oven to 325°F. Lightly spray 8×8×2-inch baking pan with nonstick cooking spray; set aside.

2. Combine oats, almonds and wheat germ in small bowl. Combine orange juice, honey and cinnamon in another small bowl. Pour juice mixture over oat mixture; mix well.

3. Spread mixture evenly in prepared pan. Bake 20 to 25 minutes or until toasted, stirring twice during baking. Remove from oven. Transfer mixture to sheet of foil to cool completely.

4. Cut 3 strawberries in half for garnish. Slice remaining strawberries. Combine yogurt and vanilla in medium bowl. Layer sliced strawberries, yogurt mixture and granola in six dessert dishes or martini glasses. Garnish with strawberry halves.

Makes 6 servings

Prep Time: 10 minutes
Bake Time: 20 to 25 minutes

Honey Granola with Yogurt

Spicy Roasted Chick-Peas

Nutrients per serving:

Calories: 264
Carbohydrate: 33g
Calories From Fat: 40%
Total Fat: 12 g
Saturated Fat: 2 g
Cholesterol: 0 mg
Sodium: 730 mg
Dietary Fiber: 7 g
Protein: 7 g

1 can (20 ounces) chick-peas
3 tablespoons olive oil
½ teaspoon salt
½ teaspoon black pepper
¾ to 1 tablespoon chili powder (to taste)
⅛ to ¼ teaspoon ground red pepper (to taste)
1 lime cut into wedges

1. Preheat oven to 400°F. Rinse and drain chick-peas thoroughly in colander under plenty of running water. Shake until fairly dry.

2. Combine chick-peas, olive oil, salt and black pepper in large baking pan that will hold chick-peas in single layer. Bake 15 minutes or until chick-peas begin to brown, shaking pan twice to brown evenly.

3. Remove pan and season with chili powder and red pepper to taste. Bake an additional 5 minutes until dark golden red. Serve with lime wedges.

Makes 4 (¼-cup) servings

Spicy Roasted Chick-Peas

Fresh Fruit with Creamy Lime Dipping Sauce

Fruit is the healthy way to satisfy your sweet tooth. Choose fruit in a rainbow of colors and you'll get a good range of nutrients, too.

2 tablespoons lime juice
1 small jicama, peeled and cut into ½-inch-thick strips 3 to 4 inches long
2 pounds watermelon, rind removed, and fruit cut into ½-inch-thick
    wedges 2 to 3 inches wide
½ small pineapple, peeled, halved lengthwise and cut crosswise into wedges
1 ripe papaya, peeled, seeded and sliced crosswise
    Creamy Lime Dipping Sauce (recipe follows)

Combine lime juice and jicama in large bowl; toss. Drain. Arrange jicama, watermelon, pineapple and papaya on large platter. Serve with Creamy Lime Dipping Sauce. Garnish as desired. *Makes 12 servings*

Nutrients per serving:

Calories: 65
Carbohydrate: 15 g
Calories From Fat: 5%
Total Fat: <1 g
Saturated Fat: 0 g
Cholesterol: <1 mg
Sodium: 23 mg
Dietary Fiber: 1 g
Protein: 1 g

Creamy Lime Dipping Sauce

1 carton (6 ounces) vanilla-flavored nonfat yogurt
2 tablespoons minced fresh cilantro
2 tablespoons lime juice
1 tablespoon minced jalapeño pepper*

*Jalapeño peppers can sting and irritate the skin; wear rubber gloves when handling peppers and do not touch eyes. Wash hands after handling.

Combine all ingredients in small bowl; mix well.

Fresh Fruit with Creamy Lime Dipping Sauce

Black Bean Salsa

This salsa is packed with protein, fiber, phytochemicals and delicious flavor. It's also great as a side dish with chicken or fish, on top of a mixed green salad, or wrapped in a tortilla.

1 can (14½ ounces) black beans, rinsed and drained
1 cup frozen corn, thawed
1 large tomato, chopped
¼ cup chopped green onions
2 tablespoons chopped fresh cilantro
2 tablespoons lemon juice
1 tablespoon vegetable oil
1 teaspoon chili powder
¼ teaspoon salt
6 corn tortillas

1. Combine beans, corn, tomato, green onions, cilantro, lemon juice, oil, chili powder and salt in medium bowl; mix well.

2. Preheat oven to 400°F. Cut each tortilla into 8 wedges; place on ungreased baking sheet. Bake 6 to 8 minutes or until edges begin to brown. Serve tortilla wedges warm or at room temperature with salsa. Garnish with lemon wedges and additional fresh cilantro, if desired. *Makes 6 servings*

Nutrients per serving:

Calories: 161
Carbohydrate: 31 g
Calories From Fat: 18%
Total Fat: 4 g
Saturated Fat: trace g
Cholesterol: 0 mg
Sodium: 351 mg
Dietary Fiber: 5 g
Protein: 8 g

Summertime Fruit Medley

This medley of summer's succulent fruits tossed with amaretto will dazzle your guests. They can enjoy seconds of this low-calorie, low-fat dessert.

2 large ripe peaches, peeled and sliced
2 large ripe nectarines, sliced
1 large mango, peeled and cut into 1-inch chunks
1 cup blueberries
2 cups orange juice
¼ cup amaretto *or* ½ teaspoon almond extract
2 tablespoons sugar

Combine peaches, nectarines, mango and blueberries in large bowl. Whisk orange juice, amaretto and sugar in small bowl until sugar is dissolved. Pour over fruit mixture; toss. Marinate 1 hour at room temperature. *Makes 8 servings*

Nutrients per serving:

Calories: 126
Carbohydrate: 28 g
Calories From Fat: 3%
Total Fat: <1g
Saturated Fat: <1 g
Cholesterol: 0 mg
Sodium: 2 mg
Dietary Fiber: 3 g
Protein: 1 g

Black Bean Salsa

Nutrients per
serving:

Calories: 47
Carbohydrate: 6 g
Calories From Fat: 16%
Total Fat: 1 g
Saturated Fat: <1 g
Cholesterol: 7 mg
Sodium: 120 mg
Dietary Fiber: 1 g
Protein: 3 g

Berry Good Dip

Add a double dose of fresh fruit to your day with this dip made to pair with fruit dippers.

8 ounces fresh or thawed frozen unsweetened strawberries
4 ounces fat-free cream cheese, softened
¼ cup reduced-fat sour cream
1 tablespoon sugar

1. Place strawberries in food processor or blender container; process until smooth.

2. Beat cream cheese in small bowl until smooth. Stir in sour cream, strawberry purée and sugar; cover. Refrigerate until ready to serve.

3. Spoon dip into small serving bowl. Garnish with orange peel, if desired. Serve with assorted fresh fruit dippers or angel food cake cubes.

Makes 6 (¼-cup) servings

Cook's Tip: For a super quick fruit spread for toasted mini English muffins or bagels, beat 1 package (8 ounces) softened nonfat cream cheese in small bowl until fluffy. Stir in 3 to 4 tablespoons strawberry spreadable fruit. Season to taste with 1 to 2 teaspoons sugar, if desired. Makes 6 servings.

Berry Good Dip

Rosemary-Scented Nut Mix

Nutrients per serving:

Calories: 108
Carbohydrate: 2 g
Calories From Fat: 88%
Total Fat: 11 g
Saturated Fat: 2 g
Cholesterol: 2 mg
Sodium: 37 mg
Dietary Fiber: 1 g
Protein: 2 g

Here's a snack that's full of protein, fiber, folate and healthy fats. Just wait until you smell the aroma coming from your oven!

¼ teaspoon red pepper flakes
2 tablespoons unsalted butter
2 cups pecan halves
1 cup unsalted macadamia nuts
1 cup walnuts
1 teaspoon dried rosemary, crushed
½ teaspoon salt

1. Preheat oven to 300°F. Melt butter in large saucepan over low heat. Add pecans, macadamia nuts and walnuts; mix well. Add rosemary, salt and red pepper flakes; cook and stir 1 minute.

2. Pour mixture onto nonstick jelly-roll pan. Bake 15 minutes, shaking pan occasionally.

Makes 32 servings

Savory Pita Chips

Nutrients per serving:

Calories: 108
Carbohydrate: 18 g
Calories From Fat: 18%
Total Fat: 2 g
Saturated Fat: 1 g
Cholesterol: 4 mg
Sodium: 257 mg
Dietary Fiber: 0 g
Protein: 5 g

These are simple to make and a crunchy scoop for bean dips, spreads and salsas. They're also good crumbled and used as a topping for mixed green salads.

2 whole wheat or white pita bread rounds
Nonstick olive oil cooking spray
3 tablespoons grated Parmesan cheese
1 teaspoon dried basil leaves
¼ teaspoon garlic powder

1. Preheat oven to 350°F. Line baking sheet with foil; set aside.

2. Using scissors, cut each pita bread into 2 rounds. Cut each round into 6 wedges.

3. Place wedges, rough side down, on prepared baking sheet; coat lightly with cooking spray. Turn wedges over; spray again.

4. Combine Parmesan cheese, basil and garlic powder in small bowl; sprinkle evenly over pita wedges.

5. Bake 12 to 14 minutes or until golden brown. Cool completely.

Makes 4 servings

Rosemary-Scented Nut Mix

Great Zukes Pizza Bites

Zucchini fills in for the crust to make a low-carb snack loaded with real pizza flavor.

1 medium zucchini
3 tablespoons pizza sauce
2 tablespoons tomato paste
¼ teaspoon crushed dried oregano
¾ cup shredded reduced-fat mozzarella cheese
¼ cup shredded Parmesan cheese
8 pitted ripe olives
8 slices pepperoni

1. Preheat broiler and set rack 4 inches from heat.

2. Wash zucchini and trim off ends. Slice ¼ inch thick on diagonal to make 16 slices. Place zucchini on wire rack over nonstick cookie sheet.

3. Stir pizza sauce, tomato paste and oregano together in cup. Spread scant teaspoon of sauce over each zucchini slice. Toss together mozzarella and Parmesan cheeses in small bowl. Top each zucchini slice with 1 tablespoon cheese mixture, pressing down into sauce. Arrange 1 olive on top of 8 pizza bites. Place one pepperoni slice on each remaining 8 pizza bites.

4. Place cookie sheet under broiler and broil 3 minutes or until cheese melts and zucchini is tender. Remove from broiler and serve immediately.   *Makes 8 servings*

Nutrients per serving:

Calories: 75
Carbohydrate: 3 g
Calories From Fat: 60%
Total Fat: 5 g
Saturated Fat: 2 g
Cholesterol: 10 mg
Sodium: 288 mg
Dietary Fiber: 1 g
Protein: 5 g

Great Zukes Pizza Bites

Chocolate Fondue with Fresh Fruit

Nutrients per serving:

Calories: 177
Carbohydrate: 7 g
Calories From Fat: 80%
Total Fat: 16 g
Saturated Fat: 10 g
Cholesterol: 57 mg
Sodium: 55 mg
Dietary Fiber: 1 g
Protein: 2 g

3 tablespoons unsweetened cocoa
1 cup heavy cream
4 ounces (½ cup) cream cheese, cut in chunks
3 tablespoons and 1 teaspoon sugar substitute (sucralose-based)
½ teaspoon vanilla
24 green or red seedless grapes
12 small to medium strawberries, halved, or 6 large strawberries quartered

1. In a small saucepan or fondue pot over low heat, combine the cocoa with ½ cup cream and whisk to mix completely while heating. When cream-cocoa mixture is hot and thick, add remaining cream and the cream cheese and cook, stirring constantly, until mixture is smooth and thick. Add sugar substitute and vanilla, stirring to mix.

2. Transfer mixture to a holder with warmer candle and keep warm over very low heat. Arrange strawberries and grapes on a plate. Provide each guest with a 7-inch long wooden skewer or a fondue fork for dipping.   *Makes 8 servings*

Tip: Substitute fruit in season for the grapes and strawberries.

Raspberry Smoothies

Nutrients per serving:

Calories: 143
Carbohydrate: 28 g
Calories From Fat: 4%
Total Fat: <1 g
Saturated Fat: <1 g
Cholesterol: 2 mg
Sodium: 88 mg
Dietary Fiber: 6 g
Protein: 8 g

1 cup plain nonfat yogurt
1 cup crushed ice
1½ cups fresh or frozen raspberries
1 tablespoon honey
2 packets sugar substitute *or* equivalent of 4 teaspoons sugar

Place all ingredients in food processor or blender; process until smooth. Scrape down sides as needed. Serve immediately.   *Makes 2 servings*

Chocolate Fondue with Fresh Fruit

Nutrients per serving:

Calories: 89
Carbohydrate: 2 g
Calories From Fat: 67%
Total Fat: 7 g
Saturated Fat: 3 g
Cholesterol: 40 mg
Sodium: 87 mg
Dietary Fiber: 1 g
Protein: 5 g

Shrimp Paté

½ **pound cooked peeled shrimp**
¼ **cup (½ stick) unsalted butter, cut in chunks**
2 **teaspoons dry vermouth or chicken broth**
1 **teaspoon lemon juice**
1 **teaspoon Dijon mustard**
¼ **teaspoon ground mace**
¼ **teaspoon salt**
⅛ **teaspoon ground red pepper**
⅛ **teaspoon freshly ground black pepper**
½ **cup chopped pistachio nuts**
2 **large heads Belgian endive**

1. Combine shrimp, butter, vermouth, lemon juice, mustard, mace, salt, ground red pepper and black pepper in blender or food processor. Blend to a purée. If mixture is too soft to handle, refrigerate 1 hour.

2. Spread pistachio nuts on sheet of waxed paper. Gently form mixture into an 8-inch log. Roll in nuts to coat. Chill 1 to 3 hours. Separate endive into individual leaves and serve with shrimp log. *Makes 12 (2-tablespoon) servings*

Variation: Spoon shrimp paté into serving bowl and sprinkle with pistachio nuts.

Shrimp Paté

Ricotta Cheese & Blueberry Parfaits

Antioxidant-rich blueberries lend their tartness to this pretty dish that's great as a snack, breakfast or dessert.

> 1 cup whole milk ricotta cheese
> 1 tablespoon powdered sugar
>   Grated peel of 1 lemon
> 1½ cups fresh blueberries

1. Combine ricotta cheese, sugar and lemon peel in medium bowl; stir well.

2. Place 3 tablespoons blueberries in each of 4 parfait glasses. Add ¼ cup ricotta cheese mixture; top with another 3 tablespoons blueberries.   *Makes 4 servings*

Variation: Sprinkle top with some chopped pecans or slivered almonds.

Nutrients per serving:

Calories: 145
Carbohydrate: 12 g
Calories From Fat: 49%
Total Fat: 8 g
Saturated Fat: 5 g
Cholesterol: 31 mg
Sodium: 55 mg
Dietary Fiber: 2 g
Protein: 7 g

Savory Zucchini Stix

Try this healthy alternative to French fries. While you're munching consider the fact that zucchini provides some vitamins A, B6, C and folate and a lot less fat and carbohydrate than a small serving of fries.

>   Nonstick olive oil cooking spray
> 3 tablespoons seasoned dry bread crumbs
> 2 tablespoons grated Parmesan cheese
> 1 egg white
> 1 teaspoon reduced-fat (2%) milk
> 2 small zucchini (about 4 ounces each), cut lengthwise into quarters
> ⅓ cup spaghetti sauce, warmed

1. Preheat oven to 400°F. Spray baking sheet with cooking spray; set aside.

2. Combine bread crumbs and Parmesan cheese in shallow dish. Combine egg white and milk in another shallow dish; beat with fork until well blended.

3. Dip each zucchini wedge first into crumb mixture, then into egg white mixture, letting excess drip back into dish. Roll again in crumb mixture to coat.

4. Place zucchini sticks on prepared baking sheet; coat well with cooking spray. Bake 15 to 18 minutes or until golden brown. Serve with spaghetti sauce.

Makes 4 servings

Nutrients per serving:

Calories: 69
Carbohydrate: 9 g
Calories From Fat: 26%
Total Fat: 2 g
Saturated Fat: 1 g
Cholesterol: 6 mg
Sodium: 329 mg
Dietary Fiber: 1 g
Protein: 4 g

Ricotta Cheese & Blueberry Parfaits

Creamy Strawberry-Orange Pops

Nutrients per serving:

Calories: 97
Carbohydrate: 17 g
Calories From Fat: 4%
Total Fat: <1 g
Saturated Fat: <1 g
Cholesterol: 1 mg
Sodium: 139 mg
Dietary Fiber: 1 g
Protein: 6 g

Make these with the kids to enjoy on sweltering summer days. Vary the fruit and yogurt flavors to your taste.

> 1 container (8 ounces) strawberry-flavored sugar-free yogurt
> ¾ cup orange juice
> 2 teaspoons vanilla
> 2 cups frozen whole strawberries
> 1 packet sugar substitute *or* equivalent of 2 teaspoons sugar
> 6 (7-ounce) paper cups
> 6 wooden sticks

1. Combine yogurt, orange juice and vanilla in food processor or blender. Cover and blend until smooth.

2. Add frozen strawberries and sugar substitute. Blend until smooth. Pour into 6 paper cups, filling each about ¾ full. Place in freezer for 1 hour. Insert wooden stick into center of each. Freeze completely. Peel cup off each to serve.

Makes 6 servings

Soy Milk Smoothie

Nutrients per serving:

Calories: 147
Carbohydrate: 22 g
Calories From Fat: %
Total Fat: 3 g
Saturated Fat: g
Cholesterol: 0 mg
Sodium: 80 mg
Dietary Fiber: g
Protein: 8 g

> 3 cups plain or vanilla soy milk
> 1 banana, peeled and frozen (see tip)
> 1 cup frozen strawberries or raspberries
> 1 teaspoon vanilla or almond extract
> ⅓ cup EQUAL® SPOONFUL*

*May substitute 8 packets Equal® sweetener.

• Place all ingredients in blender or food processor. Blend until smooth.

Makes 4 servings

Tip: Peel and cut banana into large chunks. Place in plastic freezer bag, seal and freeze at least 5 to 6 hours or overnight.

METRIC CONVERSION CHART

VOLUME MEASUREMENTS (dry)

⅛ teaspoon = 0.5 mL
¼ teaspoon = 1 mL
½ teaspoon = 2 mL
¾ teaspoon = 4 mL
1 teaspoon = 5 mL
1 tablespoon = 15 mL
2 tablespoons = 30 mL
¼ cup = 60 mL
⅓ cup = 75 mL
½ cup = 125 mL
⅔ cup = 150 mL
¾ cup = 175 mL
1 cup = 250 mL
2 cups = 1 pint = 500 mL
3 cups = 750 mL
4 cups = 1 quart = 1 L

VOLUME MEASUREMENTS (fluid)

1 fluid ounce (2 tablespoons) = 30 mL
4 fluid ounces (½ cup) = 125 mL
8 fluid ounces (1 cup) = 250 mL
12 fluid ounces (1½ cups) = 375 mL
16 fluid ounces (2 cups) = 500 mL

WEIGHTS (mass)

½ ounce = 15 g
1 ounce = 30 g
3 ounces = 90 g
4 ounces = 120 g
8 ounces = 225 g
10 ounces = 285 g
12 ounces = 360 g
16 ounces = 1 pound = 450 g

DIMENSIONS

1/16 inch = 2 mm
⅛ inch = 3 mm
¼ inch = 6 mm
½ inch = 1.5 cm
¾ inch = 2 cm
1 inch = 2.5 cm

OVEN TEMPERATURES

250°F = 120°C
275°F = 140°C
300°F = 150°C
325°F = 160°C
350°F = 180°C
375°F = 190°C
400°F = 200°C
425°F = 220°C
450°F = 230°C

BAKING PAN SIZES

Utensil	Size in Inches/Quarts	Metric Volume	Size in Centimeters
Baking or Cake Pan (square or rectangular)	8×8×2	2 L	20×20×5
	9×9×2	2.5 L	23×23×5
	12×8×2	3 L	30×20×5
	13×9×2	3.5 L	33×23×5
Loaf Pan	8×4×3	1.5 L	20×10×7
	9×5×3	2 L	23×13×7
Round Layer Cake Pan	8×1½	1.2 L	20×4
	9×1½	1.5 L	23×4
Pie Plate	8×1¼	750 mL	20×3
	9×1¼	1 L	23×3
Baking Dish or Casserole	1 quart	1 L	—
	1½ quart	1.5 L	—
	2 quart	2 L	—

Acknowledgments

**The publisher would like to thank
the companies and organizations listed below for the use
of their recipes and photographs in this publication.**

Birds Eye® Foods
California Poultry Federation
Equal® sweetener
McIlhenny Company (TABASCO® brand Pepper Sauce)

Recipe Index

General Index